The Reminiscences of Frank Gillard (Huntsman): With the Belvoir Hounds, 1860 to 1896

Cuthbert Bradley

Nabu Public Domain Reprints:

You are holding a reproduction of an original work published before 1923 that is in the public domain in the United States of America, and possibly other countries. You may freely copy and distribute this work as no entity (individual or corporate) has a copyright on the body of the work. This book may contain prior copyright references, and library stamps (as most of these works were scanned from library copies). These have been scanned and retained as part of the historical artifact.

This book may have occasional imperfections such as missing or blurred pages, poor pictures, errant marks, etc. that were either part of the original artifact, or were introduced by the scanning process. We believe this work is culturally important, and despite the imperfections, have elected to bring it back into print as part of our continuing commitment to the preservation of printed works worldwide. We appreciate your understanding of the imperfections in the preservation process, and hope you enjoy this valuable book.

THE REMINISCENCES OF
FRANK GILLARD

THE SPORTSMAN'S LIBRARY

Edited by Right Hon. Sir Herbert Maxwell, Bart, M.P.

The Life of a Fox, and The Diary of a Huntsman.
  By T. Smith.

A Sporting Tour. By Col. T. Thornton.

The Sportsman in Ireland. By A Cosmopolite.

Reminiscences of a Huntsman. By the Honourable
  Grantley Berkeley.

The Art of Deer-Stalking. By William Scrope.

The Chase, The Rod, and The Turf. By Nimrod.

Days and Nights of Salmon-Fishing in the Tweed.
  By William Scrope.

Library Edition, uniform in size with this volume.
  Handsomely Bound, 15s. a volume.
  Large Paper Edition, £2 : 2s. a volume.

THE NEW YORK
PUBLIC LIBRARY

ASTOR, LENOX, AND
TILDEN FOUNDATIONS
R   L

FRANK GILLARD AND SLUGGARD, 1872.

THE REMINISCENCES

OF

FRANK GILLARD

(HUNTSMAN)

WITH THE BELVOIR HOUNDS

1860 to 1896

BY

CUTHBERT BRADLEY
"WHIPSTER," OF "LAND AND WATER"

LONDON
EDWARD ARNOLD
Publisher to the India Office
37 BEDFORD STREET
1898

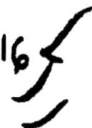

PREFACE

I HAVE hunted the line for forty seasons and more, and now I am asked by the rising generation of sportsmen to speak to it, and am reminded that it is a trait of the beautiful Belvoir blood that they can say plenty about it. Well! the memory of a lifetime spent as huntsman in the Dukes of Rutland's service is a very pleasant one, and has sped by far too quickly. It is a long way to cast back, and was never a favourite practice of mine when I carried the horn. Forrard, hark, forrard! must ever be the watchword of the chase, and as memories of those who spent their happiest moments with hounds come quicker than the pen will spring to the touch, Mr. Cuthbert Bradley is kind enough to guide that for me. Besides, I am reminded that on one occasion I broke my leg when driving a unicorn team, proving the old adage, "Every cobbler should stick to his last," therefore it is better that the practised pen and pencil of another sportsman, who has employed both during twelve seasons' sport with the Belvoir, should lead the gallop over these pages.

My feelings prompt me to dedicate this volume to the memory of my late master, Lord Charles Cecil John Manners, Sixth Duke of Rutland, as a slight token of unchanged regard and esteem. The kind personal feeling and interest always shown by the house of Manners towards me during my long tenure of office as huntsman to the family pack, has been an inspiration to excel so far as in me lay. To encouragement from the late Duke of Rutland I owe the habit of keeping a continuous record of the doings of hounds in the field through all my time, to which fact this book owes its origin, and I venture to hope that the anecdotes and sayings recorded therein of a succession of generations of sportsmen who have made Leicestershire famous will be read in no unkindly spirit, but will keep their memory green for many a year to come. Amongst those whose remarks in print I value greatly and have kept for reference when discussing hounds, are those of Mr. G. S. Lowe, Captain Pennell Elmhirst, Plantagenet, and Phantom, of the *Field* newspaper, who spent many an hour on the flags with me at Belvoir. The writings, too, of Whipster of *Land and Water*, and Tally-ho of the *Grantham Journal*, I gratefully acknowledge; whilst through the kind permission of Mr. Basil Nightingale, the proprietors of *Land and Water*, and *Baily's Magazine*, many of the illustrations appear here.

The memory of my hounds is very dear to me; their individuality has left a lasting impression on my mind like those of human friends, which only death can cancel. It was beautiful to have to hunt such hounds!

F. G.

BELVOIR KENNELS,
1896.

Facing page 1.

Yours truly
Frank Gillard.

CHAPTER I

EARLY DAYS

A Tribute to Fox-hunting—Frank Gillard's Fame as a Hound-Breeder—The Belvoir and the Brocklesby—The Points of the Belvoir Blood—Frank Gillard's Qualities—His Early Life in Devonshire, and Arrival at Belvoir—The Sixth Duke of Rutland and Lord Forester—Mr. Henry Chaplin, M.P., Master of the Burton—Anecdotes—Lord Forester and old Will Goodall—Huntsman to Mr. John Chaworth Musters, the South Notts and Quorn—Mr. Musters' horse Valesman—The hunters Lady Grey and Methodist—Colonel Burnaby, M.P.—Mr. Tailby, M.F.H.—Sporting Parsons: the Rev. H. Houson, the Rev. Desborowe, Rev. Thomas Heathcote, Rev. Waters, Rev. King, Rev. T. Bullen, Rev. John Calcraft, Rev. R. Sharpe, the Rev. W. Newcome, Rev. J. P. Younge, Rev. Banks Wright, the Rev. G. Carter—Verses by Mr. Parke of Stragglethorpe—Fathers of the Hunt.

SPORT AND AGRICULTURE

AMONG the pleasantest recollections of a pleasurable life, our days with hounds stand out as red-letter days in the calendar of the memory. There is no satisfaction like a good day's sport. George Whyte Melville said, "After a good day he felt as if he had done a good action." Fox-hunting shapes our life's course, and the annals of any great pack keep ever green the sayings and doings of a long line of sporting ancestry of whom we may be justly proud. The ardour with which sport is pursued defies the hand of time, and though the leaden wings will eventually cramp even fervour, nothing can rob us of the pleasant memories of the past. The subject of this memoir might well echo the old Latin sentiment,

> Be fair or foul, or rain or shine,
> The joys I have possessed, in spite of Fate, are mine.
> Not Heaven itself upon the past has power,
> But what has been, has been, and I have had my hour.

For on the scroll of illustrious huntsmen the century has seen, no name stands out in clearer relief than that of Frank Gillard, whose privilege, business, and we may unhesitatingly say, pleasure, it was to hunt the famous Belvoir hounds for the sixth and seventh Dukes of Rutland during a period extending over a quarter of a century. In these days of keen competition, when the utmost skill and attention is bestowed upon the breeding of foxhounds, it was no small attainment on Frank Gillard's part that he kept the pack up to that concert pitch of excellence, so that they are acknowledged by all the *première* pack of the day. We may appreciate the respect in which his fame was held by all houndsmen, when we note the fact that in one month during the summer as many as twenty-five masters of hounds paid their yearly pilgrimage to the ducal kennel at Belvoir.

Every kennel in the kingdom looked to Belvoir blood for improvement to its own. It is, in fact, as hard to get away from in foxhound breeding as that of Waxy or Birdcatcher amongst race-horses; and there are few kennel men who will not admit that a dip into it has been of great service to them. Ancient history tells us that the kennel was established in 1686 by the first Duke of Rutland, whose life, from the invigorating influence of the chase, was prolonged to the patriarchal age of eighty-three. The kennel lists and pedigrees date from the year 1750; and though the annals of the famous Brocklesby hounds are a few years later, the Belvoir can claim to be the most fashionable pack to-day. The exchange of courtesies, as regards sires, between these two celebrated kennels has been almost continual, so that their blood must be looked upon as nearly identical. Neither is there much difference in the style of the hound bred, though at Belvoir twenty-three inches is the standard of height, whilst at Brocklesby twenty-four inches is the limit. Another peculiarity of the Duke of Rutland's kennel is that they have been very particular with regard to colour, adhering to a rich black, the purest white, and bright tan, so that the latter colour has passed into a recognised quality amongst foxhounds, known as "the Belvoir tan." That there has been interbreeding, not in-breeding, is beyond a doubt, as there are signs of it in the fact that hounds from Belvoir improve all other packs, but it is very rare that hounds from other kennels improve Belvoir. The kennels that did improve the ducal lines were those possessing a large amount of the blood from which the Belvoir is said to have originated, the Fitzwilliam and the Brocklesby being two noticeable instances. It has been a great point not to breed from kennels with a variety of blood in them, and whenever there was such an experimental trial, the produce was seldom of a sufficient Belvoir type to get an entry. No pack has risen to a state of high repute when there has been a constant change of huntsmen. The Belvoir have been fortunate with but four huntsmen in a hundred years, and to this fact they owe their position as the greatest pack of foxhounds in the world.

A very striking feature of the Belvoir pack is their strong family likeness, their high-class and wonderful evenness, which is quite unapproached elsewhere. The kennel stands almost alone in having depended entirely on its own breeding for more than seventy years. No hounds have been purchased during that time, and the rule to breed from only the best working hounds has proved a sound one—good qualities cultivated through many generations being transmitted to their offspring. There may be diversities of opinions, or rather of taste, concerning size and colour in foxhounds, but there can be but one standard as regards beauty of outline, and the very important formation of shoulders, backs, loins, thighs, legs, and feet, which are so captivating and characteristic of the beautiful Belvoir blood.

For twenty-six seasons Frank Gillard ruled the

destinies of this interesting pack, retiring when the Duke of Rutland resigned the mastership in 1896. The form of the popular Belvoir huntsman is familiar to two and three generations of Leicestershire sportsmen, and regarded as the pink and the pattern of his calling, a gentleman of his profession, whose authority on hound-breeding was *nulli secundus*, and his ability to judge young hounds was sought by every kennel in the kingdom. Frank Gillard spent such a long tenure of office under the shadow of Belvoir Castle, that he seemed to form a feature of its surroundings—a typical Duke's huntsman, with the manners and bearing befitted to so high an office. A plucky horseman, he had a marvellous knack of always keeping with his hounds in the field, his head ever accompanying him over the fence, at which his heart had preceded him. For twenty-six seasons he led a hunt remarkable for its size and zealous riding, with nerve unshaken or ardour abated by many accidents and reminders of time. No day's sport was too long for him; he maintained all the traditions of his predecessors, Goosey, Goodall, Cooper, and Lord Forester, drawing covert just so long as daylight lasted, no matter what the distance back to kennels might be. Strength of constitution has ever been a characteristic of Belvoir hounds, and akin to it their reputation for being able to put in better work in late evening than in early morning. Ill-bred hounds tire at four o'clock in the afternoon, the tail is very apparent, and bad shoulders then come to grief if asked to race over ridge and furrow.

The sound of Gillard's musical voice was most inspiriting, and his horn was warranted to charm the very foxes from their earths. Such was cheery Frank as we knew him, a dapper man with a keen eye and iron gray hair, brisk as a bee in all his movements, accomplishing a gigantic day's work because his heart and soul were in it. An hour or two spent in the kennels with him talking over hound lore, in which, like his predecessors at Belvoir, he was so learned, made old time fairly gallop for his listeners.

Devonshire was Gillard's native county, where he was born in the year 1838, and until eighteen years of age had only occasional days with hounds. His father was kennel huntsman to a pack near Exeter, and from him he inherited the love of the chase, his first appointment being to a pack of harriers which had been presented by Squire Buck to Captain Willet. The kennels were at Monkleigh, North Devon; the pack were beautiful dwarf foxhounds, which hunted hare three days a week, turning their attention to otter in the summer. Unlike hare hunters in general, Gillard declined to "cast back," and in 1859 cast aside the green coat in favour of the scarlet, on taking the position of second whipper-in to the Hon. Mark Rolles' hounds, the Stevenstone. One season was spent pursuing the Devonshire foxes, and then came the chance to wear the red velvet collar and ride second whip to the Belvoir. "The spring of 1860 saw me whipping-in to the Duke of Rutland's hounds," said Frank, taking up the story, "I date everything I can back to that year. My late master, the sixth Duke of Rutland, had succeeded Lord Forester in 1859, and for three seasons I was second whipper-in, and then promoted to first, filling that position for another four to the Belvoir. The late Duke and Lord Forester were two of the keenest sportsmen I ever met, and even when hounds had run well and killed two or three foxes handsomely, they would draw again as long as daylight lasted. Often they were the only two left of the big Leicestershire fields, for they never turned their horses' heads homewards until dusk. We hunted frequently six days a week,—five with our own, and one with the Quorn, Cottesmore, or Burton. At that time Mr. Henry Chaplin, M.P., was master of the Burton, and one of the best amateur huntsmen of his day. He used to say he hunted eight days a week, for he would sometimes have two packs out in one day. Will Goodall, junior, was at that time third whip to Mr. Chaplin, and when I became huntsman to the Belvoir in 1870 he came to me as first whipper-in."

The late Duke when Marquis of Granby was fond of riding four-year-olds, and on one occasion found himself at Brant Broughton at the end of the day, very wide of home. After the last gallop Colonel Forester and the Marquis of Granby were asked by Parson Houson to go to his house at Brant Broughton to refresh. It was late in the evening, and Colonel Forester, as was his wont, declined to stop anywhere with his horse after a day's hunting, but the Marquis of Granby accepted the proffered hospitality of so good a sportsman as the parson. By the time he started again for Belvoir it was quite dark, and when the private gate to the drive at Stubton was reached it was locked, but he managed to rouse up the lodge-keeper, who warned the Marquis not to attempt to ford the river at that time of night. However he did, although there was a good stream on. In those days the country was not inclosed, and by Sedgebrook the bridle-road was lost in the darkness, and the night was spent with a tired horse wandering about until three o'clock in the morning, when a light in a cottage window came as a welcome beacon. Belvoir was reached at five o'clock, and the Marquis kept his appointment as usual with hounds that morning. On another occasion the noble master of the Belvoir had the ill luck to lame his horse when out with the Cottesmore by Gunby Warren, and he walked by the side of him all the way back to Belvoir. These two fine sportsmen never knew when they had enough fox-hunting, and a story is told of Lord Forester during his mastership and Will Goodall. "Where shall we go now, Goodall?" asked Lord Forester. "To the kennels, my Lord, I think the hounds have had enough," replied Will, after a hard day's work. "Have you been out with the Quorn?" asked the master. "No, my Lord," replied Will. "Well, I noticed those hounds were fresh at the end of the day; if these are tired you had better in future breed from them."

In 1867 promotion came to Gillard when Mr. John Chaworth Musters asked him to be kennel huntsman to the South Notts, and the farmers of the Belvoir Vale presented the young whipper-in with a silver hunting-horn on his leaving them. "The memory of my three seasons under Mr. John Chaworth Musters is a very pleasant one, for he was the finest of sportsmen and the truest of friends," said Frank of his old master. "Though Mr. Musters rode seventeen stone, no man went better; and I was the means of supplying him with his best horse, Valesman, a big brown blood hunter which I bought from Mr. Bland, who lived in the Vale of Belvoir. At first Mr. Musters did not like the horse, and said to me, 'You think so much of him, let's see you ride him!' I did so, and we started a seven mile point from Colville Wood, and killed on the Nottingham and Mansfield road. Valesman carried me splendidly, and I said to Mr. Musters, 'I hope you will never want to ride him again, for I do not want a better to carry me!' However, he got to like the horse in time, and when we migrated to the Quorn country no one could catch Mr. Musters on Valesman up and down the hills. From that time he changed his style of horse, and always advocated blood. At the dispersal sale of the Quorn Hunt horses, Valesman was bought by Mr. Henry Chaplin, who became very fond of him, and though he often sent him up for auction with the rest of his stud, he always bought him in, and was said to have spent hundreds in doing so. Two of my best mounts at this time were greys, Lady Grey and Methodist; the mare came from Mr. Corbett Holland, and was such a clipper over a country that Sir Frederick Johnstone said no money would stop him buying her. However, she unfortunately met with an accident in the stable and had to be destroyed. The horse Methodist was bought from old Mr. Wilders of Croxton, who was of that persuasion. He was made by his son Stephen, who was a light weight and a most determined horseman. In a good run of fifty minutes from Widmerpool to Piper Hole Gorse the horse carried me splendidly, and jumped the river Smite, old Mr. Sherbrooke calling out, 'There is no one in the same field with the Methodist'; and he *was* a brilliant horse, being subsequently sold for three hundred guineas.

"In Leicestershire I had a good friend in the late Colonel Burnaby, M.P., who lived at Baggrave Hall. He used to ask me to his house to talk about hunting, and would show me 'his blood-stained clothes and great treasure won in battle.' That was about the time that the evergreen Mr. Tailby hunted a pack of hounds in high Leicestershire; and he took some awful falls, breaking nearly every bone in his body. He had a way of catching hold of the back of his saddle when jumping a fence, and this was, I think, often the cause why his falls were attended with such serious results, because he could not get clear of his horse."

A sign of the times in the sixties was the number of sporting parsons who could claim honours in any country, and kept good studs of hunters. The price of wheat was up in those days and tithes were correspondingly high; but bad times and great Church reforms have banished the hunting parson, for where a dozen sporting divines were in evidence forty years ago there is but one left to pilot the way to-day. The finest horseman of a party who rode with the Belvoir and Quorn was the Rev. H. Houson of Brant Broughton, who was difficult to beat over a country. Parson Desborowe of Welborne, too, was a wonderfully hard man to shake off, and the Rev. Thomas Heathcote of Lenton was another fine sportsman who kept a good stud of hunters and planted a fox covert. The Rev. Waters of Dunsby was a frequent combatant across country, and when he moved over the borders into Nottinghamshire he still continued to hunt up to the time of his death, at a ripe old age. Others who will be remembered are Parson King of Ashby, Parson T. Bullen of Eastwell, and the Rev. John Calcraft of Haceby, who enjoyed much sport with one horse and went prodigious long distances to meet hounds. The Rev. R. Sharpe of Colsterworth was another fine horseman, and very eloquent in the pulpit. An all-round sportsman was the Rev. "Billy" Newcome, rector of Boothby for fifty years, and up to eighty years of age he rode, fished, and shot with the best of them. A contemporary of Mr. Newcome's was the Rev. J. Parker Younge of Wilsford, who bred some good horses and followed the hounds regularly up to his seventy-sixth year. He was also a capital shot and fly fisherman, remembered by the rising generation cramming along across country with his coat flying open in the most boisterous weather. Parson Banks Wright, too, would go like wildfire for twenty minutes, no matter how big the country might be; but in the pulpit he would stay for thirty odd minutes when the text was to his liking. The Rev. George Carter of Folkingham was another who has passed away from us, enjoying the sport thoroughly with four of his family.

The prowess of the Rev. H. Houson has been immortalised in verse by Mr. Parke of Stragglethorpe Hall, who in his time followed the Belvoir and Burton packs, besides contributing to sporting literature under the *nom de plume* of Nemo. The following verses were written by him after the death of the Rev. H. Houson, who was familiarly known as "the Doctor," and noted for the cleanliness of himself and horse. These verses were afterwards reprinted at the wish of his old friend, Colonel John Reeve of Leadenham House, and were largely distributed amongst hunting men :—

Amid all the scenes and joys of the chase,
In vain shall we look for one well-known face;
One slight compact form, on a tall rat-tailed mare—
How comes it, my friends, that the Doctor's not here?
Alas! our good parson's long season is o'er,
He has come to a check, we shall see him no more.
Brant Broughton's sad bells have rung forth their lament,
For as thorough a sportsman as e'er followed scent.
Those thin hands, now cold, which tho' wrinkled with age,
Might have given a wrinkle to many a sage;
So light, they the tenderest mouth ne'er distressed,
Yet so firm, that the hardest their power confessed;
In vain did high breeding rebel 'gainst their sway,
It might chafe, it might struggle, it yet must obey.

Weaver's Lodge, Lenton Pastures, or famed Ropsley Rice
Shall no more echo gaily his clear ringing voice;
Ne'er again his gay talk, as he trots by our side,
Shall dispel the fatigue of a long homeward ride.

Ah! how oft, so returning, our friend have we seen,
From his hat to his boots all unsullied and clean
As if—when the snow, or the winter's cold rains,
With mire had bestrewn all the fields and the lanes—
From his person attendants, concealed from the view,
Interposing, averted the mud as it flew!
Be that as it may, did we only look round
On the rest of the "Field" and the horses, we found
We could trace on their breeches, and boots, and array,
Upon what kind of soil they had ridden that day;
Whether Stubton's stiff loam, or bleak Stapleford's peat,
Or the heath's stony plain, had been spurned 'neath their feet.
One had thought that our friend had discovered that well,
Long sought for by sages—and of marvels they tell,
That removed all the weakness of age, and, forsooth,
Renew'd in the frame the full vigour of youth.
No such well had he sought, or much less had he found,
But he owed his old age and his stamina sound
To the genuine love for that sport which alone
In old England's fair land in perfection is known.
Long, long may it flourish; may foxes increase.
But earthed, may the Rector of Broughton find peace.

Of the fathers of the hunt still with us Sir W. E. Welby-Gregory takes precedence, Major Paynter being another staunch supporter, and Mr. John Earle Welby as fine a horseman as ever rode to hounds. The rising generation are indebted to Mr. Welby for giving them a book of poems, *Lays of the Belvoir Hunt.* Another knight of the pen and the pigskin is Mr. William Pinder of Barrowby, who commenced hunting in the thirties, and to-day is known as "Phantom" of the Field, the oldest hunting correspondent. Then we have Mr. John Nickolls of Sleaford, blooded in 1836 by Goosey on Caythorpe Heath, and he still likes a quick thoroughbred horse, sitting him as gaily as he did in his prime forty years ago. Amongst the sturdy yeomen born and bred on Lincolnshire soil, known throughout England wherever agriculture and sport are discussed, we have Mr. R. Bemrose and Mr. T. Casswell, both "rum ones to follow, bad ones to beat." And we might name a score more Nestors of the hunt, who give colour to the saying of the North American Indians, that "days spent in the chase do not count in the length of life."

The late Will Goodall, sen.

CHAPTER II

SPORT IN THE SIXTIES

The Origin of Frank's Diary—Blowing the Duke's Horn for the first time—About Hunting-horns—A Pattern Horn—Colonel John Reeve of Bulby Hall—Sir Thomas Whichcote—Mr. Chaworth Musters and his Ancestors; his Prowess in the Field—The Quorn and Belvoir countries compared—Fatal Accident to a Quorn Whipper-in—Mr. John Coupland succeeds Mr. Musters to the Quorn—Mr. Gaskin of Sysonby Lodge—About the Planting and Keeping of Fox Coverts—Advice given to Frank Gillard by Mr. Musters and the Duke of Rutland.

MR. J. CHAWORTH MUSTERS, M.F.H.

"NULLA dies sine linea"—"there is no day without a line"—is strictly applicable to hunting, and might with reason be adopted as a family motto by the house of Gillard. The age when letter-writing was a cultivated art is a thing of the past, but Frank Gillard began his career when hunting correspondents and newspaper reporters were hardly known, so that it became a duty as well as a pleasure for him to handle the pen every evening after hunting, to inform his master the Duke of Rutland. To this fact the diaries owe their origin; literally all through his career it was with him "no day without a line," and the twenty-six volumes form a unique and unbroken record of hounds and those who played a prominent part in the world of sport. Memory is but a treacherous jade, but with facts and figures set down at the moment it is possible to conjure up the scenes of the past, and pass them before the mind in stately sequence, recalling the sayings and doings of two and three generations of sportsmen. Our own part has been the result of half-hours snatched with pen and pencil in the mid-current of stirring events, during ten seasons' sport with the Belvoir hounds and Frank Gillard. In this way we have been able to follow the line in memory by familiar scenes, country, and fences, filling in the background to his story.

To carry the horn for the Belvoir has always been considered the topmost rung in the ladder of fame by all the professional talent, and we trust it will be so to the end of the chapter. Therefore it was a befitting start for Frank to commence his narrative with an allusion to his hunting-horn.

"The first time I handled the horn for the Sixth Duke of Rutland's hounds I was a second whipper-in, in the year 1860. It was seven o'clock, and so dark in that big covert, Kirby Wood, that the Duke struck a light to see the time. The only other horseman left was Mr. George Drummond, who had lost one of his coat-tails coming through a fence. Hounds were screaming along, for the wood was full of foxes, and James Cooper, the huntsman, was lost in the thicket, so the Duke turned to me and said, 'You second whip must do the best you can to stop hounds, take my horn, for I must be off home.' After blowing his Grace's horn and hallooing I got the bulk of the pack round me, though it was too dark to count them, and we started back for kennels twenty miles distant. That was the first time I had the honour to blow the Duke of Rutland's hunting-horn, and when his death occurred in March 1888, after thirty years' mastership, the present Duke of Rutland, Lord John Manners, came down to the kennels with that hunting-horn in his pocket, and said, 'My brother wished me to bring you this horn, Frank, and I am sure no one will value it more than you!'" Tears came into Gillard's eyes as he narrated the story, which it was plain to see was most heartfelt. "No man could have wished for a kinder master than the noble Duke, who was always so considerate and interested in the doings of his hounds."

"What notes you could get out of your horn, Frank, you gave it quite a language of its own; if you had not chosen fox-hunting as a profession you ought to have been a musician!" we said, determined to lead our subject back to the line, and if possible get him on a gossiping scent. "Well, you see, I had a musical pack to play up to, for the Belvoir always had plenty to say about it when they spoke to a fox," replied Gillard, brightening up, "I was fortunate, too, in getting suited with a horn, which is half the battle," he added modestly. "I must tell you the story of how I came by my hunting-horn, for I used it the whole time I was huntsman, and it went many times to London as a pattern to be copied for other masters and huntsmen. It was made of copper, which always gives a better note than silver, and it came into my possession when I whipped-in to the Belvoir. I was hunting up lost hounds one evening at Aswarby, and had occasion to call on an old fox-keeper and odd man about the place employed by Sir Thomas Whichcote. At one time in his life he had hunted hounds in the north of England, and he could give the best ringing view halloo that I have ever heard. When hounds were drawing the Aswarby coverts the old fellow was sure to be there making the welkin ring with his screams, to the great delight of Sir Thomas. When I went to see him he showed me his hunting-horn, and I thought at once that it had a good note, and got him to let me try it. It was a longish copper horn, easy to blow and full of music. 'You have got no further use for it,' I said, 'you may as well give it to me, I may be huntsman some day if I am lucky!' But the old man would not hear of it, and it ended by my giving considerably more for the old horn than I could have bought a new one. Directly Cooper the huntsman tried it, he wanted to buy it from me, but I never would be persuaded to part with it, and when I went to the South Notts as huntsman to Mr. Chaworth Musters, he was so pleased that he had it copied for his own use, and when I left his service presented me with the same pattern in silver."

Just as the old war-horse instinctively cocks his ears at the sound of the bugle, so had Frank Gillard roused the memories of the past as he clutched his old hunting-horn, for scenes and faces crowding before him. "Hey! they were fine old sportsmen in those days, and seemed to enjoy their sport more than they do now! Though possibly memories of fox-hunting resemble port, in that they improve by keeping. Ways of living and thought have altered as time goes on, but they were good old days, nevertheless! What sport we did have; to be sure it was all fox-hunting then, no one ever thought about preserving game! When I was whipper-in to the Belvoir it was my duty to go the round of the coverts in the spring-time to look up the number of litters and get to know the earths, for fox-keepers were few and far between. The large tract of woodland from Aslackby to Grimsthorpe swarmed with foxes, and I used to hack over to these woods, spending two or three days hunting through them. I remember after one of these visits I rode on to Bulby Hall, to report to Colonel John Reeve, who lived there, and he asked me in to have 'a refresher,' as I had more than twenty miles to ride back to Belvoir kennels. He loved playing a practical joke, and when I said, 'I must be starting homewards,' he replied, 'Oh, you cannot possibly go to Belvoir to-night, your horse has been suppered up and the stablemen have gone home with the key. Come and shoot some rats with me!' However, I was more than content to look on whilst he handled the gun, and keeping my eyes open, I saw a chopper lying in the wood-shed and picked it up. 'What are you going to do with that?' he asked. 'Unlock the stable-door,' I replied. It had the desired effect, I got my horse without any further trouble; but he dearly loved a joke, and would turn rats down in a room when the ladies were about, wearing those big hoop crinolines. Another fine old Lincolnshire sportsman was Sir Thomas Whichcote of Aswarby Park. It may safely be said that for half a century he was the most prominent figure with the Belvoir hounds, and in their palmy days too! He rode one of the finest studs of hunters ever seen in the country, and in his younger days was an undefeated horseman. Always a hard, zealous rider, the Melton division delighted to journey to such fixtures as Weaver's Lodge to take Sir Thomas on over his own country, and it was no unusual sight to see two and three four-in-hands come to the meet full of riding talent. Half Sir Thomas's stud were stabled at Grantham, and he would drive any distance with a fast trotting horse to hunt on the Leicestershire side, returning to Aswarby again that night. After the death of his first wife, which happened in the fifties from the result of a carriage accident, Sir Thomas never again hunted in scarlet. He belonged to the good old school, and was regarded as one of the fathers of the hunt. My old master, the late Mr. Chaworth Musters, was another of the fine old English gentlemen born and bred for sport, for I am sure his happiest days were spent with hounds. I went to him as huntsman to the South Notts in 1867, with the understanding that he would take a better country as soon as one became vacant, and two seasons later we migrated with his pack to the Quorn. Mr. Chaworth Musters came of a long line of sporting ancestors, and in a letter to me, dated December 10, 1871, he wrote: 'My grandfather began to hunt hounds about 1805, and his last pack were sold at Colwick in 1845. He used to hunt with his father's hounds—my great-grandfather—which were kept at Colwick, but whether he ever hunted them himself or not I do not know. He hunted first of all and certainly last of all in this country, the South Notts, the same which I hunt now, and which his father hunted before him. He also hunted the Pytchley two or three seasons, the Badsworth one season, the Southwold several, and, like Colonel "Jack" Thompson, the Atherstone.' Old Mr. "Jack" Musters, the grandfather, lived in the days when there were giants in the land, the golden age as it is called, and, like Squire Osbaldistone, he was very active and fond of feats of strength. On one occasion he made a bet that he would jump in and out of twelve sugar-casks placed all in a row in Nottingham market-place, and I believe he accomplished the feat. It was his delight to pound the field and get away with hounds all by himself. To ensure this, he would sometimes have a bagman turned down over a wide river, and a second horse waiting for him on the far bank, to gallop away over the vale of Whatton."

"In November 1868, owing to the death of Lord Hastings, who had held the mastership of the Quorn for two seasons, Mr. John Chaworth Musters succeeded; and the season of 1868-69 was a very good one for scent and consequently for sport. Mr. Story of Lockington used laughingly to say, 'It would be a pity if Mr. Musters could not show sport, considering that he had three huntsmen in his establishment besides himself, namely, myself to hunt the high country; Bob Machin, late huntsman to the Rufford, to whip-in; and John Goddard, who, after hunting the Quorn hounds and Mr. Tailby's, undertook the management of the stud at Quorn.' Having hunted both countries, I think the Quorn is easier to ride than the Belvoir, because there are very few ditches and very little grass in any of those. Since my time the ox-rail has practically disappeared, a strand of wire taking its place, but when the timber was up you wanted a bold, well-bred horse who could extend himself to get safely over. When the Quorn country is wet it gets very boggy, and sucks horses in owing to the nature of the soil."

"I must tell you of a singular and terrible accident which happened to my whipper-in when at Quorn. His name was Onion, and he was a keen promising servant. As the weather was very hot in the autumn of that year, we went out with hounds at three o'clock in the morning to catch the dew, and we took them to Garenden Park, close to Loughborough, the property of Mr. de L'Isle. After spending a long morning showing them the deer, so as to break the young hounds from giving chase, I decided it was time to turn homewards as the sun was getting very hot. Suddenly Onion saw amongst the thorn bushes a white stag grazing, and it was lame from an injury to one of its hocks. 'Do let the hounds have a look at him!' said Onion, and he was so keen and excited about it, that at last I turned round and said, 'Where is it? but we have done quite enough!' The moment I said so, he galloped his horse round the thorn bushes to set the deer going, though I shouted to him, 'Stop, stop! don't go on!' But it was no use, he seemed crazed about this white stag. The next moment I heard a crash, and going to see, found his horse had cannoned against the stag as they met round the thick clump of thorns, both were down, and Onion lay stretched senseless on the ground. I got him into a sitting posture, which is always the best thing to do in cases of concussion, and held him up until a doctor arrived. Mr. de L'Isle sent down ice and stimulants, and had a tent erected, for it was impossible to move him, but the poor young fellow died that night in his red coat and boots where he fell."

Referring to the records of the Quorn Hunt at this time we find that Mr. Musters's health unfortunately proved unequal to the work after two seasons, and the expense was greater than he could afford to continue, so that he was obliged to give up the country, though much pressed to go on hunting it with a subscription. The hounds were lent for one season, 1870-71, to Mr. John Coupland, and they were hunted by Jem MacBride; after which Mr. Coupland bought the Craven hounds, and Mr. Musters took his own back to Nottingham.

"Another of the old school of sportsmen whose going days were over just as I appeared on the scene in Leicestershire was Mr. Gaskin, who lived at Sysonby Lodge, a hunting-box on the Kettleby and Melton road. The old gentleman knew every yard of the country with gates and gaps, so that he could trot about and get a bird's-eye view of all that was going on. With him rode a second horseman armed with a hatchet and saw; and directly they came to a fence that had been mended up, he would say, 'John, here is one of our gaps made up. Clear it all out, clear it all out at once!' Instead of a hunting-crop he carried a thick oak walking-stick, and if his horse would not stand still whilst his servant was reducing the fence, he would crash it down on his head, shouting, 'Whoa, won't you stand still!' In his younger days it was said he went well to hounds, thoroughly enjoying the ride, but when he was reduced to trotting about to look on at the rising generation negotiating a strongly fenced country, he would set his teeth and grin with delight, exclaiming, 'Look at the lunatics, John! look at them!'"

"Time flies," continued Frank, musingly. "I have lived long enough to see many of the best-known fox coverts grow up from saplings to tall trees. I might mention Casthorpe covert by Belvoir, which was planted by the late Duke of Rutland to blot out the view of a fallow field from the Castle, as he liked to see nothing but grass. Then there is Sherbrooke's covert, about which Lord Forester had to be consulted as to the site, and Mr. Sherbrooke paid for the planting of it, some twelve acres or more of thorn and gorse. The gorse soon sprang up, but the thorns took twenty years or more before they were good covert. When I came as huntsman to the Duke's country one of the first things I took in hand was the improvement of the fox coverts, which had been sadly neglected, the sticks had been chopped down and laid, which is the worst possible plan, because they are full of rotten thorns, very bad for the hounds to get amongst; so I had them all cleared out and burned. When Mr. Henry Chaplin hunted the Burton country, he had all his coverts brushed, and very good it made them. Young thorns should be topped just as long as you can get a man to go amongst them, if not they grow up like kidney-bean sticks, harbour starlings, and no grass will grow at bottom. Thorns and grass grow well together, and make the best of fox ground; old thorns soon spring up again when chopped down, but newly-planted thorns take a long time to get a start, and privet wants frequently topping or else it soon grows out. In conclusion," Gillard remarked, as he put the old hunting-horn back again on to the mantelpiece, where it stands as an ornament with several other trophies of the chase, "if I have been successful and enjoyed a good time, I owe much to the kindly advice given to me at starting by my dear masters, who were my best friends until death removed them. Mr. Musters used to say, 'Frank, we must hold the candle to the end, play the game out whatever it may be,' and the Duke of Rutland often said to me, 'Make as many friends as you can, Frank, and as few enemies, and then life is sure to run smoothly with you.'"

Mr. John Coupland, M.F.H.

CHAPTER III

SEASON 1870-71

The Hunting View from Belvoir Castle—Appointment of Huntsman to the Belvoir—Letters of Congratulation—Will Goodall, junior, First Whip—The Institution of the Hound Van—The Kennels at Ropsley—James Cooper, late Huntsman—The Duke of Rutland's Visit to the Kennel—Dick Christian's Story of the Duke's Leap—The Duke as a Master—Mr. George Lane Fox's Letter to Mr. Tom Parrington—Frank's First Entry in the Diary, Aug. 23, 1870—Osbaldeston Furrier—The Belvoir and Cottesmore Hunts join in the Field—The Duke takes a heavy Fall—Mr. Tom Hutchinson picks him up—A Day of Disaster—Sir Watkin Winn's "Royal" and John Walker in his Kennel—A good Run, and Mr. Henry Custance asks for the Brush—H.R.H. the Prince of Wales has a Day—The Field out.

THE BELVOIR HOUND VAN.

BELVOIR and fox-hunting are almost interchangeable terms, for no history of the one can possibly be complete without frequent mention of the other. A Duke of Rutland may stand at one window of his dining-room and overlook twenty parishes, each of which bears a name that is associated with some brilliant episode in hunting history. The topmost turrets of Belvoir Castle command views on every side over the far-famed fields of Leicestershire and Lincolnshire, where the mightiest Nimrods of modern days have delighted to disport themselves. The county hunted by the Belvoir embraces every description of ground, extending on the west from the Trent to the German Ocean on the east, reaching from Leadenham on the north to Melton Mowbray on the south, distance across as the crow flies, thirty miles. The past history of the Belvoir Hunt can be summed up in a very few words, a fine old Conservative institution, hunted for over two hundred years at the expense of a succession of Dukes of Rutland, under the management of huntsmen who have been acknowledged as the best of their day. In a little under one hundred years but four huntsmen have been at Belvoir kennel, viz. Goosey, Goodall, Cooper, and Frank Gillard, filling the post successively from 1816 to 1896, all following the same system of breeding in the kennel, maintaining the high traditions of the pack.

We find Frank at Quorn in the spring of 1870, and scarcely had he settled himself in the saddle under the mastership of Mr. John Coupland, than the Belvoir were in want of a huntsman. At first there was some little difficulty in terminating the engagement with Mr. Coupland, but directly the late Duke of Rutland expressed a wish that Gillard should be his huntsman, he was graciously released. Letters of congratulation were addressed to Gillard on his appointment from a very numerous acquaintance, and amongst the hard-riding fraternity and covert-owners there was great rejoicing, the letters from Lord Forester, Mr. John Welby, and others being sacredly preserved by their recipient. His Grace the Duke of Rutland wrote from his seat in Scotland, May 1870: "I am much indebted to Mr. Coupland and gentlemen of the Quorn Hunt for releasing you, and I shall be very glad of your services. You know it is a place for regular hard work, as the distances are long and I hunt five days a week." Sir Thomas Whichcote, one of the hardest men that ever rode to hounds, wrote from Aswarby Park, Lincolnshire, "I cannot resist giving a line of congratulation, and I trust Providence will spare you many a long year to fulfil the proud position of huntsman to the kindest master of the noblest pack of hounds in England. I intend to purchase three more hunters for next season. Young Goodall writes me word the Duke has been kind enough to appoint him first whip; I think you will find him sharp, active, and attentive." The first whip referred to in the letter was Will Goodall, the son of old Will Goodall who had a numerous family, and hunted the Belvoir for nearly twenty years, meeting his death by falling upon his own hunting-horn, which he had thrust into the side pocket of his coat. Young Will's first experiences were in the stables at Aswarby Park, where Sir Thomas Whichcote paid for his education, and taught him to ride; he then "entered to hounds" as second whip under George Carter. From there he got promotion with Mr. Henry Chaplin, master of the Burton, coming to Belvoir as first whip in 1870. Springing from a family to whom "hunting a pack of hounds" comes as naturally as finding game does to a setter, he proved himself a brilliant whipper-in and subsequent huntsman to the Pytchley.

Complaints were made in Cooper's time that beautiful as the Belvoir hounds were in their work, they did not say enough about it, and it was the one thing that Gillard fancied faulty when he came as huntsman. The kennel was full of Senator (1862) blood. Cooper swore by him and everything that he got; his was the most fashionable strain. Senator was by Singer out of Destitute; Singer by Comus out of Syren, by Mr. Drake's Duster (1844) out of Sprightly, by the Grove Singer. Destitute was by Sir Richard Sutton's Dryden out of Tuneful, by Trouncer out of Skilful, by Grove Stormer. The two special qualities Senator transmitted to his stock were nose and drive. His own sister Destitute had the best nose to work a line down a road that Frank Beers ever saw a foxhound possess. Then all the Senators could drive at any pace, and old Jack Morgan said, at the time he had a good many of them in Lord Galway's pack, "They *do* get their hackles up when a fox is sinking."

There was a hound, called Wonder, in the kennel with a voice like a bell, and he did not fail to use it at the right moment. For this quality Gillard used him freely, although he was not of the Senator line, being the son of Chanticleer, son of Chaser, son of Brocklesby Rallywood, brought to

Belvoir in 1850 by Will Goodall. Wonder's dam was Willing, a noted bitch by Rallywood, son of Brocklesby Rallywood or Vaulter family. Both, it will be seen, trace to the same source through a whole decade of chase history down to the great Furrier several times, and then to a bitch called Comely, by Lord Monson's Conqueror out of Red Rose, who lived about the year 1785. The kennel was full of Senator blood, so that Woodman and Warrior—the sons of Wonder-Susan—two of this season's entry, were just sufficiently far enough away from that strain to give Gillard a chance to still further accumulate this famous blood so full of Duster, without inbreeding. It was no easy task to breed Belvoir hounds, and one cannot help admiring the judgment with which all the strains are picked up to such standard points as the Drake Duster (1844) or Osbaldeston Furrier. No animal of any sort whatever has been bred to in the same persistency as can be traced to Osbaldeston Furrier. He was the best hound of his day in the opinion of all hound-breeders. Warrior, it will be seen, was quite a Belvoir bred hound, as his pedigree does not get away far, and is confined to Belvoir, Brocklesby, the Grove, and the Drake Duster, whose dam was got by Factor, the son of Mr. Saville's Carver. So in Warrior there were two hits to Duster, three to Carver, two to Rallywood, and two to Senator. Warrior eventually sired Weathergage, 1876, who sired Gambler, 1884.

The strength of the kennel when Gillard came was sixty-seven couple, but was reduced by five couple as soon as the vanning to distant meets became an institution.

It was Lord Forester's original idea to have a hound van to take the pack on to the distant fixtures of twenty miles and more. Both Will Goodall and Cooper preferred instead half-way kennels at Ropsley, but these were abandoned when Gillard came, and a van was instituted, to the great saving of wear and tear both to hounds and hunt servants. Many a time in Gillard's younger days when whipping-in, turning to Ropsley at the end of the day meant farther to go for the hunt staff, and by the time the pack were kennelled there, it was nearly midnight before Belvoir was reached, or there was a chance of changing wet clothes. Well might it have been said of the Belvoir, that one day's hunting with them was equal to two in the provinces. Cooper had an attraction at Ropsley, because he was courting his future wife, the daughter of the landlord of the Fox's Brush Inn.

The noble master placed the greatest confidence in Frank Gillard's abilities, leaving it to him to carry on the correspondence and business generally of the hunt. The whole internal machinery of so vast and important a hunt as the Belvoir was practically worked by one man for a quarter of a century, and on such good lines that the kennel occupied the premier position by general consent.

Few things interested the Duke more than a chat with his huntsman about hounds, in the sanctum at the kennels, known as "The Duke's

Room," where the celebrated sires and favourites of his pack were drawn for inspection, and he would dwell long in silent contemplation on their beautiful symmetry and colour. A corner of this room at the kennels was railed off so that the hounds should not touch the noble master's gouty leg, aggravated by severe accidents in the field. When young, the Duke could hold his own across country with the boldest and best, and delighted to play a conspicuous part with such bold spirits and brilliant performers as Asheton Smith, Lord Forester, Lord Jersey, Sir Charles Knightly, Mr. Green, Sir Thomas Whichcote, and Lord Wilton. It was Dick Christian who used to tell how his Grace once jumped Croxton Park wall near the entrance gates, and pounded every pursuer. "It's nigh six feet and a tidy drop on the other side. Will Goodall and none of them would have it!" Unfortunately, a series of severe falls crippled him considerably, and in 1868, during a smart run from Casthorpe covert, he had a very heavy fall on his head, when jumping a stake-and-bound fence, the result of the accident being that with all the will of younger days he was after that physically incapable of riding up to hounds. What he could do in early days as Marquis of Granby will always place him in the first rank of those whose performances in the field belong to the period known as the "golden age of fox-hunting." A courteous bearing and manner distinguished the Duke, and though a hard rider, full of enthusiasm that danger could not daunt, he had always a marvellous control over the impetuous spirits of which a Belvoir field was so largely composed. Yet his government was marked by the gentlest suasion, and in anything stronger than an ironical rebuke he was hardly known to indulge. Seldom interfering with the pack in the field, he never gave his huntsmen a direct command, preferring rather to turn his order into a request. Conservative to a degree, he delighted in upholding all the famous traditions of the family pack, and when discussing any subject relating to hunting, qualified his opinion by saying, "I think Lord Forester would have done so!" Politics he did not trouble much, but his few speeches in the House of Lords on Protection, which he always upheld, were short, vigorous, and to the point. Such was the master who ruled the destinies of the Belvoir, and whose service Gillard found so congenial and conducive to aspire to excellence. The liberality with which hunting affairs have all through been conducted at Belvoir Castle never degenerated into mere display; indeed, many provincial establishments were more conspicuous for the lavish scale of their expenditure. Nothing was spared that could help to make the pack thoroughly efficient or sustain its high reputation, and all reasonable claims for damage were promptly satisfied.

Every day has its line recorded in the diaries of twenty-six seasons' sport, kept religiously by Gillard. The death of every one of the 2709 foxes slain during that period is mentioned. Here is the first entry, characteristic of many

BELVOIR CASTLE.

thousand others, all of which might be used to conjure up a pleasant memory of the past. It was Mr. George Lane Fox who said very truly in a letter to his old friend, Mr. Thomas Parrington, the promoter of foxhound shows, "If a man is once a real sportsman, and loves hound and horse, he will, when age prevents him from taking an active part, still continue to delight in hearing of the sport that hounds show and which others are enjoying." If that be true, a debt of gratitude is due to Frank Gillard for keeping so consistently a record during the whole of that time, which forms a history of the men and manners in the world of sport. The writing is scrupulously neat and clear, and reads as follows :—

"*August* 23*rd*, 1870.—Commenced cub-hunting, found a good show of cubs at old Church Wood (Woolsthorpe), hounds running from fox to fox one hour and twenty minutes, killing three cubs. *Remarks.*—The harvest was very early, but owing to the dryness of the weather we could not begin sooner. It rained yesterday afternoon for five or six hours. Owing to it falling unexpectedly we had not got the earths stopped; in consequence, it was half-past nine before we made a start, rather an unusual hour for the first morning! The day was dull. Wind, S.W. Fair good scent. Foxes killed, 3. To ground, 0. Hounds out, 84 couple. I rode the chestnut hack mare."

On the last day of September the meet was arranged for half-past ten at Belvoir to suit his Grace, who was out for the first time with his two friends, Sir Francis Grant, P.R.A., and Mr. Parker Gilmour, who were staying at the Castle, whilst Mr. Chaworth Musters, as was his wont, slept the night at the kennels, the guest of Frank Gillard. Scent was not very good, but the young entry distinguished themselves by Three Queens, where the ground was much foiled by fur, and doing so greatly pleased the Duke. Ferryman and Woodman were first away on the line of their fox, after running through Harston pastures, whilst Fleecer afterwards distinguished himself by carrying the line from Harston to Hallams Wood, where the pack effected their second kill.

A curious incident in a day's sport at the end of November is related with an afternoon fox from Newman's Gorse, which beat hounds after a good hunt up to Saxby. When the hunt was returning by Freeby Wood the Cottesmore were seen running into it, leaving with a point for Waltham, where the huntsman was told of a fox being shut up in a stable at Welbournes, which he promptly demanded and gave to the hounds. The fox had been captured an hour before, and was undoubtedly the Belvoir fox, for he was as stiff as a stake, and one hound was seen to follow him on in the direction of Waltham. The Duke of Rutland and most of the field joined in with the Cottesmore, and followed them to Waltham, thinking they were with the Belvoir. A few days later his Grace took a bad fall, owing to his horse jumping short at a brook by Carlton Scroop, and first to render aid was Mr. Tom Hutchinson, one of the hardest men to hounds of the yeomen brigade. "Oh, that brute of a horse, your Grace," he exclaimed, "I'll cut his throat; he's not fit to live." "No, no! Mr. Hutchinson," replied the Duke, who always excused his horse on every occasion, "it was not his fault." "But I will cut his throat, your Grace, I will," persisted the good Samaritan, who was always very determined and resolute. Possessing a marvellous control over a horse, Mr. Tom Hutchinson was one of those who seem to be able to make them do anything, and they all knew this, when he was on their backs that they must do their best. Many are the wonderful stories told of his celebrated cob Jack, who could top over anything his own height, and it was a lesson to watch his master ride at a big place, giving each hand a hurried lick so as to get a better grip of the reins as he measured his distance and sent him at it.

A day of disaster happened on February 14th, when hounds were in Belton Park, for though several foxes were afoot they were so headed by foot people that little good could be done, and then to crown all, the huntsman's horse kicked an old hound, Sportsman, in a gateway and killed him on the spot. Sportsman was a lemon-coloured hound by Sir Watkin Winn's Royal, whom old John Walker, the huntsman to that kennel, said "that there was never such another hound as Royal living"; he was always singing his praises, and so Cooper used him at Belvoir. Frank tells the story of how when a youth, whipping-in for the Hon.

Mark Rolle in Devonshire, he was sent to Sir Watkin Winn's kennel to bring away a draft of twenty-six couples. "Are the hounds ready, sir?" asked young Frank of old John Walker on his arrival, quite expecting that he would start the homeward journey by the next train. "No, they are not, young man, and won't be for another week, you go and help my whips in the kennel!" During his stay he learnt much from the old huntsman which was very useful to him in after-life, for John Walker was hard to beat at his calling. But to get back to our day's hunting and its misfortunes from which we have somewhat digressed: Will Goodall, the first whip, got his horse so fast in a ditch near Jericho Wood that he had to be dragged out by a farm team, and the second whip's horse was so dead beat that he had to be left the night at Foston. No one was left to help Frank home with the hounds at night except Cooper, the ex-huntsman, who was out on a pony.

The best day of the season was February 15th, from Croxton Park, and a capital scent enabled hounds to race a fox to the left of Wymondham past Woodwell Head, straight through Gunby Gorse to Morcary Wood on Cottesmore domains. A few fields from the Great North Road hounds were close to their fox, and it looked fifty to one on a kill. So sure was Mr. Henry Custance, the famous jockey, blazing along on his favourite horse Doctor, that he said to Gillard, "Give me the brush, will you?" "Oh, dear, I wish you had not asked me," replied Frank, "for now we shall not kill him!" "Oh, but they can't help doing so, he's crawling about just in front of them," argued Custance. "It's bad luck to ask for a brush before it comes to hand," replied Frank. So it proved on this occasion; a fresh fox jumped up in the huge forest, and led hounds out past Mickley Wood, to the east corner of Witham. Instead of entering the covert the cunning old customer ran along the outside, and crossing the Great North Road by North Witham, hounds were brought to slow hunting, but working it out with great perseverance, reached Gunby Warren and effected a kill. The run lasted upwards of three hours, the distance was not less than fifteen miles, and no one rode more consistently than the late Duke.

A very fast dart, for which the beautiful Belvoir are so famous, happened from Ingoldsby Wood with a straight-necked February fox. Taking the line of coverts Boothby Little Wood, Humby and Ropsley Rise, he crossed the Bridge-end Road, ran past Welby, and they pulled him down in the open near to Gipple, after racing for thirty-five minutes, distance seven miles. Five couple of hounds, with Benefit leading, got away in front of the others, and the pace throughout was so great that they were never caught.

March 15th was made memorable by the presence of H.R.H. the Prince of Wales on a visit to Sir Frederick Johnstone at Melton Mowbray. The choicest coverts of the Belvoir were reserved for the occasion, namely, Coston and Newman's Gorse, but, alas! the ground was hard as iron and there was a total absence of scent! On the Pytchley side the same morning the ground lay four inches deep in snow, but the Duke's territory, on the contrary, was a foot deep in dust, and in spite of Gillard's untiring efforts no sport resulted. Amongst a large and distinguished field out to meet the Prince were Colonel Kingscote, Master of the Horse, Colonel Ellis, equerry, Mr. Knollys, private secretary, Sir Frederick Johnstone, Lord Grey de Wilton, Mr. Gilmour, Messrs. Behrens, Captain Boyce, Mr. Henry Chaplin, Mr. Ernest Chaplin, Captain Coventry, Lord Calthorpe, Colonel Forester, Major Paynter, Captain the Hon. Henry Molyneux, Captain Riddell, Captain Barclay, Captain King, Captain Pennell Elmhirst, and Mr. Chapman.

The season's sport was much hindered by weather with hard going at the commencement and finish. There was a long stop for frost, and the cold was so intense that twenty-six degrees were registered in the Belvoir gardens on the last day of the year. The number of hunting days was 116, the number of foxes killed 140, and 48 marked to ground.

FORRARD AWAY.

CHAPTER IV

Seasons 1871-72 and 1872-73

The Hunt Stud—The Mare that taught Mr. James Hutchinson—Jumping Gates—The Hunters Black Charley and Culverthorpe—Old Tom Chambers—Mr. Ferrand—Sir Thomas Whichcote's Stud—A Visit from Mr. Chaworth Musters—A Morning's Cubbing in Flood with Mr. Algernon Turner only—The Belvoir catch a Blankney run Fox, and two Opinions about it—Colonel the Hon. H. H. Forester—H.R.H. the Prince of Wales at Croxton Park—H.R.H. clears a prostrate Farmer—H.R.H. apologises—A wet Day in Lincolnshire—A good Day and Mr. George Drummond—Frank Beers from the Grafton—The Hound Grafton Silence.

"MY stud of horses for five days a week was ten or twelve, and the Duke was never very particular to a horse or two," said Gillard, as he revived the memory of many an equine acquaintance. "I was a nice weight, eleven stone three pounds, and amongst my lot were some of the best I ever rode, for we were capitally mounted. Five of those that I had at this time were bought for the Duke; they all came from

Mr. 'Bob' Chapman of Cheltenham, and the figure was always the same, £350 apiece. During the seven seasons that I was whip to these hounds we were only allowed one horse a day, and we had to arrange with one another that whoever got away with hounds in the morning had to go on up to the huntsman through the run, the one left behind bringing on the tail hounds. It was a hard day's work for one horse, but it is astonishing what a well-bred one can do, and we liked it better than did Lord Henry Bentinck's servants, who were over-horsed with three or four a day at about 300 guineas apiece. The Burton Hunt horses were so full fresh that the men could not ride them to turn hounds quickly, and they gave them more falls than did our slaves. Goodall the first whip was allowed two, and he was a hard bruising horseman. One of those that he rode was a chestnut mare, bought of Mr. Bedford, the Grantham tanner, and I always say that she taught Mr. James Hutchinson to ride. His father before him, tall in build, with snow-white hair, was a splendid man across country. I remember him jumping a very wide brook by Garthorpe, and the singular point about it was that I never saw this place jumped by any one else except his son James some years later, when riding the particular chestnut mare we were speaking about. Hounds swam over the brook, and you may always be sure it is a big place when you see them swim, and as I turned to the left for the ford I saw Mr. James Hutchinson sail down to it and get well over, exactly where his father had it, of which fact he was in ignorance until I told him. On another occasion he gave me a lead on this mare over a locked gate near Folkingham, so we knew something about her, you see, when she was brought to carry the first whip. She finished her career breaking her back in a wide brook near Folkingham. Talking of jumping gates, that seems to have gone quite out of fashion, yet at one time of day there were plenty who never thought of stopping to open one. I have seen the late Duke of Rutland, when hounds were running, take half-a-dozen gates in succession. As a matter of fact, a hunter had to be a good timber-jumper in those days, when ox-rails were more general in Leicestershire and the big bullock pastures of Lincolnshire."

The cubbing time was a good one with a scent most mornings, so that hounds were out thirty-seven times, accounted for fifty-six foxes, besides marking fourteen to ground. Amongst the good days this season that of January 3rd stands out for mention, lending itself for narrative. Melton Spinney supplied the fox, who ran with a point for Brentingby Spinney, where a shepherd cur joined in chase and nearly spoilt the run. From Goadby Gorse it was a regular race of thirty minutes to the kill in Croxton Park, and out of the large field Sir Frederick Johnstone was certainly the foremost. With the evening fox from Freeby Wood hounds ran by Saxby nearly to Woodwell Head, where they were stopped by darkness after running well for fifty minutes. There were lots of falls and tired horses, but the pride of place belonged to

Lord Wilton, who was first from find to finish. Although there was a sharp frost in the morning, scent was very good in spite of the ploughs carrying. "I rode Culverthorpe and Black Charley," Gillard records, "and both carried me well, especially the latter, who, when he got to Woodwell Head, had lots of gallop left in him." Black Charley was a very stout horse and great jumper. He was bought for the Duke's own riding from Mr. Chapman, but was a bit too gay, for which reason he was passed on to me. Culverthorpe was a good-looking chestnut, ridden by Cooper the huntsman, and in those days when whipper-in to him, I had to hunt the hounds on several occasions when he was laid up, and old Tom Chambers was the only one to turn hounds. It was poor old Tom's fixed rule never to jump a fence under any pretence whatever, so I had pretty well to run the whole show, but was singularly lucky, as it happened to be a very good scenting season. On one of these particular occasions, when I was riding Culverthorpe, we found a fox in Nightingale Gorse and ran him hard to Burton Plantation, where he had to surrender his brush. Just by the Flowerpot Inn, at the Burton cross-roads, hounds sighted a fresh fox running heel way, and immediately gave chase. We had just jumped into the road, but having no whipper-in, I turned old Culverthorpe short back over the fence, extended him for two fields and got to their heads, lifted them back on the line of the hunted fox, and killed him handsomely. A great friend of the Duke's, old Mr.

Ferrand, noticed the incident, and congratulated me on what he considered a very smart performance. This old gentleman used to stable his stud of hunters at the inn at Belvoir, and as he was often away for weeks together, Lord John Manners, the present Duke of Rutland, used to ride them when he liked, and very well he went to hounds in those days. In the field old Mr. Ferrand was quite a character, very jolly and noisy, singing out, 'Forrard, forrard!' as he rode along at the tail of the hunt, quite oblivious of the fact that there were no hounds in his immediate neighbourhood to cheer along. However, it was one of his fond illusions that every hound in the pack knew him, and many a time was he chaffed by the Duke and his friends when he accompanied them to the kennel."

The Lincolnshire breed of foxes have always been noted for their stoutness, and we find a great day's sport recorded on January 16th from King's Gorse by Culverthorpe, hounds travelling at a good fair pace over the ten lordships of Culverthorpe, Oseby, Haydour, Dembleby, Aunsby, Scott Willoughby, Newton, Osbournby, Threekingham, and Folkingham, where they killed him near the big gorse after a run of one hour and forty minutes. Again, when hounds met at Haverholme Priory, five-and-twenty miles distant from kennels, and every mile of the journey done by road, they started a stout fox from Eveden Wood, and killed him by Swarby after a splendid gallop. Sir Thomas Whichcote certainly had the best of it all the way, and told Gillard afterwards that it was the best gallop he had seen since Goosey's days. The squire of Aswarby rode the best of cattle, all being big bang-tailed horses as nearly thoroughbred as possible, looking as if they were cast in the same mould. Old Tom Wincup was the stud groom at Aswarby, and he was most successful in the art of conditioning hunters, so that there were few studs to equal that of Sir Thomas Whichcote's in excellence, and many of their portraits from the brush of the elder Ferneley are to be seen hanging on the walls of the dining-room at the Hall to this day.

During the month of March, when the hours of sunlight lengthen out, the opportunity is generally taken by strangers from a distance to enjoy a hunt with a neighbouring pack. Amongst those who came to enjoy a good day's sport from Cottam Thorns and the Normanton coverts were Mr. George Fitzwilliam and his huntsman George Carter, also Mr. Chaworth Musters, who was able to congratulate Frank on a good performance after an old dog fox who led the pack for one hour and fifty minutes before he was caught. Just at this time the famous master of the South Notts was out of harness, which enabled him to have a day or two with the Belvoir, and on these occasions he always put up with Frank, discussing many a good day's sport with him. To be in the service of four excellent masters does not fall to the lot of many in a lifetime, but Frank Gillard is one of those who can own to this, and perhaps illustrates the old adage that "A good master makes a good servant."

Bullard

The last day of hunting this season was April 12th, and the game was played out, for the weather was hot, the ground hard, and scent nil. The number of days hounds went out was 134, being stopped 16 days for frost, accounting for 110 foxes, marking 61 to ground.

Season 1872-73

A very early start from kennels was always the rule on cub-hunting mornings, to reach the outlying coverts perhaps twenty miles distant. The stablemen were up before cock-crow, and the crack of a whip under the huntsman's window about 3 A.M. was the signal for all in the kennels to be astir. On the morning of October 21st the outlook must have been most uninviting, for after a time of drought the flood-gates of heaven had opened, and rain fell in torrents from 1 A.M. to 2 P.M. Fair weather or foul hounds always kept their appointment, and by 6 A.M. twenty-nine and a half couple were rousing the echoes in Sherbrooke's covert. Half the country was under water in the vicinity of the covert, so quickly had the floods risen, but a litter of cubs were set afoot, and after a hunt lasting one hour, a nose was secured for the kennel board. The next find was in Hose Gorse, from which covert an old fox with the pack close after him was set going, running over the Canal Bridge nearly to Kaye Wood, where he turned by Harby, coming back by Piper Hole Gorse and Goadby Bullimore to Melton Spinney. The whereabouts of the

Melton brook was completely hidden by the flood in the low-lying meadows, and the hunt staff, who were only mounted on hacks, had the greatest difficulty to keep the pack in view. Fortunately hounds turned on the line of a fresh fox, swimming back over the Melton brook and were promptly stopped. The field out on this desperate wet morning was certainly a select one, the only other horseman beside the hunt staff being Mr. Algernon Turnor of Stoke.

The opening meet on the 1st of November was at Leadenham House, and, unfortunately, a fox possessed with the spirit of mischief led the pack for a mile up the railway towards Caythorpe, where they met an express when running hard. All but one hound, Durable, turned, and she was cut to pieces by the express. As extra trains were running for Lincoln races, the scene was promptly changed to the heath country.

On November 11th, after meeting at Staunton, the pack viewed a fox going into Cottam Thorns, and it was one the Blankney hounds had run from Coddington Plantation. The Belvoir promptly took up the chase, ran him out by Elton, and killed in the open by the road-side between Staunton and Cottam. On being told that another fox had been seen running into Cottam Thorns a return was made to that covert, which was found full of Mr. Chaplin's hounds, who had run in, only to find it tenantless, and to hear that the Belvoir had made a meal of their fox. A deputy master acted on this occasion for Mr.

Chaplin, with Harry Horton as huntsman; and directly he met Gillard in the central ride he tried to pull him by the leg: "It's all right, Frank, we've killed our fox after a rattling good gallop!" "Yes," replied Gillard, "he looked very stiff, but your hounds have not killed him." "Well, we soon shall, for they have just marked him to ground in the covert," went on the master, determined not to be bested. "I'm afraid they won't do that," replied Gillard, "for there is only one earth in the covert, that's artificial and stopped safe enough. I'm afraid you've made a mistake and been running some of those old hares, for we killed your fox stiff as a stake half an hour ago."

In a good gallop during December the Melton brook was crossed, and Colonel the Hon. H. H. Forester, one of the fathers of the hunt, went in for total immersion. He was known to his intimate friends as "the Lad" on account of his sprightly appearance, and over a country was hard to beat, though somewhat handicapped by wearing glasses. Especially is this the case in foggy or wet weather when it is almost impossible to see at all with the glasses dimmed by mist, and on one occasion the Colonel set his horse at an unjumpable fence, which he refused in the last stride, much to the surprise of the rider.

The visit of the Prince of Wales to Belvoir as the guest of the Duke of Rutland makes this season a memorable one, for he enjoyed three days' sport with hounds on the Leicestershire and Lincolnshire side of the country. On March 5th an enormous field of over five hundred horsemen assembled at Croxton Park to give His Royal Highness a befitting welcome, so glad were they

H.R.H. THE PRINCE OF WALES INSPECTS THE BELVOIR.

to see him honour the fair pastures of Leicestershire with his footprints, and before the visit was completed he commemorated the occasion by planting some gorse for a future fox covert near to Baggrave. The meet was by the old ruin known as Croxton Park, the remains of what was once a residence or sporting lodge of the Rutland family, the habitable portion of which now shelters the widow of poor old Will Goodall. Very punctually to time the party from the Castle rode up with the Prince of Wales, amongst them being Lord George Manners, the Earl of Wilton, Lord Calthorpe, Mr. Parker Gilmour, Mr. Henry Chaplin, M.P. To the regret of every one, the noble master, the Duke of Rutland, was prevented from appearing in the saddle owing to an attack of gout. The elder school of sportsmen were represented by Lord Wilton, Mr. Parker Gilmour, Lord Scarborough, Colonel Forester, Mr. Micklethwaite, Mr. Sherbrook, Mr. Hardy, the Rev. T. Heathcote, and Mr. Westley Richards. Amongst the younger men fifty might have been picked out in a run to show the way to an ambitious stranger, Lord Grey de Wilton, Sir Frederick Johnstone, Captain T. Boyce, Major Tempest, the Hon. H. H. Molyneux, Lord Carrington, Mr. H. Chaplin, and a host of top sawyers, including a strong detachment from Mr. Tailby's hunt with the noted rough-rider of that day, Dick Webster. Nor must we forget the large body of those who don the yeoman's mixture, who, though seldom allowed to retain second season hunters, are generally there or thereabouts when hounds run. At the head of these we must place Mr. Burbidge of Thorpe, Mr. Wood of Market Overton, and Mr. William Pinder of Barrowby. Such is a sample of the large body of sportsmen who welcomed the Prince, and with them he chatted pleasantly for half an hour before hounds threw off. These special days so often turn out badly for sport, which is frequently marred by the crowd, and on this occasion the sun was hot, scent was a vanishing quantity, foxes ran short, and the crowd was everywhere. The find was in Freeby Wood; hounds then rattled their fox by Brentingby, crossed the Melton brook, and turned into a nice country, a line for Goadby village, where fresh foxes jumping up spoilt all chance of an orthodox finish. By the afternoon the day clouded down, and a good gallop resulted from Coston covert, hounds racing hard for Woodwell Head, bowling their fox over in the open by Edmonthorpe, and Gillard had the honour of presenting the brush to the royal stranger. The horse ridden by the Prince was a superb chestnut, and carried him right up to hounds over a stiff line of country, in spite of a large thrusting crowd, and the difficulties caused by one or two self-constituted pilots. At one fence a farmer took a fall just in front of the Prince, who, unable to check his horse, cleared the prostrate form, but he immediately pulled up, and riding back to the fallen horseman expressed his regret. To this day the incident is remembered and appreciated by sportsmen who love fair play, for selfish indifference is too often, we fear, characteristic of a hard-riding Leicestershire field, whom Whyte Melville described as "fierce as hawks, jealous as women." On the following day the Prince met hounds and a large field at Newton Bar to sample the Lincolnshire side of the country. Unfortunately the weather was bad, and got worse as the day advanced. A fox found in Folkingham big gorse led hounds over one of the worst lines of deep plough country across to Heckington, so that His Royal Highness abandoned the chase, and went to lunch at Aswarby Hall with Sir Thomas Whichcote.

A singular and terrible accident happened on one of the latter days of March, when hounds were hunting a fox in Belton Park. A blinding snowstorm came on, and while Mr. Clark Cole of Fulbeck was facing it, his horse jumped on one side to avoid coming into collision with a tree, pitched his rider against the trunk, killing him on the spot.

One of the best days of the season resulted from Bottesford on a good scenting morning at the end of March. The find was in Normanton Little Covert, and hounds ran hard nearly to the Debdales, crossed the Great Northern Railway and the river Devon by Mussons Gorse, running through Shipman's Plantation to Woolsthorpe Wharf, where they pulled him down after a blazing forty minutes. "I never saw hounds run a fox harder," was the remark Frank set down against the day, "and he turned short several times, but they were able to turn equally short on his line." A great run followed in the afternoon, lasting till darkness set in, and only Mr. George Drummond was left of the large field of the morning. This keen sportsman, who had a fine stud of hunters stabled at Grantham, was cousin to the Duke; he was full of ride, and hard to beat over a country. When hacking home at night with hounds, which was often his wont, he would say, "Well, Frank, who has had the most falls to-day, you or I?"

A hard day's sport with a fox round Melton put a finish to the season, and only wanted blood to make it excellent. The weather was very hot, and at six o'clock the pack came to a full stop by Welby Holt, with only Mr. A. V. Pryor and the Hon. H. H. Molyneux left out to help Gillard with the pack into Melton, for both the whippers-in were left behind looking up missing hounds. On this day Frank Beers, the huntsman from the Grafton, was out on a hack to watch hounds in their work, and buy some of the draft. The Grafton kennel dipped very freely into the Belvoir blood, paying as much as £80 for a single hound. About this time the crack of that kennel was Silence—the name was enough to hang him—by Statesman out of Garland, and he proved one of the finest sires the Grafton ever produced, and had a numerous family, over one hundred couple.

Taking all things into consideration it was a good season of 186 days, with only 11 days' stop for frost. The number of kills was 98, and 57 were marked to ground.

VENGEANCE, BY GAMEBOY—VANITY.

CHAPTER V

Seasons 1873-74 and 1874-75

Sir Francis Grant, P.R.A., in the Field and at Work—Leicestershire Sport compared with Lincolnshire Sport—Will Goodall, junr.—Sir Frederick Johnstone and Mr. "Chicken" Hartopp—Hunters Tom Day and Lady Grey—Lord Wilton leads the Field—William Blakesborough, Whip—Death of Lord George Manners—Mr. Richard Norman and Lord Forester—The Empress of Austria has a Morning's Cub-hunting—Her Beagles in Austria—Thirty-eight Days' stop for Frost—Red-Letter Days afterwards—A Fall taken by Captain Riddell—Lord Wilton and Lord Grey de Wilton at Timber.

ONE of those who hunted from Melton at this period was Sir Francis Grant, President of the Royal Academy, considered the handsomest man that rode to the three packs in his day. Related to the Duke of Rutland by marriage with Miss Norman, he was a constant visitor at Belvoir, spending many an hour on the flags with Gillard. Perhaps of all the pictures and portraits he painted, none is more widely known than that of the "Melton Hunt Breakfast," a hunting picture which vies in interest with Mr. Ferneley's scene at Barkby. Doubtless it was a labour of love for the artist himself, who though a heavy weight, and by no means lucky in horse-dealing transactions, was seldom far from the finish of a good thing, and at times pounded the field. On many occasions Gillard sat as model, when Sir Francis was painting a large picture of a kill with hounds, and it was generally agreed that the central figure of a fat huntsman holding the fox above his head spoilt the contour of the group, he was therefore painted out, and Frank went day after day to Melton to stand as model for the new figure. "A great honour to have been chosen as the subject for the brush of so distinguished a painter!" we suggested. "It was terrible hard work holding up that fox, I can tell you; by Jove it was an awful bore, and I should not like to have to do it again!" replied Gillard, shaking his head. Sir Francis Grant was just as fond of shooting as he was of hunting, and very often walking about some coverts the Duke had given him, on more than one occasion omitting to stop the earths when hounds were expected, so that the huntsman was compelled to write rather strongly on the subject. In reply he sent a pencil drawing of himself mounted on an old pony, riding out at the dead of night with a spade under his arm and a lantern tied to his stirrup iron. Written underneath was, "Is this the sort of thing you want me to do?"

The best sport this season appears to have been on the Lincolnshire side of the country, and somewhat indifferent in Leicestershire owing to short-running foxes. So good an authority as Brooksby has said, when summing up the merits of the two sides of his Grace's kingdom, "Real sport—and nothing but the sport—being the primary object, we are inclined to concede that such is more likely of attainment on the Lincolnshire than the Leicestershire side of the Belvoir country. For in the former division the ground is, at least here and there, equally favourable; the hounds are the same, while the foxes are undoubtedly better. In the one you have a local field of reasonable dimensions and less ardent aspirations; in the latter you have a swollen field, a jealous—no, let us say, a zealous crowd." When hounds visited the Caythorpe Plantations and Reeves Gorse on the extreme northern Lincolnshire boundary they found them alive with foxes. On the line of a good old dog they led the way over a country from the Beacon Plantation to Normanton hilltop, where they turned on to the heath land by Sparrow Gorse, bowling him over in the middle of a large grass field near Rauceby High Wood, after making a nine-mile point. Again, on November 19th, after meeting at Croxton Park, a good gallop resulted from Newman's Gorse, hounds going away close at the brush of their fox. Past Freeby village and Thorpe Arnold, with a sharp turn to Brentingby Wood, the time was thirty minutes, and all the way hounds were a field or two ahead of the hard-riding division. Without dwelling long in Brentingby Wood he led the way back at a reduced pace by Freeby to the starting-point, where they rolled him over. Altogether the run lasted 50 minutes, and the distance was 8 miles.

Will Goodall, the first whip, was one of the hardest that ever crossed a saddle, and as keen as mustard for sport; he would go from morning to night without taking bite or sup. Gillard would often remonstrate with him on the folly of doing so, but could never persuade him to carry a flask or food, as he always declared that he never felt the need of it, and had so strong a constitution that he could fast with impunity. Alas, poor fellow! he tried himself too high in his attempts to keep weight down, and in all probability sowed the seeds of the fatal disease that cut him off in the prime of life. On one occasion, when returning home at dusk with hounds after a very hard day, he pulled an armful of peas from a stack, shelling them as he went, being ravenous, nor would he stop in spite of warnings. The consequence was he was seriously ill afterwards, and laid up in the kennel for several days. On December 6, after meeting at Stoke Rochford, a great gallop is recorded with an outlyer into the heart of the Cottesmore country. After passing Burton Coggles he turned for Lobthorpe, took a direct line for Morkary Wood, over a stiff bit of desolate grass country. Disdaining shelter, he crossed the North road and turned straight for Greetham, which was reached in one hour and forty minutes. Several foxes were afoot, but sticking well to the line of the hunted one, they followed him on through Woolfox Plantation, and ended up by marking to ground in Exton Park, near to the keeper's house. The distance hounds ran as measured on the map was 22 miles.

One of the best known of the Melton division was Sir Frederick Johnstone of Westerhall, who with his brother did more skylarking than anybody, except Mr. "Chicken" Hartopp. But the Johnstones should be good horsemen, for the crest of the family suggests life in the saddle, being a winged spur with the motto, "Nunquam non paratus." It is said to have originated from the lady of the house serving up a clean spur on a dish when the last bullock was killed—a hint to spur over the border and fetch more from Cumberland or Westmoreland. A convivial spirit with Lord Waterford, Sir Frederick was always full of ride, and ready for a good thing with Belvoir, Quorn, or Cottesmore. When looking through the locker of his memory Gillard brought to light the following story, going back to the days when he carried the horn for the Quorn:—"We were sailing away with a breast-high scent across those great bullock pastures by Asfordby, and all the timber was up. I was riding one of my best horses, Tom Day, a wonderful fencer, and we cleared a wide place with an ox-rail on the far side, and I think it was one of the biggest I ever jumped! Sir Frederick Johnstone was close up, banging along over all those big fences, and as he followed on, I looked round, for I knew he had got something to do. His horse caught the single rail as he landed, sending it flying through the air right back over the head of his rider. He rode up afterwards to me and said, 'I shall buy your horse and the gray mare Lady Grey when Mr. Musters sells the Quorn horses at the end of the season.' I must tell you Lady Grey was a flyer every one wanted to buy, and on one memorable occasion she carried me in a clinking gallop. We found our fox at John o' Gaunt, and crossed the Twyford brook on the south-east side of the station, made a seven-mile point, and only rode over one field of plough, pulling our fox down on the hillside by Dalby Hall. Lord Wilton led the field all the way; we jumped the last fence side by side and saw hounds race into their fox; he said, 'Frank, that is the best gallop I ever saw,' and he had seen a few in his time! Well, I must tell you that as I set the gray mare's head for the Twyford brook, Henry Custance, who was riding on my left hand, shouted out, 'It won't do, Frank, it won't do!' However, I did get over, though it was a wide place, and I don't know what became of him, for the pace was too good to inquire. When the hunt horses were sold, Tom Day did not make a very high figure, for he had a game leg, but it did not make much odds to him, for he threw it away as soon as he set going, and I think he was one of the best horses to gallop on through the deep that I ever sat on. Unfortunately Lady Grey got pricked with a fork in the elbow-joint two days before the sale, and joint oil starting to run, Mr. Musters had her destroyed. Sir Frederick Johnstone told me afterwards that a thousand would not have stopped him from buying her."

Frost visited us in February, but the first day out we had a quick thing from Clawson Thorns to Piper Hole Gorse. Ascending the hill to this covert took the wind out of our horses, but when we reached the table-land we were able to keep the pack in view, racing all the way to Knipton, where they marked to ground after a regular burst of forty minutes. It being but a small earth, we dug, and two others besides were found lying up at the end of it. The first was given a start, and hounds ran hard to Croxton Banks, where they unfortunately changed; but on hearing that one of the other foxes was still in hand, we had him turned down, and a regular race of fifteen minutes resulted, until he saved his brush by getting to ground.

A mad dog was destroyed at Leadenham, so the district was given a wide berth by hounds in consequence, and the fixture changed during February to Haverholme. It was on this day that the afternoon fox from Newton Wood gave a splendid gallop by Scot Willoughby, Osbournby hill-top, Aswarby, nearly to the Thorns. With the pack close at him he doubled back to Osbournby, and was rolled over after going racing pace for thirty-five minutes. Hounds were a field ahead all the way, and those nearest to them were Sir Thomas

Whichcote, Major W. Longstaffe, and Mr. John Hardy.

On March 21st, with the evening fox from Melton Spinney, one of those fast spins occurred for which the Belvoir are so famous. After crossing the Melton brook close to the town, they ran at a great pace to Thorpe and Scalford, where there was a welcome check, for the pace had been a cracker. Following on to Waltham, it had to be given up, for there was no more daylight. Those who stayed to the finish were Major Tempest, Captain King, Mr. Chaplin of Brooksby, and his brother Mr. William. "We only wanted blood to have made it a first-rate day," was Gillard's verdict.

The number of hunting days this season was 188, including cubbing, and 105 foxes were killed.

Season 1874-75

A change in the staff this season was caused through Will Goodall being offered the Pytchley horn by Earl Spencer, and in his place came William Blakesborough, who had turned hounds seven seasons for Lord Eglinton. He remained but one season at Belvoir, and then went to hunt Lord Middleton's hounds.

The rider of the pale horse was very busy this season, and made many gaps in the ranks of the veterans; before the year had run its course the hunt deplored the loss of Lord George Manners, Mr. Richard Norman, and Lord Forester. For

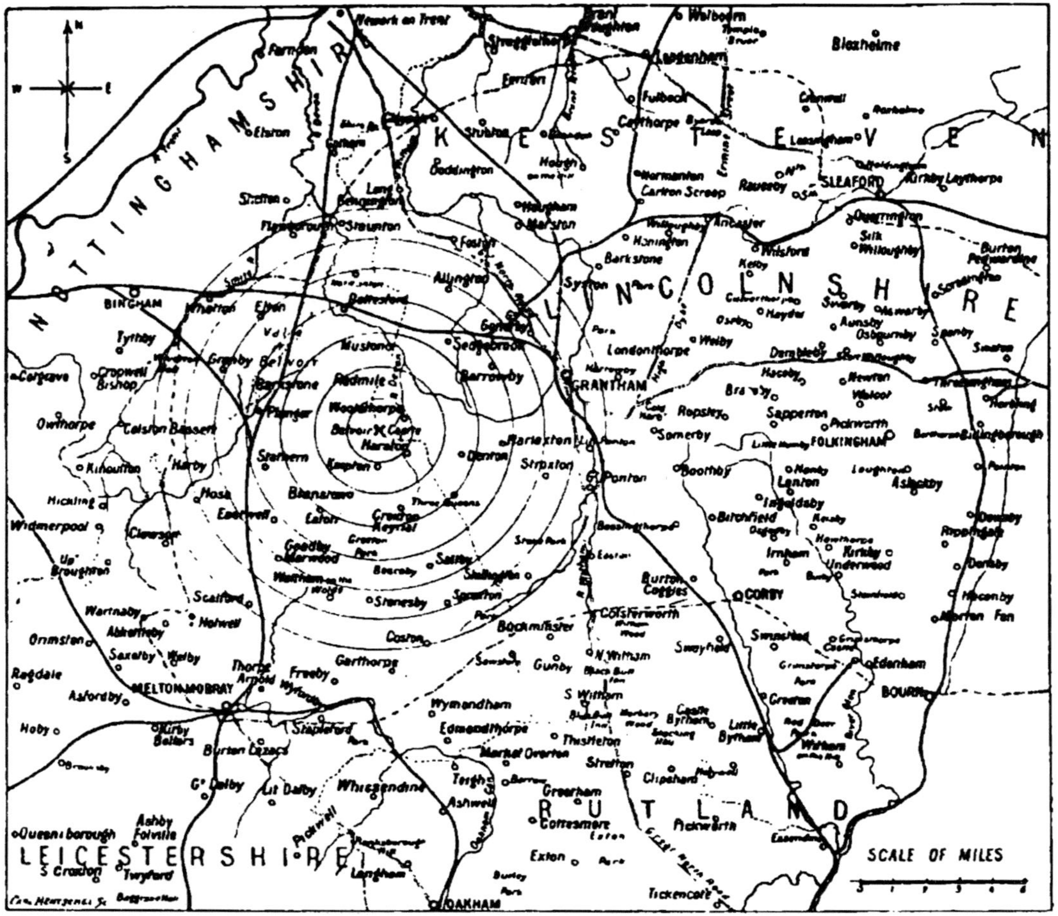
NOTTINGHAMSHIRE
KESTEVEN
LINCOLNSHIRE
LEICESTERSHIRE
RUTLAND
Newark on Trent
BINGHAM
GRANTHAM
SLEAFORD
FOLKINGHAM
MELTON MOWBRAY
OAKHAM
CORBY
Belvoir Castle
Knipton
Harston
Denton
Barrowby
Bottesford
Colsterworth
Ancaster
Woolsthorpe
Redmile
Croxton Kerrial
Long Bennington
SCALE OF MILES

THE NEW YORK
PUBLIC LIBRARY

ASTOR, LENOX AND
TILDEN FOUNDATIONS
R   L

twenty-seven seasons did the Right Hon. John George Weld, 2nd Lord Forester, rule over the Belvoir, acting as a warming-pan between the masterships of two Dukes of Rutland, retiring in 1857. His mastership dated back to the palmy days of fox-hunting; he was the very centre of a brilliant group of sportsmen, and most impatient of the presence in the field of town-bred sportsmen. Lord Forester rode out all his time, and towards the last had to be helped into the saddle, but once in it he could go with the best. No man ever had a better innings at hunting, for he dropped into the mastership of the best pack at a most favourable period, held it for an unusual length of time, and made the most of it. The hunting spirit has run high among the Foresters for centuries, and he was one of the last of the old school of aristocrats of whom Thackeray's Esmonds were a type. On his marriage with Lady Melbourne, widow of the Hon. Frederic Lamb, created Lord Beauvale, he was presented by the Belvoir Hunt with a splendid piece of plate, representing a fox in a tree, with figures of the leading members of the hunt grouped round, an incident which occurred in Croxton Park, 1851, also depicted by Sir Francis Grant, R.A. On the reverse side were the names of the subscribers—the Duke of Rutland, Marquis of Granby, Earl Winchilsea, Lord John Manners, Lord George Manners, Lord Willoughby de Eresby, Lady Marion Alford, Right Hon. R. A. C. Nisbet Hamilton, Sir. J. C. Thorold, Sir T. Whichcote, Sir M. J. Cholmeley, Sir Glynne Earle Welby, Sir

H. Bromley, Sir R. G. H. Clarges, General Reeve, General Mildmay Fane, Colonel J. Reeve, Colonel H. Fane, Colonel P. Dundas, Rev. Thomas Heathcote, Mr. John Litchford, Mr. A. Wilton, M.P., Mr. W. E. Norton, and twenty-eight others.

One morning at the end of September, during the cub-hunting season, Gillard received a mysterious wire asking him to change the fixture from the Lincolnshire side of the county to nearer Melton. After much wire-pulling it turned out to be no less illustrious personage than the Empress of Austria, and of course a royal request amounted to a command, so the meet was changed from Boothby to Three Queens at 8 A.M. The Empress duly arrived with her suite of four gentlemen and a lady, having chartered a special train from London to Melton that morning. This was the first occasion that the Empress of Austria enjoyed a day's hunting in England, and after looking about for a house in Leicestershire without being successful in her search, she betook herself to Cheshire. On her morning's cub-hunting with the Belvoir she wore a tall hat and rode a good-looking bay hunter, a present from the late Lord Dudley, who was said to have given a long figure for him. The Empress remarked, after casting a very critical glance over the pack of twenty-three and a half couple, "Why, you have all lady hounds out this morning!" This was a fact, but an exception to the rule which was for a few small dog hounds to always run with the lady pack, and Gillard was surprised that it was noted so quickly.

Amongst the Empress's suite was Count Botazzi, who had hunted from Melton before, and came for the express purpose of piloting her Majesty; however, he declined the honour at the last moment, saying that he was indifferently mounted, and did not know the country well, requesting Frank to do so, warning him to mind where he led, for the Empress was sure to follow. The morning's sport was a good one, for after finding in Herring's Gorse, a nice spin resulted by Saltby to Hungerton, where the pack were beaten by scent. With the second fox from Sproxton Gorse they ran hard over the heath-land country to Denton, where they pulled him down after a nice spin of twenty-five minutes. The Empress rode in workmanlike style, being greatly delighted when she saw the fox rolled over and was presented with the brush. After the hunt she returned to kennels, inspected all the hounds, expressed a wish to see the hunt horses, gardens, and Castle—in fact, did all the sights of Belvoir before realising that she was ready for luncheon after so strong a morning's exertion. As the Duke of Rutland was away from Belvoir, Frank and Mrs. Gillard entertained the Empress and her suite in their parlour. To answer all her questions about the sporting pictures and hunting trophies which adorned the walls was quite a pleasure, and while doing so her host attempted to open a bottle of soda water for his royal guest. Alas, it is never safe to do two things at once! the result being the cork flew out sooner than was expected, and to Frank's horror the Empress of Austria was saturated with the contents of the bottle. However, she good-naturedly laughed heartily at the accident, and so did all her suite. On her return to Austria she commissioned Gillard to buy a pack of beagles, the best that money could find. It took a whole summer to execute the commission, and a lawsuit was only just missed with a wild Irishman who insisted on sending a lot of red lurcher terriers. At last twelve couple of twelve-inch beagles were found, bright with Belvoir tan, and smart as new sixpences. Before sending them away they were hunted, and good to follow was their beautiful cry, Frank Gillard, Junr., taking them over, being entertained right royally during a week's stay in Austria. The Empress, delighted with her new purchase, found a good hare for them and started a hunt. Very quickly they outdistanced the field who were on foot, at the finish the Empress being the only one left going, and she threw aside first one garment, then another, until in her enthusiasm to keep them in sight she landed in the middle of a drain. Ponies had to be procured to catch the runaway pack, and they were never used again as foot beagles, being much too fast.

The opening day of the season was delayed on account of the hard state of the going, and hounds stopped hunting in the middle for thirty-eight days of frost. After the break up, a big day occurred on January 6th from Piper Hole Gorse, a good fox facing the river Smite as bold as a lion. Hounds went away close at his brush and pressed him so hard that he ran nearly in a straight line to Widmerpool Inn, which was reached in forty-five minutes without a check. After heading through Kinoulton Gorse he endeavoured to reach the main earths at Owthorpe borders, but these were fortunately stopped, so he turned away, struggling gamely on to Cotgrave Gorse, and though it looked fifty to one on the chances of a kill, the friendly shades of night threw her pall over the scene, allowing a right good fox to live to run another day. The distance hounds ran was not less than 13 miles, and it was a very severe day for horses, many of the Melton men having to leave theirs out all night in the Widmerpool country.

Another red-letter day of this season was on January 16th, when a fox was started from Burton Sleighs, the neutral covert on the borders of the Cottesmore country. The line was by Easton, past Swayfield Wood, through Mickley Wood, over Witham Common. The pack raced for fifteen minutes as if they were sighting their fox, but, unfortunately, by Witham they changed on to the line of a fresh one, who led the way by Holywell, the pace being so good that tired horses were to be seen standing like landmarks all over the face of the country. Although the hunted one was viewed 50 yards in front of hounds, he just managed to crawl into Grimsthorpe Park, where he beat them, spoiling a fine hunting run that only wanted blood to crown it.

All through January and February the pack

ran hard and straight day after day, accounting for their foxes in capital style. Amongst these good things was the fast spin of thirty-five minutes from Elton Manor, ending with a kill in the open; and again from Leadenham, when hounds were running for two hours from fox to fox, being stopped at dark with all the horses reduced to a trot. A fine run of one hour and thirty-five minutes occurred from Nightingale Gorse, ending with a kill in the middle of Syston Park. The first forty-five minutes of this gallop were accomplished without a check. On February 13th, from Stoke, hounds had a very hard day, running incessantly for six hours, and at last three and a half couple slipped away, ran their fox into Grantham town, where he was captured by some boys, but died before hounds could get hold of him. Great sport was supplied from Goadby Gorse with a fox who led the way at a terrific pace in the direction of Melton Spinney, changing his course for Stonesby Ashes, ending with a mark to ground in Buckminster Park. Foremost of a large field was Major W. Longstaffe, mounted on one of Mr. George Drummond's stud. Captain Riddell, Mr. Samuda, Colonel the Hon. H. H. Forester, Captain the Hon. H. H. Molyneux, and Mr. Corbett Hollands. There were few more ardent followers of hounds than Captain Riddell, the gallant ex-officer of Lancers and most accomplished horseman. Gillard tells a story of how on one occasion in a good run the field got pounded, until Captain Riddell saw a gate in the corner which he soon had off its hinges, letting him into a cattle-pen surrounded by five-foot timber baulks. The straw in the yard made the run at it as springy as a feather bed, so that, hard man as the gallant officer was, his judgment prompted him to turn away from the fence. Just as he pulled his horse round, old Lord Wilton crossed his bows, and lifted his horse in splendid fashion out of the crew-yard over the rails. This was too much for Captain Riddell, and he attempted to follow the lead, his horse breasting the top rail, turning a complete somersault on to the top of his rider. The landing was on a rough cart track, and those who saw it made sure the rider was crushed to death under his horse, but to their surprise both sprang up and set going again at once. The old Lord Wilton could top over strong timber in a marvellous way, and his son Lord de Grey was nearly as good.

The number of hunting days this season was 128, the number of foxes killed 125, and 43 marked to ground.

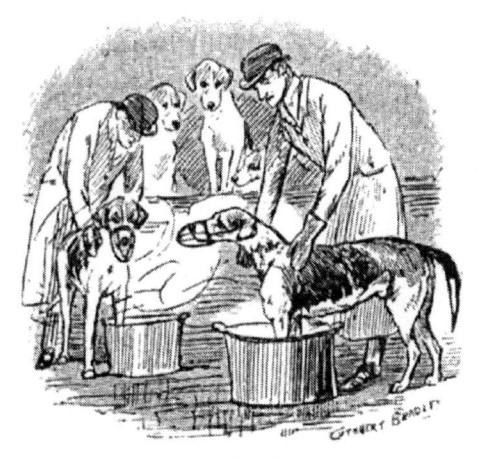

AFTER THE DAY'S WORK.

CHAPTER VI

SEASON 1875-76

Belvoir Blood and Competition—"Gillard's Compound"—Alfred Orbell Whipper-in—Gillard's Opinion on digging out Foxes—The Rev. "Billy" Newcome of Boothby and Mr. Banker Hardy of Grantham the last Home—A Run in the Fens piloted by Mr. F. Smith—Lenton Church Spire—Cuthbert Bede's Pen—Peck, the second Whipper-in, has an awkward Experience—Mr. Micklethwaite on Sport and Marriage—The Gray Horse Sluggard—Retrenchment and Subscription from the Lincolnshire Side—Fox killed in a Brewing Tub at Sleaford—Mr. Tom Oliver—A good Day in Leicestershire, and Miss Miles in the Field and on Paper.

THE FOX ON THE KENNEL.

AN annual puppy show in the summer is adopted by most kennels throughout the kingdom, but the old order at Belvoir was never to enter into competition on their own flags, or those of Peterborough. Occupying the premier position by general consent, the Duke's kennel had no occasion to contest. Yet at Peterborough the beautiful Belvoir blood won the ribbands for other packs who had dipped into it, and many a time have we seen cheery Frank's face lit up with a smile as he watched the hounds of his own breeding catch the judge's eye. There was no doubt that the Senator strain was the most fashionable blood at this time, winning this summer at the Alexandra Palace Foxhound Show for both the Quorn and Brocklesby kennels.

As many as one hundred couple of puppies were sent out to walk every season from Belvoir, many going to the tenants on the Derbyshire estate as well as Leicestershire and Lincolnshire. A good start in life was insured for each puppy sent out from kennel, a label bearing his name and pedigree accompanying him, together with two bottles of medicine for distemper and jaundice, with full instructions when to use it, and a small gilt spoon in which to measure the same. Consequently the mortality amongst puppies was reduced to a minimum, and the fame of "the Gillard compounds" for distemper is to-day known world wide.

This season Alfred Orbell was promoted to the position of first whipper-in, a duty which he performed with great credit, being quick to turn hounds, and a nice weight, 9 stone 7 lbs. The cubbing time was one of the best on record, especially during October, when several nice preliminary gallops with stout cubs in the open resulted. During the second and third weeks of September, when the weather was so hot and dry, the Belvoir woods afforded excellent schooling ground for the young entry, so that in forty-three mornings' work thirty-three brace were offered up on the altar of learning.

When a discussion was raised on the question of digging out foxes, we drew Gillard on the subject. "No one hates it more than I do," he replied. "I should say that after November 1st in each year, for the last twenty years, not more than a brace in a season have been dug out. In the cubbing season, however, when foxes go to ground like rabbits morning after morning, it is ruinous to a pack of hounds; but to help them to get a fox out not only makes them keen in their work, and steady from riot, but it thus teaches them to mark their fox to ground. In the regular hunting season, for various reasons best known to the master and the huntsman, it is sometimes necessary to dig. Depend upon it, after a fox beats hounds by going to ground, he will follow up his cunning, and if one hole is stopped he will find another. I should, therefore, with the help of a terrier, or by other means, bolt him from drains and such like places."

The season was remarkable for wet and windy weather, hunting being stopped ten days in December, ten days in January, and three in February. Of good days' sport recorded, that of November 12th, from Kirkby Underwood, resulted in two fair gallops over an excellent woodland grass country. The day was a hard one for horses, both whips being left behind to hunt up missing hounds, and the distance back to kennels was not less than 20 miles as the crow flies. "It was a pity we had not more daylight to have enabled us to kill our fox," Gillard remarks against the day, "for it looked fifty to one on our doing so had we not been compelled to whip off in the big woods, and I never saw hounds so glued to a scent or so determined not to be stopped. Mr. John Hardy, the Rev. W. C. Newcome, and Major W. Longstaffe acted as my whippers-in, helping me to get hounds back to Grantham, where the van was awaiting us." No day was too long for the veteran Mr. "Banker" Hardy, who was one of the mainstays of the hunt; he kept a stud of good hunters at Grantham, rode them hard, and enjoyed the sport thoroughly. His great friend was the Rev. "Billy" Newcome, and the two were very often the last to bid the huntsmen good-night, for they never thought of going home until hounds did. Mr. Newcome was a well-known figure with the Belvoir hounds for half a century, being all that time Rector of Boothby. After hounds he was a fearless rider, possessed of iron nerves, though not a finished horseman; he frequently went pounding along with a slack rein, and at different periods of his career came in for some serious crumplers. A contemporary of Sir Thomas Whichcote at Eton, he was born the same year, 1813, and passed away in the winter of 1896.

A run down into the fen country when it rides deep is always a stiff day's work, and on December 28th, after meeting at Rauceby Hall, a great gallop resulted from Summers Plantation to Howell, two or three miles below Haverholme. Darkness stopped hounds at the finish, but the line they ran could not have been less than 20 miles, the distance back to Belvoir was 30 miles, so that the hunt horses put two days' work into one on this occasion. The big fen-land drains are quite unjumpable, and Frank tells how he trusted himself to the pilotage of a fen-land farmer, Mr. Fred Smith, who, when he came to a single plank bridge, dismounted and ran over, swimming his fen-bred horse across the drain. Quick as thought, the huntsman had his horse in the stream at the same time, and with the lead got him the right side; but Mr. Joseph Wilders, who delayed to follow, got his horse stuck, and it looked at one time as though he would have to leave him there. The fox was killed by a solitary, outlying cottage, where lived a man blessed with twelve children, and they had never before seen a foxhound or scarlet coat, being quite out of civilisation.

On December 29th a good gallop of an hour and fifteen minutes was enjoyed from Hose Gorse, over the vale straight from Sherbrooke's Gorse, crossing the Smite, running by Hickling and Kinoulton through Kaye Wood to ground in a tunnel under the road by Hose Lodge. For a ring this was a first-rate performance, and all over a charming country, which for fencing is warranted to satisfy the biggest glutton that ever crossed a saddle.

The spire of Lenton church on the hill has

The Brocklesby Rallywood.

come into the landscape background of many a famous run, besides being the steeple for the annual hunt chases. When it was restored by the Rev. Thomas Heathcote in 1875, he asked the Duke of Rutland for a subscription. "Why should I subscribe to a church that is not on my property?" asked the noble master of the Belvoir hounds. "Because it is such a good landmark when your hounds run," replied the fox-hunting vicar; and the Duke promptly sent £5 towards the restoration of the spire. At Mr. Heathcote's death in 1883, the Earl of Ancaster, patron of the living of Lenton, presented it to my father the Rev. E. Bradley, better known as Cuthbert Bede, author of *Verdant Green*, and though not a follower of the chase, his pen contributed many a note on hunting lore and Belvoir Hunt history. Under the shadow of Lenton church spire hounds met the last day of the year, and started a fine fox from Heathcote's covert, running a fast ring to ground by the Folkingham rifle butts. The second gallop was from the Little Gorse, and proved a fast forty minutes over a charming hunting country, ending with blood. The first point was for the Big Gorse and Walcott village; then swinging round through Heathcote's covert, he went straight away past Laughton to a drain below Dowesby willow-bed on the edge of the fens. A terrier to bolt him was procured from Mr. Tom Casswell of Pointon, that well-known sportsman and distinguished agriculturist, who was brought up in the Southwold country, where more farmers have entered to sport than in any other county in England. A large dog-fox he proved to be when pushed out by the terrier, and a stout one too, for hounds had raced from find to finish. Those nearest to the pack were Sir John Thorold and his two brothers, Captain Cecil Thorold and Major Charles Thorold, also Mr. Beaumont of Irnham. Amongst the farmer division, Mr. James Hoyes of Hanby was most prominent, and he was tremendous over a country, though seldom mounted on a second season hunter.

New Year's Day was spent in the saddle, and the ground was terribly deep after a heavy rain. The scene was in Leicestershire, and hounds whipped off in darkness near Hose with no one left to help Gillard home, till he met his second whipper-in Peck, near Harby. At the end of three seasons' service with the Belvoir, Peck left to become huntsman to Count Larish's pack in Bohemia. An awkward experience once happened to him when riding a hack home from Grantham in the dark after a very long day's hunting. It was in the days of toll-bars, and when stopping to pay at Denton his hack was so fidgety that he got down to count his change by the light of the lamp. An over-officious limb of the law lying in wait for a chance to distinguish himself sprang out of the darkness, seized the hack, and told Peck that he was drunk. The whipper-in was so offended at the base insinuation that, without further ado, he went for the policeman and blacked both his eyes. The end of it was the handcuffs were forced on to poor Peck, and he was marched back to the lock-up in Grantham, red coat, top-boots, and all. He had the sympathy of all who knew him, and it was some little satisfaction to know he had punished the policeman, though he made himself amenable to the law by doing so.

A brilliant gallop of fifty minutes came off from Aswarby Thorns on January 25th, hounds racing over the park, forward by Swarby and Aunsby, through Dembleby Thorns, Nightingale Gorse, and Haceby coverts, straight as a rocket. On the far side of Sapperton Wood, near to Pickworth village, the leading hounds were but a few yards behind their fox, and a kill looked a certainty. Directly this good fox found the pack so close at his brush, he turned sharp down wind, and immediately all trace of scent vanished. Those who held good places in the run were Sir Thomas Whichcote, Major Longstaffe, Mr. John Welby, Mr. John Hardy, and Mr. F. Searson. Amongst the school of old sportsmen who were to the fore at this period was Mr. Micklethwaite, who had rooms at Grantham, over White's the saddler. The old gentleman was quite a character, wearing a red flannel jacket over his scarlet coat, and nearly always riding a roarer. It was his custom never to go first at a fence except every one else was pounded, and it was a case of in or over. If he got the right side he would wait to see how they followed on, enjoying the fun. There was no occasion to read the newspaper when Mr. Micklethwaite came out hunting, for he was always full of the news, and proclaimed it in a loud voice, so that half the field might know what he was talking about. Starting life in the navy, it had always been his ambition to hunt five days a week in Leicestershire if riches would allow, and the wherewithal coming to him in middle life, he carried out his wish after retiring from the service. His seat on a horse was a very loose one, and he summed up his enjoyment by the number of falls he took. "Capital day's sport, took five falls, and enjoyed myself thoroughly!" was often a remark he would make to Gillard as he shogged home with him at dusk. On one occasion his friend, Mr. "Banker" Hardy, said to him, "Micklethwaite, did you see how well Captain 'Doggy' Smith jumped that gate?" "Where, where, tell me which gate," said the old gentleman, keen as mustard, as he turned his horse back and sent him at the gate indicated, with the result he cut every bar out of it. He once said to Gillard, "My friends say that I ought to get married, what do you think about it, Frank?" "Well, sir, to speak from my experience of ten years of married life, I think it is the best thing that can happen to a man!" "Well, Frank! you see you've probably got a wife who can sew your shirt buttons on for you, or, for all I know, can make a shirt. Now, if I married, it would be to some fine lady who would want to spend £50 on some Bond Street milliner's finery, and then where would my hunting be? No, Frank, I am better single!" The stories told about this cheery old sportsman and his doings are many, and one of his cracking falls made him go light-headed for a time, that when he got back to London, he shocked his many friends by jumping out of a window. He turned up again at covert side all right next season, and said, "Frank, I made one of the biggest jumps I ever made in my life this summer, three stories high! I don't suppose I was right in my head, it ought to have killed me, but it did not!"

February as usual this season brought its quantum of good sport, and on the 2nd hounds ran a fox very hard from Croxton to Easton Park, where he beat the pack by scaling the wall after making three attempts, falling back twice. The web-like foot of a fox enables him to take hold of a wall and get over a high one where a hound cannot follow.

Frank had an interesting recollection of a favourite gray horse Sluggard, who carried him well for eleven seasons, and only gave one fall. When a four-year-old the horse belonged to a small farmer, who was often three sheets in the wind, and used to hunt twice a week, jumping over every mortal thing, no matter whether hounds ran or not. The horse's tail had never been pulled or squared, and he lived in a crew-yard where a besom and duck-pond constituted all the grooming he ever got. "I wish you would buy that horse to carry me, Mr. Musters," Gillard often said to his master; but Mr. Musters's reply was always, "I don't know what the deuce you will want me to buy you next, Frank!" When the Borough Hill chases came off at the end of the season, Sluggard was entered in the Farmer's race, which he won easily, and then that good sportsman Mr. Brewster of Denton bought him, but could only get second in one or two chases. At last when Gillard returned to Belvoir he got Sluggard into the hunt stable. The only fall he gave in eleven seasons was by Wymondham in a good gallop, and Frank always said it was his fault, not that of the horse. Finding the crowd were rather too close to his heels when riding him at a wide open gully, he changed his purpose, and asked him at the last moment to jump some stiff timber at the side. The result was Sluggard came end over end, and in the melee his bridle slipped off; Lord Aylesford followed, and seeing that the huntsman had a damaged shoulder and could not raise his arm, he caught the horse for him and got his bridle on. Sluggard was a tricky horse to ride until you knew him, for he threw his head up and down as he approached a fence, but was safe as London when left to it. On one occasion when Blakesborough, the first whip, rode him, he turned up at the end of the day with two fearful black eyes where the horse had hit him with his head.

A succession of bad seasons for agriculture caused the shoe to begin to pinch all those whose income was derived from land, and the expense of hunting a pack of hounds five days a week over such an enormous extent of country became too great a burden even for the noble owner of Belvoir.

When talking the matter over the Duke suggested, as a means of retrenching, to hunt four instead of five days a week. This proposal Gillard begged should not be entertained, preferring rather to hunt six days a week as long as he had breath in his body to do so. "But, Frank," said the Duke in his usual kind way, "you must remember that we all get older!" A rough estimate of the cost of hunting the Lincolnshire side of the country was drawn up, and a meeting of gentlemen took place at Belton Park with Lord Brownlow in the chair on February 22nd to consider the matter. A subscription of £1500 a year was immediately forthcoming to meet the expenses of the poultry and damage fund, with the proviso that Gillard was not to be interfered with, and all responsibility rested with him when the Duke was not in the field. The hunt then continued the even tenor of its way to the day of the Duke's death.

A curious finish to a smart gallop occurred with the evening fox on Leap year day this season. The find was in Sir John Thorold's plantation, and hounds fairly raced, leaving Cranwell to the right, turning to Holdingham covert away to Sleaford, where they killed in Miss Peacock's brewing-tub after a capital twenty-five minutes. When crossing the valley below Cranwell, the horse Gillard was riding swerved from some sheep-trays, and jumping at the netting, got completely wound up in it, rolling over, smothering his rider in the most tenacious clay, so that it was necessary to be well scraped before he regained the free use of his limbs. When Miss Peacock's garden was reached at Sleaford, Frank was on foot helping hounds to discover the whereabouts of their fox, which had vanished amongst the out-buildings. Hearing muffled sounds and a great splashing, he found Dutiful worrying the fox single-handed in the brewing-copper. One of the horses ridden by the huntsman on this day was a five-year-old bay mare Primrose, the property of Mr. Tom Oliver of Walcott, a pair of fifteen stone blood ones, own brother and sister, bred by him, being on price to the Duke for £700. However, the deal did not come off, and the horses subsequently went for a much lower figure elsewhere. In those days Mr. Oliver was flourishing; for they were the prosperous days of farming, and he had a stable full; even to-day, in spite of hard times, the spirit of the chase is not quenched within him, for he is to be seen on foot following the hounds, leading a couple of varmint-looking terriers ready for any emergency.

Towards the end of the season, when hounds were running in Belvoir woods, a vixen was viewed carrying a cub in her mouth, and the pack were promptly stopped. On another occasion a hunted fox was seen by Gillard to sit down and extract a thorn from his foot, as if he cared nothing for danger; but instances of vulpine cunning are so numerous and well known.

The season's sport concluded with a good day in Leicestershire, April 12th, which we reproduce from Frank's own diary. "Owing to a heavy snowstorm we failed to do any good with our morning fox, but at five o'clock a good one was set going from Bescaby Oaks. First he took a turn over Croxton Park, then away past Sproxton Thorns and through Coston Covert. Up to this point the pace was very severe, though the field kept pegging along, and after getting clear of the last-named covert, hounds raced past Wymondham, bearing to the left for Woodwell Head. At Coston Covert and Sproxton Thorns I lifted the pack forward on to the line of our fox as he left the covert, and so lost no time, but Woodwell Head being a bigger covert, I had to let them carry the line through. This they did without dwelling there, and by the time we galloped to the south end, the pack were streaming away towards Cottesmore Gorse, just skirting it as they ran round by Teigh, and killed near Edmondthorpe in the dry canal. It was after seven o'clock when we killed, and the distance as the crow flies from Croxton Park to Cottesmore Gorse is ten miles. The mask was presented, instead of the brush, which was a poor one, to Miss Miles, who went well on one of the Duke's horses. Those who were up at the finish were Major Longstaffe, Mr. John Hardy, Mr. Turner Farley, Mr. James Hutchinson, Captain King, and the Rev. J. Mirehouse. All the horses were beat, and a call was made at Mr. Pochin's house for gruel." The next day the Duke had a description of the run written by Miss Miles which pleased him very much, especially as she described Gillard taking a

86 HUNTING REMINISCENCES

cropper at a blind fence, and he had forgotten to admit it.

The number of hunting days this season was 189, and the foxes killed 131, with 61 marks to ground after November 1st.

HUNTING THE LINE.

CHAPTER VII

Season 1876-77

John Bull's Top-boots—Catching a Lamb-stealer—Thomas, Earl of Wilton, Social Whip to the Quorn—Turkish Bath for Hunters—Mr. Little Gilmour, Prince of the Heavies—Sir George Wombwell—The Messrs. Behrens—The Butcher in Blue—The Hound Weathergage entered—Belvoir and Brocklesby Entries—Will Goodall and Rallywood in 1850—Distinguishing Points of the Belvoir Pack—Weathergage's Pedigree—Mr. Burbidge of Thorpe and his Fox Covert—A Kill in Staunton Churchyard—Lord John Manners across Country—Sir Beaumont and Lady Florence Dixie—Major Whyte Melville—Captain Pennell Elmhirst—Melton Spinney—The longest Run of the Season—Lord Carrington—The best Day of the Season—The Horse Melon—Presentation of Plate to the Sixth Duke of Rutland, and his Speech.

SWEPT OVER EVERYTHING IN CHASE.

TWENTY-SIX seasons is no considerable period when marking the flight of time, yet in the history of a pack of hounds it gives a record of many changes in the way we live and conduct our sport. When Gillard commenced to hunt the Belvoir hounds, a fine old generation of sportsmen were passing away, and the present fathers of the hunt were winning their spurs over the fields of Leicestershire. The fashion then with the sturdy yeomen of his Grace's kingdom was to walk about in high boots with brown tops from one week's end to the other, in the same way that the typical John Bull is represented to us to-day. Two of the last of this race were Mr. Wood of Market Overton and Mr. John Ashbourne who lived near Croxton, both first-class sportsmen. Gillard tells a story of the latter at the time he whipped-in to Cooper. It was the spring of the year, and Mr. Ashbourne asked the Duke of Rutland and Lord Forester to look inside his barn to see a long string of lambs hanging up. "Well, what has happened to them?" asked Lord Forester. "I only want to show you, my lord, what a good time the foxes have had, not to complain about it!" replied Mr. Ashbourne. "Don't be too sure that it is our foxes!" went on Lord Forester. "Draw a waggon into your field to-night and watch with your men. If a fox comes—shoot, for a lamb-stealing fox ought not to live. Shoot him or whatever comes!" The plan was carried out that night; the marauder appeared at the lamb's pen, the shepherd fired, and was much surprised to find that he had killed no fox, but his own thieving dog.

The leader at Melton was Thomas, Earl of Wilton, one of the last of the old school of aristocrats; and Egerton Lodge, the abode of hospitality when once the threshold was passed, was by no means an easy place to get the entrée. No one could have filled the post of social whip to a subscription pack like the Quorn as did the old Earl, who successfully steered the hunt through troublesome times. Lord Wilton kept a large stud of hunters, and was the first to introduce the Turkish bath in his stables, which is considered advantageous for conditioning hunters. Then there was Mr. Little Gilmour, as cheery and full of spirits as a schoolboy home for his holidays. He was a great favourite at Melton as well as at Belvoir, and nobody worshipped him more than his stud groom, old Charley Wells, who used to swear by him and his contemporary Sir George Wombwell. The Prince of the Heavies, as Mr. Little Gilmour was called, if we give full credit for the extent to which he was handicapped by weight, surpassed either Sir Francis Grant or Lord Wilton. These were both large-framed, heavy men, but Gilmour could give either of them a couple of stone at least, and was always superbly mounted. The Messrs. Behrens stabled forty horses, so Melton was full. A well-known character of the Melton Hunt was Morris "the butcher in blue," mounted on an old hunter, going gallantly across country, thereby winning all the custom from the hunting division.

The most favoured sires among the stud hounds this season were Whynot—1870—in his eighth season, a wonderfully good son of Senator—1862—and Woeful by Wonder—Susan. His shoulders were perfection and his wise gray face full of intelligence. The seven-year-old Royal, son of the younger Rallywood, the light-faced Admiral and Albion in their fifth season, the four-year-old Barrister and two-year-old Rockwood, were all good ones who left the mark of high lineage in many a subsequent entry. Saffron in his seventh season was the most favoured of the Senator race, though the six-year-old Firebrand, by the same sire, from Frolic, and his brother Brusher, were in great favour. Three and a half couple among the best of the hounds in their first season were by Saffron and also many beautiful whelps. Warrior—1879—by Wonder was the sire of nine and a half couple in the pack this season. Of all the sires, however, none were so generally admired as Fallible—1873—a three-year-old son of Milton Furrier and Prophetess. His bright black tan coat, supple, muscular limbs, clean shoulders, deep, full chest and ribs, and shapely head, showed true foxhound style in every line. In later years, possibly, the Fitzwilliam got a bit too coarse and big for the Duke's hounds, but Fallible proved an exception, for he was as near foxhound perfection as possible, and he proved of the greatest use to Belvoir. His reputation would have been lasting if it had ended when he got Stainless—1881—a hound said to be incomparable by Mr. Chaworth Musters. He certainly was a beautiful hound, his colour, neck, shoulders, and general contour being so perfect. Stainless did good service for his own kennel as well as the Cottesmore, and in his seventh season was much damaged from being ridden over.

This season, in the entry of 16½ couple was the famous Weathergage by Warrior the son of Wonder, and his dam was Royalty, by Rambler, son of Senator. In Gillard's opinion Weathergage was the best hound in every part of a run he ever saw, and he combined nose, drive, tongue, and devilry in breaking up a fox, which he transmitted to all his get. Weathergage was not a taking-looking hound, being flat-sided and three-cornered in appearance. His ribs were deep and his neck was short; so mean did he look, that Gillard treated him as the ugly duckling of the pack. "I did not breed from him at first; but when I saw what beautiful stock he got in other kennels—for he never sired anything so mean-looking as himself, I started to get a kennel full of the sort." His voice was beautiful—he had only to speak and the whole pack would fly to him, trusting it. It is quite different when a bad hound speaks, the rest know; they only cock one ear as much as to say "You fool and babbler!" Weathergage always seemed to know which way to cast, and carrying a line down a road he was unsurpassed. He did this on the last time he ever hunted, enabling the pack to kill their fox handsomely.

The Belvoir always crossed well with the Brocklesby and *vice versa;* three couple out of seventeen, Lord Yarborough's entry this season, were by Belvoir sires. If all the strains belonging to these two great kennels could in any way be summed up, it would be found that a vast amount of hunting in this country is indirectly indebted to them. Numerous kennels have been entirely formed from Belvoir and Brocklesby drafts, or by the kind privilege allowed to sportsmen by the Dukes of Rutland and the Earls of Yarborough in the services of stallion hounds. It is not too much to say that these kennels are of national importance to masters of foxhounds generally, therefore the condition of the great packs and how the entries have been made up each successive season, must be a source of great interest. Such entries as they always were too! with Belvoir walking a hundred couple of puppies a year, and Brocklesby nearly the same number, whilst from this prodigious choice just seventeen couple was the selected few that each kennel put on.

The standard of 23 inches, to which Will Goodall reduced the pack on his accession to power, has been maintained, and the work, breeding, and beauty of Lord Yarborough's Rallywood, who came to Belvoir in 1850 when an old hound, has been transmitted to his present descendants. Will Goodall said of him: "This is a most beautiful short-legged dog, exceedingly light of bone, but with beautiful legs and feet; he was considered by the late Will Smith to be one of the best-bred hounds in the Brocklesby kennels. Rosebud, his dam, worked until she was ten years old, and was never known to do anything wrong—was perfection in her work, and everlasting." Brocklesby Rallywood's age did not prevent Goodall from sending fifty-three couple of puppies by him out to walk the next season. It has always been admitted that to Rallywood, Belvoir owes greatly the staunch and staying qualities of its hounds. "The Druid" tells us that, "when he died, in 1853, twelve years old, he was buried in the centre of a flower-bed in Will Goodall's garden, and a red currant tree now blooms over his remains." His blood is diffused through every fashionable foxhound pack in England, and portraits of him by the elder Ferneley hang in the smoke-room at Belvoir Castle, and the Rev. Cecil Legard's home at Cottesbrooke, Northamptonshire.

The wonderful evenness of appearance is quite unapproached in any other kennel, for a Belvoir hound is a marvel of beauty and putting together. It was always a matter of comment and admiration when strangers viewed the pack at covert side, to see their sheen of coat and polished appearance, groomed as they were like thoro-breds. Gillard's kennel management has never been surpassed, and gives colour to the story that any hound seen making his own toilet by scratching himself in public, was instantly drafted to the provinces.

Amongst the days of note this season was the run from Burbidge's Covert on November 8th, and amongst those to see it drawn was its faithful custodian Mr. Burbidge of Thorpe. This good sportsman rode out his title as "father of the hunt" on less than half-a-dozen mounts, he was tall and thin with white hair, never rode more than nine stone, and was the beau-ideal of a light weight. He will always be remembered as the owner of a famous gray whose doings in the field have been commemorated in verse by Tom Markland. The veteran was consulted by the Duke on matters connected with the chase; and when the nearest vulpine stronghold to Melton was planted, it was called Burbidge's Covert, with sufficient reason too, for he tended it, overcame difficulties arising from the floods, and did all he could to make it a sure find. Hounds left with a point for Burton Lazars and Great Dalby, crossed the steeplechase course, and ran their fox to ground at Twyford. This was a good hunting run of one hour, scent was never very good, but hounds made the best of it. Old Warrior and his son Wellington, with Patience and Finder, distinguished themselves in maintaining the line, for the fox ran 50 or 100 yards on every road he crossed.

On December 4th from Belvoir a good hunting run resulted, the find was at Muston Gorse, and hounds ran a bee line by Debdale's Covert, Allington, and Bennington to within a field of Cotham Thorns, where he turned and was killed in the porch of Staunton Church. The parson, Mr. Staunton, was a hunting man, and quickly on the scene when the fox was brought out into the roadway for the final ceremony. On this day Lord John Manners, subsequently seventh Duke of Rutland, went wonderfully well, although the going was terribly deep. It was a rare scenting day, and though the run was all the way on plough, hounds raced as if it had been grass. The distance from Muston Gorse to Cotham Thorns is 8 miles, 14 as hounds ran, and the time just over two hours.

WEATHERGAGE, BY WARRIOR—ROYALTY, 1876.

Facing page 94.

THE NEW YORK
PUBLIC LIBRARY

ASTOR, LENOX AND
TILDEN FOUNDATIONS

A note of regret stands against the day's sport of December 6th, when Gillard had the misfortune to stub his good horse Brilliant, and though lame, he jumped the Melton brook. The floods were out and Sir Beaumont and Lady Florence Dixie jumped it well at a very wide place. This was a period before Lady Florence wrote condemning fox-hunting, and there was not a lighter weight or more determined horsewoman in the shires. Her mounts all had to go when she was up, and if they did not know how, she very soon taught them, being able to plant a refractory horse down each shoulder with a hunting-crop better than many men.

The day before Christmas a fall of $13\frac{1}{2}$ inches of snow occurred, but a rapid thaw setting in, there was practically very little delay. In so extensive a kingdom as that hunted by the Duke of Rutland a soft spot could always be found—some locality where the going was possible, for the nature of the soil varies so considerably that frost will not touch the sheltered vales when the upland country may be hard as a road. Gillard knew his ground well, and averaged less days in kennel for a stop than any other huntsman in England. Although snow blocked the fences of Leicestershire, hounds had nothing to hinder their sport over the barren tract of stone-walled country out by Byard's Leap.

Another good day was seen from Goadby, and this time hounds ran from the Bullamore to Harby Hills, where the fox dipped down into the vale running by Long Clawson. Up to this point the pace was first-rate, but after that it was hard work to keep the line to Willoughby, on the Wolds, where they killed this good old fox in the middle of the village, making a good finish to a fine run of one hour and thirty-five minutes, distance 13 miles as hounds ran. Those who kept with the pack were Lord Grey de Wilton, Sir Beaumont and Lady Florence Dixie, Mr. John Welby, Mr. A. V. Pryor, Mr. E. Chaplin, Mr. Cecil Samuda, Captain Pennell Elmhirst, and his brother of the pen, Major Whyte Melville. On the long list of those who have seen sport with the Belvoir, no name stands out in bolder relief than that of George Whyte Melville, soldier, novelist, poet, and sportsman, by birth and natural instincts. The two great objects of his life at this time were, as he said of himself, "the pig-skin and the pen"; his days were devoted to hunting, and his evenings to literary work. Happy the man who had George Whyte Melville for his companion on the homeward ride after a day's hunting, and he often came to Gillard at the finish to express his enjoyment at the excellence of the sport.

Amongst coverts that have established a reputation for being a safe draw, Melton Spinney may be reckoned one of the best, and on January 20th it responded well to the call. No doubt the fox roused was the one that had been run on many occasions before, for he pointed as usual for Melton, then wheeled round for Brentingby Spinney and Freeby Wood, going at a rattling pace forward to

Saxby, and they killed him at Thorpe Arnold, close to old Mr. Burbidge's house, after a capital gallop of one hour and seventeen minutes.

The longest run of the season came two days later, when they found in Easton Wood, and went away at speed past Stoke Park, a ring into Witham Wood running hard for quite an hour, getting their fox dead beat. Unfortunately a fresh-found one jumped up in front of the pack and took a line from Burton Sleigh to Lenton village, crossing the brook, through Keisby Wood without a pause, and on to Aslackby village, pointing for the fen country. Here the pack were within fifty yards of him, but a flock of sheep interposed and obliterated scent. The pace to this point was very fast, and tired horses were standing about all along the line. Continuing on past Dowsby, hounds went straight over the fens, and this good fox beat them near the Forty Foot Drain. It was a wonderfully fine run over a splendid line of country, for hounds only passed through one covert from the start, and that was Keisby Wood. The time from leaving Easton was two hours and twenty minutes, the distance as the crow flies is not less than 14 miles.

Another great day on the Leicestershire side came on January 24th, after drawing Coston Gorse, when hounds went streaming away on the line of a good fox towards Garthorpe, passing to the left of Wymondham, running zigzag to Woodwell Head, through this covert and down the hill to Market Overton. Turning for Cottesmore a shepherd dog coursed him, causing a slight check, and the pack divided by Burghley Wood. With the main body Gillard held on to Greetham Wood, where the run ended, for the whipper-in came on with the information that the hunted fox, stiff as a stake, had entered Burghley Wood. This fine run lasted one hour and seventeen minutes, and those to the front all through were Lord Grey de Wilton, Lord Carrington—one of the smartest and best to hounds, who, the following season, became Master of the Cottesmore,—Lord Wolverton, and Mr. Beaumont Lubbock.

The best run of the season, combining pace and distance, was on February 20th, from Colonel Willson's Gorse by Brandon, hounds going over that fine country below Fulbeck and Leadenham to Wellingore Gorse—in the opinion of the late Sir Thomas Whichcote the biggest line to ride in the whole hunt. The river Brant was crossed, and turning by Stragglethorpe, he came back to his starting-point, which was reached in an hour from the time of finding. Too game to stop, this stout-hearted one led the way for Willoughby Gorse, where Gillard viewed him very beat. Struggling on, he nearly reached Syston Park, when the pack fairly raced from scent to view, killing in the open, thus ending a fine hunting run of two hours and forty minutes. The distance hounds ran was nearly 24 miles, and the pace at times was very severe.

Though the Duke passed many a good horse on for Gillard's riding, he would never take one from him, although sometimes rather short of a suitable conveyance. Many a time would Frank say, "Such and such a horse, your Grace, would carry you well!" "Does he suit you, Frank?" the Duke would ask, in his usual kind considerate way; "if so, keep him." One of these mounts was a chestnut short-legged horse, well bred and up to fifteen stone, called Melon, and unfortunately in going through a gateway in a good run this season he got pushed on to the hasp, which tore the flesh on his ribs very considerably. Bad luck marked him down; for no sooner was he better and going strong in a run than he reared up with Gillard and fell dead as a stone by Kettleby. Frank laments his loss in the diary: "He carried me five seasons, and a stouter horse I never rode, coming out as he did twice a week."

The all-important day, which will long be remembered in the annals of the Belvoir Hunt, was April 10th, the occasion of the presentation of plate valued at 2500 guineas to the ducal Master. No fewer than 240 gentlemen and farmers of the Belvoir Hunt subscribed as a token of their esteem, respect, and grateful appreciation of the sport during twenty years so liberally provided for them. The presentation took place in the armoury room at Belvoir Castle, where a very large gathering of sportsmen and ladies dressed for the hunt met the Duke, who wore scarlet. Sir W. E. Welby Gregory, M.P., made the presentation, in the absence of Lord Brownlow, and amongst the large number present were Lord

Scarborough, the Marquis of Bristol, Sir John Thorold, Sir Thomas Whichcote, the Rev. T. Heathcote, Captain Drummond, Mr. John Welby, Mr. Algernon Turner, Sir Hugh Cholmeley, Colonel Reeve, Major Longstaffe, Mr. John Hardy, Mr. James Hornsby, etc.

His Grace, who was deeply touched, rising to reply, said, in a telling speech: "The Belvoir hounds have been in existence as a pack for more than one hundred and fifty years, and I hope that as long as ever the old Castle remains, its woods and vales will continue to re-echo their music. For a successful day's hunting we are mainly indebted to the abilities of the huntsman; and when I consider the names of those who have been huntsmen to this pack—Newman, Shaw, Goosey, Goodall, Cooper, and Gillard—I cannot be astonished that the hounds should be able to show you sport. This is a festive occasion, but even the brightest scenes have their shadows, and it is impossible on an occasion like this not to remember the faces we no longer see, the names of those we have no longer amongst us—Forester, beloved of the hunt, Lichford, Alford, Howson, and many others—who would have been amongst us this day, but that the Giver of all Good has seen fit to call them away. Though they have passed, their spirit still lives to animate and encourage us. Fox-hunting is the noblest, finest, and most unselfish sport in the world. Long may it flourish. It brings all classes together. We all rejoice together at a good run, and regret together over a bad scent. We clear the large fences together, we fall into the brook, and laugh together!"

A splendid luncheon terminated the proceedings; and the remainder of the day was spent in hunting a woodland fox.

The number of hunting days this season was 150, with only 3 days' stop for weather. The number of foxes killed was 110, and 45 were marked to ground.

"A Hunting Morn, I think."

CHAPTER VIII

Season 1877-78

A scratch Pack *v.* a thoro'bred Pack—The Business of the Summer—The blind Master from the Grove—Proof of the Pace of the Belvoir Hounds—Lord Rossmore surprises Mr. Little Gilmour—Nine of the Messrs. Hornsby in one run—The Rector of Colsterworth's Cottesmore Hunt Hat—Frank's Description of a good Hound Day—The Saffron Family as Hounds—The Samuda Pink Wedding—Another good Hound Day, Senator, Saffron and Brusher—The Hound Wellington killed on the Railway—A good Run from Melton Spinney—Lady Florence Dixie presented with the Brush—Story of Captain "Tom" Boyce receiving a Brush and Hunt Button—A good Run and Lady Florence Chaplin presented with a Brush—The Ash Wednesday Run—The Hon. H. H. Molyneux's Collection of Ash Wednesday Masks—The Horse Wing gets in the Smite—The Hose Gorse black Fox rather wide of his Home.

A COTTESMORE HAT.

IT has been seen in England that a scratch pack has never lasted more than a few seasons, and those who have been content to hunt with any sort of hounds have invariably tired of it before they have arrived at middle age. The old hunts and the veteran sportsmen have owed their existence to the celebrity of packs of foxhounds, and the greatest assistance to sport has been the enticing pleasure some people have found in forming packs and breeding hounds.

The interval between one season and the next, it can easily be realised, was no idle time for the head of the Belvoir kennel, and a week or inside of a fortnight at the nearest seaside place, so as to get salted, amounted to the year's holiday. "I was never very happy away from my hounds for long," Frank would say, "and I liked to be within hailing distance, so that I could run down in the day and see how they were getting on." Greatness has to pay its own penalty, and Belvoir of all places was looked to by Masters of hounds as the fountain-head for information. The amount of letter-writing was therefore very considerable, together with the copying out of countless pedigrees, to send to those who desired alliances for the matrons of their own kennels. The number of visiting lady hounds to Belvoir every season amounted to over 300.

Amongst those who came regularly every summer to enjoy a day on the flags with Gillard was an ex-master of the Grove who was stone-blind from the result of an accident in the hunting field. In spite of his affliction he never lost heart, and would ride out on a led horse, saying to Gillard in the most cheery way, "I'm coming to see your hounds, Frank!" No man enjoyed himself more when he was at the kennel, and as each hound was drawn for inspection, he would feel him all over most critically from head to stern, remarking, "Well, Frank, this is a nice hound if he is straight!"

His judgment was very sound, and his remarks interesting to listen to, for he had a most delicate sense of touch, and a good memory for hounds.

Cub-hunting began this season on the last day of August at Willoughby Gorse, ending November 3rd at the Rectory Covert, after 41 mornings' sport, in which 55 cubs were accounted for. "Through September the weather was moist, so we did capitally, but during October scent was bad," is an extract from the huntsman's diary.

A red-letter day was November 14th from Coston Covert, hounds racing with a breast-high scent to Woodwell Head, accomplishing the distance in 12 minutes. Gillard took the time, and so did the Rev. J. Mirehouse of Colsterworth, who was always "a good clocker." The Duke was very pleased when he heard of this brilliant burst, and remarked that it proved the Belvoir hounds were faster than in Goosey's time. The run of the afternoon too was worthy of mention, for hounds got glued to the line of a traveller from Stonesby Gorse, racing past Garthorpe to the Ashes and Freeby, ending up with slow hunting nearly to Brentingby, where darkness came on and all the horses were beat. Those left to see the finish were Lord Rossmore, Captain Candy, Mr. Richard Hornsby, jun., and the Rev. J. Mirehouse. The mention of names calls to mind incidents of the chase. On one occasion in a gallop from Old Hills to Melton, a gate served the leading division, and whilst Mr. Little Gilmour, the king of the heavy weights, was bending down with the crook of his whip under the latch, Lord Rossmore, who was a bruiser, jumped the gate, much to the astonishment of the cheery old gentleman, who in his day could find his way about a strongly-fenced country rather better than most men.

Amongst those who found it possible to have foxes as well as pheasants were Messrs. James, William, and Richard Hornsby, of Grantham, who rented the coverts about Culverthorpe at this period; and though warm disciples of the gun, a blank day in their coverts was unknown. A good story is told of a stranger, at the end of a run, who noticed that out of eleven at the finish, nine bore the name of Hornsby. "I knew they had made the town of Grantham," he said, "but I did not think they made the Belvoir Hunt as well!" Harking back to the Rector of Colsterworth, whose name we mentioned in the famous gallop from Coston Covert to Woodwell Head, we note his head-gear as being the style of hat worn by the Cottesmore Hunt in 1826. A good description is given by Mr. C. T. S. Birch-Reynardson in his pleasant anecdotes of bygone days when he says, "The tall chimney-pot hats had as much nap on them as there is wool on many a Southdown sheep's back. The hat of those days was very unlike the light silk affair that we cover our brains with in these days. But in spite of this the servants of the Cottesmore Hunt preferred them to caps, and were allowed to wear hats, making an excuse that with caps the rain got down their necks."

The incidents of a hound day as recorded in

Gillard's diary are full of interest to the sportsman, and we quote the doings of November 26th. "With the second fox from Normanton Little Covert we ran very fast, first towards Bottesford, then turned and crossed the new railway, and river Devon, going on to Orston Wind Mill, and back again by Staunton right into Bottesford village, where we killed in the street opposite Mr. Norman's house. This was a good fifty-five minutes and a very satisfactory finish, especially as our fox threaded his way through the village, making it very difficult for hounds, as is generally the case when near bricks and mortar. Those hounds that distinguished themselves were old Nero, Spinster, Crusty, Redcap, Rocket, Dauntless, and the Saffron young bitches Sanguine, Spangle, Sorcery, and Starlight. The latter especially pleased me by making hits and driving their foxes when scent served them." Old Nero had a voice that any one might distinguish and remember, there was such a ring with it. Saffron was a hound very much admired, for he was as level as ever you saw one, and his daughters were so good in their work, no day was too long for them! "It was beautiful to have to hunt such hounds," added Frank with a sigh, as he viewed in memory every hound named in the account of the day's sport.

December 12th was the "Melton Pink Wedding Day," the Duke of Rutland arranging for his hounds to meet at the House, Melton Mowbray, the residence of his cousin Colonel Markham, in honour of his daughter's marriage, Miss Cecil Markham, to Mr. Cecil Samuda; the noble master, the members

A Chat with Frank Gillard in Kennel.

THE NEW YORK
PUBLIC LIBRARY

ASTOR, LENOX AND
TILDEN FOUNDATIONS

of the Hunt, and Frank Gillard going to church in scarlet. After the grand ceremony and breakfast were over, a very large field accompanied the pack to Burbidge's Cover, where a fox was found who proved quite equal to the occasion. A crowd of foot-hunters had stationed themselves on the high ground overlooking the cover, but bold reynard swam the river and ran through their very midst. Once clear of them he took a bee line, with the hounds pretty close to his brush, away by Burton Lazars, Berry Gorse, Laxton Spinney, over the Whissendine brook, and passed the village by Ranksboro Gorse and the Punch Bowl, entering Wheat Hill planting. Here there were two or three foxes, but the pack, sticking to their hunted one, ran back by Wild's Lodge to ground near Melton; the time was an hour and fifty-three minutes. To commemorate the happy occasion the bride and bridegroom presented Gillard with a silver hunting-horn, and as they went away from Melton by train they viewed hounds with their fox running from Burbidge's Covert.

A hound day is recorded by Frank on December 17th, after meeting at Scrimshaw Mill as follows: "A good hunting run resulted from the Rectory away past Elton, where we crossed the railway by the Plaster pits. Here a fast train cut through the pack, killing a fine bitch called Novelist, but we ran on by Thorston and the Coronation Covert, marking to ground at Flintham. This was a good straight gallop at a rattling pace, distance as the crow flies from six to seven miles, and it proved a good pipe-opener for the run of the afternoon. A tough customer was set going from Normanton Thorns, and I never knew hounds run harder than they did on this occasion for the space of one hour and ten minutes. The fox was anything but a straight-necked one, the line being, first in the direction of Cotham Thorns over a stiff holding country as any to be found in the Belvoir Hunt. Farther on it was not so sticky for our horses, though I think the fences are a bit bigger as we ran by Foston, Allington, and Gonerby Moor. We hardly reached Barrowby Thorns when a turn westward took us by Sedgebrook away to Allington, but Mr. John Welby's new privet covert had not grown up strong enough to shelter him, so off he went for a tunnel N.E. side of the village. He was, however, soon bolted, and hounds bowled him over, well deserving his blood, which they thoroughly enjoyed after their very hard day. The way the pack worked from morning to night deserved great praise; they seldom required assistance, and every hound, except poor Novelist, was up at the finish. Those which I observed most during the run were Dealer, Rebel, Discord, Garland, Gossamer, Gambler, Partner, Patience, Wilful, Wenlock, Dahlia, Careful, and old Saffron." Turning to the *Field*, under the well-known *nom de plume* of Plantagenet, we read the following: "The Duke of Rutland and Frank Gillard may be congratulated on the appearance of this season's entry on paper, and the outside hunting world must see much in it to approve of, for Jack Morgan says—and I believe many others are of his opinion—that no hounds on earth can beat those with the blood of Senator in them. Turning to the Brocklesby entry we see that Nimrod Long is rather a follower of the same opinion, for he has dipped very freely into the blood. Saffron, a light-faced tan hound, now in his seventh season, is perhaps the most favoured of the Senator race. Though the six-year-old Firebrand, by the same sire, from Frolic, has been much used through the length and breadth of fox-hunting England, and all his progeny are liked. Brusher by Saffron is much like his sire in colour, but with a square and more massive head, his well-knit frame is full of the power that indicates his faculty for driving, and the activity that makes him equal to clearing any fence."

Hunting in the vicinity of a railway was always a source of great anxiety to Gillard, and he tells the story of the death of Wellington from a passing train on the line by Rauceby. It is very seldom that hounds flash straight over the metals, more often casting about, and on this occasion old Wellington went up the line with his nose on the ground, meeting the train. The engine-driver blew his whistle, and the old hound threw up his head as though he had heard a view halloa. The next second the engine killed him, much to Gillard's distress, "for he was such a good hound in his work, one of the most reliable in the pack; his voice being husky, you could always distinguish him from the rest. He spoke to fox and nothing else, so it was always safe to cheer when he was heard."

The New Year brought with it excellent sport, and on January 9th a fine gallop from Melton Spinney is recorded. A fox was immediately set going, crossing the brook in a line for Old Hills, where he turned and recrossed the railway and brook at Scalford. The navvies were at work on the new railway by Newport Lodge, and turned him so that he made his way back to the starting-point and saved his brush by shifting responsibilities on to the shoulders of a friend. It was one of the best runs of the season, and at racing pace for fifty minutes. Out of the large field of the morning very few turned up at the finish, and these were Captain Smith, Mr. John Welby on a 15-hand 3-inch blood horse, Mr. Allcard, Mr. James Hutchinson, and Mrs. Sterling.

A good Leicestershire hunt was scored on January 16th, and one of the field enjoying cross-country work as a holiday was Fred Archer, staying at Melton. The afternoon fox led the way from Coston Covert by Stonesby, hounds travelling very fast down to the brook below Waltham to within a field of Goadby Gorse, where he turned and recrossed the brook back again to Waltham. "I stopped them there," Frank records, "for I had lost both my whippers-in, and the only one left to see the finish was Mr. Micklethwaite, who had gone well all through and taken his regulation number of falls. Mr. 'Banker' Hardy also came up, and these two very kindly helped me back with hounds to kennels in the dark."

A great gallop of two hours and fifteen minutes from Goadby Gorse occurred on January 23rd with a brush at the end of it. Hounds ran fast past Waltham Rectory to Bescaby Oaks, through it without dwelling, and on by Saltby over the heath to Skillington. Here a point was made for Buckminster, ending with a kill in the open near to Stainby. The distance hounds ran was about sixteen miles, and nine as the crow flies from Goadby Gorse to where they killed. The brush was presented to Lady Florence Dixie, who had gone remarkably well, and the hunt numbered no more ardent follower. No day's sport was too long for Lady Florence, and she would come at the end of the afternoon with the request, "Now, Gillard, you will draw once again, won't you?" "I can tell you," added Frank, as he narrated the story to us, "I did not want any coaxing if there was a fox covert anywhere within reach! and as to daylight, we did not always take that into consideration if there was any light from the moon."

Leicestershire this season seemed to be the favoured side of the country, for again on February 6th a tremendously fast gallop was seen from Coston Covert by way of Wymondham, Garthorpe, Coston, Sproxton, Stonesby, Waltham, to Freeby Wood. Time to this point was forty minutes, with but one slight check by Stonesby village. One good gallop calls to mind the incidents of another, and Gillard harked back in thought to a memorable occasion when he rode whipper-in to these hounds. "We found our fox in Freeby Wood and ran round Stapleford and Whissendine village, a big ring back to our starting-point, giving us the brook to jump twice, finally marking to ground in a turf drain, from which we bolted and killed. I remember how well Captain 'Tom' Boyce went on a good-looking chestnut horse; he was a new-comer from Ireland, and the Duke of Rutland, who was also out and going well, was so delighted that he presented Captain Boyce with the brush and that night also sent him the hunt button!"

On the Lincolnshire side of the Belvoir country, the domains of Rauceby, under the fostering care of that keen sportsman and distinguished soldier, Colonel Mildmay Willson, C.B., have always held the reputation of being one of the best nurseries for foxes in the hunt. As a natural consequence, good runs to instead of from Rauceby oftener result, but February 19th saw a really brilliant gallop from Cliff Hill Covert. The line taken was by Rauceby Thorns away over the heath past Cranwell Lodge and Lord Bristol's Plantation, where hounds fairly ran into their fox a few fields short of California Covert, near Fulbeck. The brush was presented to Lady Florence Chaplin, wife of Mr. Henry Chaplin, M.P., two of the keenest and best across country, and frequent followers of the Belvoir in spite of the attractions of their own pack at Blankney. Amongst the foremost division were Miss Laura

Willson, Lord Brownlow, Sir Thomas Whichcote, Colonel John Reeve, Captain Tennant, Mons. Couturie, Mr. John Hardy, Sir John Thorold, Colonel Charles Parker, and Mr. T. Robarts.

The Belvoir Ash Wednesdays have often been records in the annals of the hunt, and in olden days the meet was always fixed for 12 o'clock by Saltby Church, just when the congregation were coming out from service. On this particular Ash Wednesday of March 11th, the meet was at Piper Hole, where a very large field were assembled to meet hounds. The wind blew very hard, and a fox from Holwell Mouth cheeked the gale at a rattling pace away over the vale, past the right of Nether Broughton. The bulk of the field were left the up-wind side of Holwell Mouth, having failed to hear hounds leave covert owing to the roar of the wind through the trees. After taking a direct line for Hickling, he wheeled round and ran between the two Broughtons, nearly reaching Old Dalby before he took a right-handed turn over the hill, after which he headed away in a straight line for Willoughby on the Wolds, where they killed him close to the village. The time was one hour after leaving Holwell Mouth, and there were plenty of applicants for a piece of this good Ash Wednesday fox when hounds broke him up. Over the chimney-piece of the comfortable hunting-box Sanham House near Melton, a brace or more of grinning foxes' masks killed with the Belvoir on Ash Wednesday, and labelled as such, are the pride of their owner the Hon. H. H. Molyneux.

A similar run in 1867 from Clawson Thorns over the same line of country, with a kill at Willoughby, is on record for the Ash Wednesday of that year.

Of the horses Gillard rode, he had many a story to tell. "Yes, Wing was a big valuable horse, full of quality and as good a shaped one as ever you saw, but he was not my horse! I never thought him quick enough! He was bought by the Duke from Squire William Wing of Market Overton, hence his name, and he carried me several seasons on the Leicestershire side. I remember on one occasion he put me down, and altogether out of a run, by jumping short at the river Smite. The banks of the river are steep, being rough with the growth of thorns, and Wing in mid-stream showed no inclination to make an effort to get out again. I began to wonder where the deuce I should be, for Tom Chambers with my second horse had gone on with hounds, not knowing that I was left behind. A Leicestershire farmer at last came to my rescue, and at once said, 'My little old mare will pull him out for you!' When he brought the mare, I exclaimed that she was only about half the weight of my horse and could not possibly be strong enough to pull him out, but he only laughed as he adjusted the end of the rope in a slip knot round Wing's neck. In a very few minutes he had my big horse high and dry on the bank, but I exclaimed, 'He's dead sure, enough,' for the rope had drawn tight and strangled the poor brute, so that he lay on the bank apparently lifeless. My farmer friend, however, laughed, and dispelled my fears, saying that he had lifted many a heavy cart horse or bullock in this way out of the stream with his little light nag mare, and until he had choked the life out of them to prevent their struggling it was well-nigh an impossibility to lift any horse safely out of a deep water-course. It turned out all right; Tom Chambers came back with my other horse, just as Wing came to life again little or none the worse, though I sent him back to Belvoir stables."

Interest attaches itself to the events of March 29th, when hounds met at Weaver's Lodge, for it was the only day this season the Duke was able to hunt with his hounds on the Lincolnshire side of the country. The pack were lucky enough to score a really good hunting run, which was quite unexpected in such dry weather. As was his wont, the Duke took up a position at the down-wind corner of Newton wood, for he delighted to view the fox away. There were no less than two and a half brace in the covert, and Gillard with the Duke viewed two brace away whilst they listened to the pack running hard in the wood with number five. When at last he did break, with hounds close at his brush, Frank exclaimed, "By Jove, your Grace, that is our Hose Gorse fox, I know him, for he looks as black as if he had been shaken out of a soot bag." The Duke laughed at the idea, quite thinking that Gillard was drawing the long-bow in his enthusiasm, considering that Hose Covert lies at least eleven miles from Newton wood as the crow flies. However, events proved that Frank was right, and the Duke admitted so when he met him next day. This fox took almost a straight line for Croxton Park, through Haydour Southings, Ropsley Rise, Ponton Park Wood, crossing the Great Northern Railway, passing to the left of the School Platts covert, where he ran out of scent. "The distance was eleven miles as the crow flies, and I knew him directly by his dark appearance, to be our Hose Gorse fox, who had, during the season, given three nice gallops from that covert, in the direction of Croxton Park. We never did account for him, so I fear that he came to a bad end." The hunting days of this season were 189, and 115 foxes were killed, with 26 marked to ground.

A SINKING FOX.

CHAPTER IX

Season 1878-79

Will Wells, Whipper-in—George Gillson's Career—George Cottrell leads for a Sovereign—A Wet Jacket—The Belvoir and Quorn Packs clash—Two good Gallops from Leadenham—Colonel John Reeves' Entree Dish—Parson Heathcote's Pudding—Brook-jumping—The good Fox of Sherbrooke's Covert—A Run to the "Forty Foot" Drain—A severe Run from Sproxton to Crown Point—A curious Accident to Mr. Alfred Cross—Good Sport—The Messrs. Frank and George Gordon—Three Foxes killed by Haverholme—The Horse Peter—Mr. Fisher of Orston.

GEORGE CARTER.

THE story of one pack of hounds must necessarily give us links in the chain of events with many another, and this constitutes some of the charm of hunting history. It is pleasant to note the early career of men who were destined to become famous later on in the world of sport, and Belvoir has always been looked to as the school for huntsmen and a stepping-stone to promotion, so that the record of the whippers-in who learnt their business and served under Gillard is an interesting one. The change in the staff this season brought Will Wells and George Cottrell to Belvoir, as first and second whipper-in. For smartness and fine horsemanship it is generally agreed that Will Wells heads the list of the many who turned hounds during the last quarter of a century, and he came from the Quorn, where he acted in the capacity of second whipper-in to Tom Firr, with George Gillson, the present Cottesmore huntsman, first whipper-in. Will Wells was the beau-ideal of a hunt servant, and quickly established himself as every one's favourite, the bruisers delighting in galloping Will, whose seat over a fence was the envy and admiration of all who beheld him flitting about a strongly-fenced country like a swallow on the wing. He possessed in a remarkable degree the rare knack of making all horses go alike, good, bad, or indifferent, such as we venture to think has only been equalled by Captain "Doggy" Smith, when he was the pride of a Leicestershire field. Both these fine horsemen—and we make no apology when we link together the names of the gentleman and the professional—were wonderfully strong in the saddle, and could see their way through a fence where there did not appear a place fit for a pigeon to fly.

We mentioned the name of George Gillson, the first whip to the Quorn this season, and promotion came to him with the offer to carry the horn for Lord Ferrers, who kept a pack of hounds to hunt the Donnington side of the Quorn country. The pack was a very good one, for Lord Ferrers began with Belvoir blood and stuck to it, but it was soon dispersed when the Quorn claimed this slice of country to themselves. When this happened George Gillson migrated to the York and Ainstry, where he remained until Mr. William Baird accepted the mastership of the Cottesmore, and his choice fell on Gillson for huntsman in 1888, to the great improvement in the breeding of that old-established pack.

The second whipper-in, George Cottrell, came from Mr. George Lane Fox, and after a season or two at Belvoir he passed on to Quorn to fill the first position of whipper-in. Possessed of a good voice, he was a plucky horseman and good servant. Many a time, to use Brooksby's words :—

> When we're jammed in a corner, the timber too strong,
> The bullfinch too thick, and our courage all gone—
> Hie! give us a lead! and over he'll flip,
> But it's little improved by the galloping whip.

Gillard called to mind a particular occasion when a locked gate, with an up-hill take off and bad landing, confronted the field. Some one said, "Now, George, give us a lead, and we'll give you a sovereign if you smash it." Cottrell, riding a mare bought from Mr. Philip Hornsby, humped his back, rammed the mare at it, getting well over without breaking the top bar, but he at once pulled up and drew the sovereign.

A succession of bad colds brought on a smart attack of gout and rheumatism which placed Gillard *hors de combat* for a few days and gave Wells the opportunity to carry the horn. When we come to think of the number of wet jackets he must have carried during his long career we are inclined to marvel that he never took permanent harm, for many a day it was eight or nine o'clock before he was able to effect a change. A good heart and a temperate life were the real secret of the preservation of health and usefulness. We are reminded of a wrinkle given by the post-boys for travelling in bad weathers which may be of service to the hunting man of to-day. A long great-coat was part and parcel of the post-boy's equipment, and when, bringing his "bounder" back, he would often sit on the apology for a seat to drive the horses. If he had got wet when riding the stage, on the return journey he put his dry coat over the wet jacket, and never feared taking cold when so doing, saying it converted cold water into hot.

The opening day of this season was November 4th, the meet being Three Queens, hounds setting a good fox going from Tipping's Gorse. Although the pack did not get away on the best of terms, they eventually settled to the line, and the farther they ran the more pace improved. The line was by Sproxton Thorns, Coston village and Coston Covert to Wymondham, where the fox was viewed just ahead, but a couple of sheep-dogs joining in the chase, spoilt the run. The pack whipped off at Woodwell Head after running well for four hours. Considerable friction was caused by the Quorn and the Belvoir meeting during a run in one of the coverts of the former pack on November 25th.

HUNTSMAN'S HOUSE AND BELVOIR KENNELS.

Facing page 122.

THE NEW YORK
PUBLIC LIBRARY

ASTOR, LENOX AND
TILDEN FOUNDATIONS

The meet of the Belvoir was at Plungar on a cold foggy morning, and after dallying with a bad fox at Harby Covert, a good one was set going from Hose Thorns, giving a regular Leicestershire burst of thirty minutes by Hickling to the Curates Gorse on Quorn soil. It was fully thirty minutes before hounds could set their fox going again from the covert where he had lain down in the thick tangle, obliterating all trace of scent. In the meantime the master came into the covert and requested that the Belvoir hounds be taken out to let the Quorn come in. Such a request was against all the canons of sport, and could only have originated after a trying morning spent with a bad scenting fox, which had been the lot of the Quorn. Gillard declined to go, saying that it was no use his being so early beaten off by such an unreasonable request, for he was sure his hounds would stick to their run fox in spite of Quorn whip-cord. The fox must have heard the squall, for the next moment Cottrell's scream proclaimed him away in the direction of Willoughby with the pack not far behind his brush. A little farther on Gillard got a view of his hunted one with back arched and brush dragging. "Is that a run fox?" he asked of Captain Pennell Elmhirst who happened to be nearest to him, and there was no gainsaying the fact, for hounds pulled him down fairly in the open before they had gone a mile. Whilst the obsequies were performed, both fields drew up, having enjoyed the sport together; so all's well that ends well, and may both packs flourish for many a day to come, enjoying excursions over the borders of one another's country.

Two good hunting runs fell to the lot of those who joined the field at Leadenham on November 26th. Colonel John Reeves was one of those who found foxes for both packs, his coverts being situated on the borders of the Blankney country. Both gallops ended with a kill, and both commenced with a thirty minutes' burst, ending with steady hunting. The first, from Leadenham Hill-top Covert, was away over the vale nearly to Wellingore by Brant Broughton to Caythorpe, where he turned and was finally killed at Fulbeck hill-top after running for two hours. The next gallop was from California Covert, hounds going away at racing pace to the left of Bayard's Leap, Lord Bristol Plantation, nearly to Dunsby Gorse, where they turned towards Bloxholm. Gillard remarks in his diary, "We checked, and a forward cast was in vain, so I held them round to Pilkington's Plantation, where we refound our fox, and he made his way back through Lord Bristol's Plantation to the starting-point California Covert. We ran through the covert, and two fields away from it hounds were at fault, evidently having overrun their fox, for he jumped up behind them and ran back into the covert, where he puzzled them for some time, creeping about in the briers. When he came to hand he was a fine old dog, and had led the pack for one hour and fifty minutes from find to finish."

Many an amusing story is told of the old squire of Leadenham, over whose lordship we have just been following the lines of two good foxes. A typical character of the old school, his sayings and doings savour more of the times of Squire Western than with the manners and customs which obtain in these "degenerate days," as it is the fashion to call them. He seldom rode hard in the morning, excepting to covert, on his hack, often turning up with a scratched face, smashed hat, and clothes all over mud. By the afternoon he would warm into activity, and could slip along over a country with the best of them. A staunch fox-preserver, in his enthusiasm for the chase it is said that he once had a whole fox served up for dinner. But a better story is told of him when a brother sportsman went to dine, and for a practical joke he had a fox's tongue garnished and sent up on a dish. Under an assumed name it was thoroughly enjoyed by the unsuspecting guest! But on this occasion he met more than a match in his old friend the Rev. Thomas Heathcote, who returned the compliment by asking the Colonel to dine, and gave him a Roland for an Oliver. A dainty dish was set before him in the shape of a tapioca pudding, of which the Colonel partook. "I am glad you enjoyed it," the host remarked, "for it was not tapioca at all, but frog spawn off my pike pond."

All through the month of December this season there was much delay for winter and rough weather, but the new year was ushered in under conditions most favourable for sport, and a nice gallop was enjoyed from Melton Spinney by way of Scalford and Chadwell, whose brook was soon having the mud stirred up by several hardy divers. How often do we not see the Whissendine or one of those winding Leicestershire brooks full of the highest-priced hunters in England, where a polo pony might jump it? A horse can jump sixteen or twenty feet of water "if he gets his foot in,"

THE FATE OF THE ROVER IS SEALED.

but how often when he comes down to twelve feet of water has he a chance given him of taking off properly? The very pace that frequently gets him over water as frequently gets him in; and horses, like human beings, are demoralised by a bad example, for let but one leader come to grief, immediately ten or a dozen more will stick their toes in, shutting up like foot-rules.

A well-known fox took up his quarters in Sherbrooke's Covert this season, and just as often as hounds shook him out he gave good runs, in all of which Captain "Bay" Middleton was fortunate enough to take a prominent position. On February 8th this good fox gave a tremendously fast spin over his usual line of country until he reached the tableland by Piper Hole, where a check occurred near to Scalford Bogs, after thirty-five minutes of the very best, saving his life. At the end of the day, when riding at timber, Lord Grey de Wilton fell, breaking his leg.

A hard day's sport on the Lincolnshire side of the country resulted on February 11th, when hounds met at Aswarby Park, and Sir Thomas Whichcote welcomed his many friends. The first run was from Moneys Gorse, hounds giving their fox a terrible doing for twenty minutes, regularly bursting him. The second fox from Burton Gorse set his mask for the fen country, and in the deep clay land, hounds quickly had the foot of horses. This fine old fellow led the way to within two fields of the famous Forty-Foot Drain, and it being impossible for the hunt staff to get across at the critical moment, he twisted out of scent and saved his brush. The tenacity of this stiff mud is proverbial, as many a shirtless strapper can testify, for he very soon learns in which corner of the hunt the horse has been by the quality and quantity of the soil he has brought away with him. Though the sport was severe, that of the next day on the Leicestershire side of the country possibly beat it for goodness and severity. The find was proclaimed from Sproxton Thorns, from which covert hounds were quickly away for Coston Covert, running like wildfire without slackening to Crown Point, where they turned for Woodwell Head. Here two or three foxes were afoot, but the pack stuck to the line of their hunted one and eventually got him away towards Wymondham back to covert again. With hounds running very keen for blood, he could never shake them off, and as a last shift to save his life, made for a drain between Thistleton and Crown Point, which he was viewed to enter with the pack snapping at his brush, after one of the fastest and severest runs on record. A terrier unfortunately killed this good fox in the drain, and he was dragged out with a hook at the end of a pole to be given to the hounds.

A large field assembled on February 19th at Leadenham House and included its squire, Colonel "Jack" Reeves, with his neighbour and contemporary, Colonel Francis Fane of Fulbeck, Mr. Henry and Lady Florence Chaplin, Sir John and Lady Thorold, Lord Brownlow, Sir Thomas Whichcote, Mr. John Welby, Mrs. Franklin, the Misses Willson, Captain Tennant, Mr. Allcard, Mons. Roy, Mons. Couturie, and Mr. Alfred Cross. Without troubling about the details of an average day's sport, we will describe a curious accident which befell the last-named sportsman, who always enjoyed his ride. Hounds had left Fulbeck hilltop, sinking the vale, and after Gillard had negotiated a stiffish fence he heard a tremendous crash behind him. Looking round, he saw Mr. Cross and his horse struggling about as they made desperate efforts not to part company. However, it was of no avail, for the next moment a riderless steed galloped by, and a top-boot stood up in the near side stirrup, just as if a leg had been inside it. Mr. Alfred Cross happily was none the worse, giving chase to his horse over a rough fallow field, which was decidedly hard going for the bootless foot.

The vein of good luck continued all through February, and one good Croxton Park Wednesday succeeded another, that of the 19th being as good as that of the week previous. The famous Burbidge's Covert was the first draw, but as Gillard remarked to us, it is a mistake to disturb a good fox covert oftener than once in three weeks. On this occasion hounds chopped a mangy one who had probably been run very hard on a previous occasion. The right article was waiting for us in Freeby Wood, and a very merry spin resulted with him as far as Thorpe Arnold, where he hid himself in a straw stack in Mr. Garner's yard, but paid the penalty of his indiscretion. The third fox was started from Melton Spinney, running by Chadwell, Freeby, and Brentingby villages to Burton Lazars in fifty-five minutes without a check. When the line was recovered the pack ran on by Freeby village, marking to ground near Brentingby with all the horses pretty well at the end of their tether. The noble master was out on this day and unfortunately knocked his leg on a gate-post when crossing the railway by Saxby Station, which, added to the complications of gout and anno domini, caused much anxiety on his behalf.

Amongst the shining lights who rode with the Belvoir at this period were the brothers Messrs. Frank and George Gordon, sons of the Rector of Muston, both hard to beat across country. The elder brother, Mr. Frank, was very good handling a young horse, he had also an eye for a hound, and took particular notice of the pack in their work. To-day his name is to be found in the working committee of the Peterborough Foxhound Show. The younger brother, Mr. George, was fond of his ride, but with him it was first or nowhere. "On many occasions I had to blow him up for getting a bit too forrard!" said Gillard, who like the recording angel has got all our shortcomings down in his book. "But you could not help but forgive him in his impetuosity, for he was a fine horseman, and could jump over stiff timber out of a road as only a good one can. His answer to me was always the same, 'You must blow somebody up, Frank, so it may just as well be me; but you know somebody ought to keep up the riding reputation of the Belvoir!' he would add with a merry twinkle in his eye. I remember on the occasion the Prince of Wales hunted with us from Hose Gorse, I galloped my horse down the tow-path of the Harby Canal to get to hounds lower down, and I saw Mr. George Gordon standing on the bridge, having slipped away ahead to get a flying start and be first man, which was his delight. Away he went, and after jumping one fence successfully he tried to jump the rails which ran down to the canal. Unfortunately for him there was a space at the end of the fence to which his horse swerved, thinking to get round it. The result was certain catastrophe, the bank being slippery and too narrow, besides the pace being far too great to attempt such a feat. Mr. Gordon and his horse went with a mighty splash into the stream, both bobbing to the surface, the rider swimming out for the bank. The horse followed him up and knocked him down as he swam, so that if we had not lent timely assistance it would have been a very awkward moment indeed. Some years later he threw up his farm, and the fates banished him to a non-hunting country. I can tell you that when he said 'good-bye' to me, he had tears in his eyes!"

The widest fixture from Belvoir was Haverholme Priory, the home of the Winchilseas, where hounds were always welcomed, and her ladyship on each occasion of their visit had a button-hole of choice flowers ready for Gillard, who submitted to the decoration with that courtly grace that always distinguished the huntsman of the ducal pack. A good day's sport was enjoyed there on February 21st, it being a singular coincidence that three foxes were slain in the vicinity of bricks and mortar. The first was killed after a nice gallop of thirty minutes from Evendon Wood to the "Old

Place," Haverholme village, the second from Sleaford Wood to Mr. Sharpe the seed merchant's nursery garden, and the third surrendered up his brush in the Bloxholme Hall gardens, where several of the hounds got badly cut by dashing through the window of a greenhouse. "I was riding old Gameboy that day, and he jumped a very wide drain by Haverholme; Will Wells tried to follow, but his horse made a mistake and fell. I always remember the spot because it is a tributary of the river Brant, and in the days when I was whipper-in to Cooper in a run from Fulbeck on the occasion of the marriage of Colonel Francis Fane, the bridegroom, who was one of the field, got a tremendous ducking owing to his horse jumping short."

The account of two more brilliant gallops over Leicestershire closes the record of this season's sport. The first of these was from Melton Spinney, "a regular clipper of twenty minutes, for we killed him close to Mr. George Norman's front door at Goadby Hall. It was a race, for hounds led horses by quite three fields down the valley towards Chadwell. I was mounted on my old roan horse Peter, a common enough one to look at, but he could both gallop and jump with the best of them, and was safe to clear a wide place, for he went very fast at his fences. I remember he jumped into the road by Hose, which is a wide place with an old water-course running alongside, and it all but put Captain 'Bay' Middleton down when he followed, for he only just saved a fall by good horsemanship.

On another occasion I set old Peter going at a wide beck by Bottesford, and just in front was Mr. John Welby, who did not stop for much in those days. However, he did not like the look of it, and held up his hand for me to stop. I might as well have tried to stop the sun in its course as turn old Peter's head when set for a fence, and he jumped it with a foot to spare. Old Mr. Fisher of Orston followed on, and I think he was the best of the farmer division to hounds that I ever knew. The last good thing of the season was in the cool of the afternoon on March 19th, after a hot and unprofitable day's sport. We found our fox in Melton Spinney and ran well with an improving scent by the brook to Scalford and Old Hills, nearly to Melton, where he turned. The pace improved with every yard of the journey as we ran by Thorpe Arnold and the Broom Cover, and we killed near Waltham Ashes, putting a good finish to a very nice gallop."

The number of hunting days this season was 112, and 101 foxes were killed.

WATCHMAN, BY NOMINAL—WHIMSICAL.

CHAPTER X

Seasons 1879-80 and 1880-81

Hunt Changes—Tea with Frank Goodall, the Queen's Huntsman—A Country equal to the Vagaries of any Weather—An awkward Accident—Smite Hill Gorse Flames head a Fox—The big Ash Wednesday Day—Mr. Alfred Brocklehurst first up—Colonel Gosling borrows some dry Clothes—A kill under a Woman's Petticoats—Frank rides a run under Chloroform—Will Wells' Horse out all night—Twelve-Hour Cubbing Mornings—Arthur Wilson, Whip—Parson Bullen of Eastwell—Wet and good Sport—Interviewing the Duke in his Bed—The Taste of a "Pug"—Blooding a fat American Gentleman—A Jackal Tooth Scarf-pin—A fast Gallop and dead Fox next Day—Lord Queensbury—Lord Doneraile, his Hounds, his pet Fox, his End—A long Run.

A Portrait.

CHANGE is the general order of things in this life, but the Belvoir Hunt for a century and a half escaped the common lot, following the even tenor of its way as a family pack under the mastership of the house of Manners. About this time a general change was effected in a comparatively small circle of the fox-hunting world within hailing distance of Belvoir, for we find Lord Carrington succeeding to the mastership of the Cottesmore on the retirement of Lord Lonsdale, Sir Bache Cunard hunting Mr. Tailbys' country in high Leicestershire, and Mr. Herbert Langham of Cottesbrooke following Lord Spencer with the Pytchley, retaining the services of Will Goodall. To mention such classic names in Gillard's hearing was a sure way to draw a good story from him. "Luck generally favours a start, and well I remember my first season with the Quorn. What good sport we had! Day after day our foxes would take a good line of country, and we continually crossed the borders of Mr. Tailbys. In these days Frank Goodall was the huntsman to that pack, subsequently leaving to carry the horn for the Queen's stag-hounds, and many a time he would say to me as I rode by his house late at night after a good run into Mr. Tailbys' country, 'You are the worst poacher I ever knew, Frank; I will shoot you the very next time I catch you in my country!' 'Give me a cup of tea and shoot me afterwards!' I used to say, for I was very fond of a cup of tea on the way home after a hard day, and I had lots of kind friends and houses of call where they would get the kettle boiling if they knew I was anywhere in the neighbourhood about dusk."

The conditions of weather will often give a clue to the sport of any particular season, and this was so in the present instance. Owing to a wet autumn, the harvest was delayed, so that it was not until the first week in September that the cubbing campaign could be started. Frost and absence of scent at the very commencement made sport moderate, proving the old saying, "A hard winter follows a wet summer." This was verified to the very letter, for hounds were stopped from December 1st to 15th, as many as 37 degrees of frost being registered in Leicestershire, after which snow fell. The first day out, December 22nd, after the break-up of the wintry blast, found the pack at Bottesford Station. To have hunted anywhere else but in the low-lying country would have been impossible, but an obliging fox started from Normanton Thorns, stuck to the vale instead of taking the high-level country, which was still unridable, so that a run lasting one hour and a half was scored by Foston, Bennington, Stubton, ending at the Thirteen Acre Plantation.

With the new year the conditions for sport improved, and a good gallop was enjoyed on the 3rd from Tippings Gorse, hounds running very hard to Stoke Rochford, where the fox was headed; turning to Sproxton Thorns, he crossed the brook by Saltby. The lead was given by Mr. Alfred Cross, and as hounds ran over the Sproxton road a postman told Frank that his fox was only a minute in front. Want of daylight spoilt the finish; but in spite of this it was a capital day's sport, "and had it been in a grass country, hounds would have run away from horses," was the huntsman's opinion. The mention of the foremost rider of this day's sport brings to mind the story of an awkward predicament he was placed in through his horse making a mistake at a trappy fence. Hounds had roused a fox in Casthorpe Covert, and the first obstacle away was a wide drain full of water, with a stake-and-bound fence on the top of a bank. The lead was given by Mr. Tom Hutchinson, whose horse popped over, climbed the bank, and got the right side of the stake-and-bound without making any fuss about it. Mr. Cross was not so successful when he attempted to follow, for after clearing the drain his horse reared up on the bank and came backwards with his rider into the water. A providential presentiment told Gillard what was going to happen, and directly the horse fell back on to the bank he was ready to seize him round the neck with both arms and hold him there, preventing his rider from drowning at the bottom of the stream. It was a very awkward position, and he had to be dragged out, being partly held down by the horse against the bank side, and in doing this his top-boots were again left behind. Mr. "Banker" Hardy, who saw the accident, always said Gillard saved a victim from a watery grave by prompt action, complimenting him on his great strength of arm to hold the horse up to the bank side for so long a time.

On January 12th, after meeting at Elton Manor, a fox was found in Whatton Hall Plantation, and setting his mask for Smite Hill Gorse, he received something of a header from the flames that leapt up from the covert, which was being grubbed up and burnt, having outgrown itself. This gorse was originally planted by Mr. Chaworth Musters when he left the Quorn country, and it was regarded as a neutral covert for South Notts and Belvoir. Ash Wednesday, always a great day with the Belvoir, this season attracted a field of over four hundred horsemen to the meet at Croxton Park. There was a bite of frost in the air that betokened a scent, and the influence of frost and rain had worked wonders on the ground. A fox was viewed by Will Wells near to Sproxton Thorns, and the information quietly given to his chief, who obtained a flying start by lifting the pack round the covert. Scoffers have been known to hint at a bagman for the Belvoir Ash Wednesday occasions, but the present knocks the bottom out of such a suggestion. For twenty-five minutes hounds screamed away by Coston, Buckminster, and Sproxton where a brace were running before the pack. On nearing Woodwell Head scent became very low, and Gillard had to render assistance, casting forward on the plough. Just at a critical moment Wells's voice came to set matters right, and away they streamed at top speed down the hill by Market Overton, going fast nearly to Barrow, leaving Teigh village on the right. Not a gate was swung, and two were jumped in quick succession, as the leading division rode as if between the flags to keep hounds in view. Mr. Hugh Lowther, now Lord Lonsdale, Mr. G. Drummond, Mr. Rhodes, Captain Pennell Elmhirst, Lord Esme Gordon, Mr. Gerald Paget, Captain Byng, Captain Arthur Smith and Mrs. Candy were piloting the way. After crossing the railway between Ashwell and Whissendine stations, the huntsman fell, and Mr. Alfred Brocklehurst getting the lead cheered hounds on, bored through a thick bullfinch, and got the treasured remains away from the savaging pack. The time of this fine run was two hours and five minutes, the first twenty-five and the last thirty being most brilliant. "When I picked myself up," said Frank, as he continued the narrative, "I found a big man in a billy-cock hat, shepherd's Sunday clothes, and a red handkerchief round his neck, pushing up against me, and as I thought putting himself unduly prominent in the group round the baying hounds. I therefore asked him to stand on one side. He laughed at me, and then I thought it was a face I knew. Sure enough it was Colonel Gosling, who, with many others, had come to grief at Coston brook early in the run, and he was hardly recognisable in a shepherd's Sunday clothes. My word, he did use to send his horses along; it was in or over with him!"

A remarkable day's sport happened on February 18th, hounds running a stout fox for over two hours from Ingoldsby Wood by Osgodby, back to Humby and Ropsley, before they marked to ground near Weaver's Lodge. To illustrate the finish we might borrow the old picture of Selby Lowndes' hounds killing their fox under an old lady's petticoats. Directly the fox bolted from a long drain down a field, he made straight for two women from the village, and they ran for the nearest fence. One managed to scramble over, but the other, who was rather stout, got astride the ditch, and hounds dashing up killed their fox in the ditch under her petticoats.

Early in March, Gillard took a heavy fall near Hose village, and dislocated his right shoulder owing to Snowstorm, a gray horse, making a mistake.

Frank continued as follows:—"One of the field happened to be Dr. Williams, and he took me off to a cottage to try to put me right. Well, he got me down on the floor, pulled and hauled without being able to get my arm in again. 'It's no use,' he said, 'I must either chloroform you or send you back home for your own doctor to attend to.' 'I'll be chloroformed here,' I said, 'for I want to get my horse and go on!' So chloroformed I was, and I never rode to such a good run in all my life, or over such a good country! When I came too again there were several people round me and all laughing, for I had given vent to my pleasure, and called out to the whipper-in 'to put them on quicker.' My shoulder was in, and I was sent back home in a trap the first time in my life, Dr. Williams remarking that he had never seen any one with stronger muscles, and the mere fact of my trying to help him had made it harder."

In consequence of this accident, Will Wells hunted hounds, and very successful he was in showing sport. On one of these occasions he was placed in an awkward position, his horse falling at the brook below Melton Spinney, and, getting away from his rider, he was not recovered until

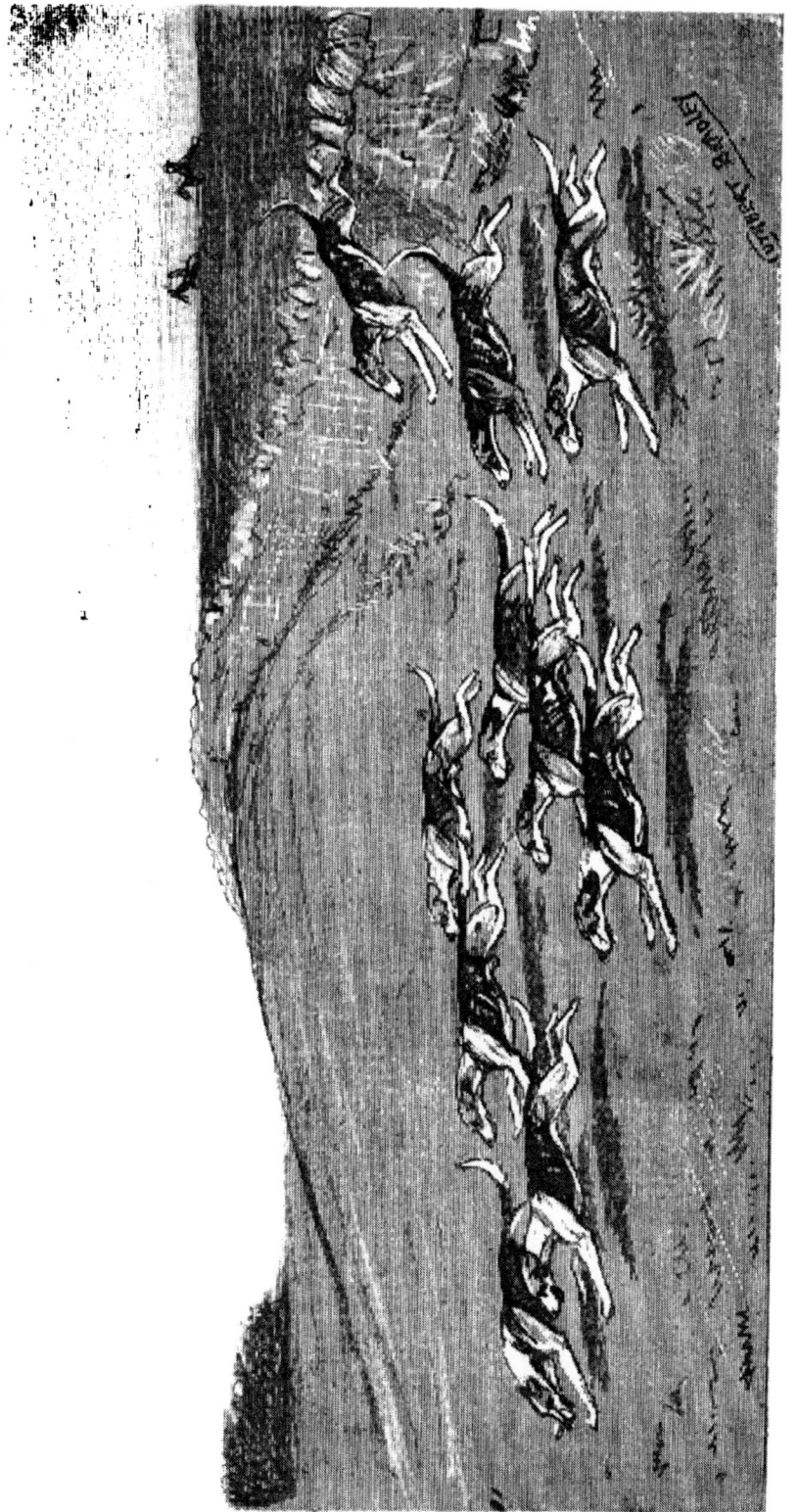

A Dart with the Belvoir.

THE NEW YORK
PUBLIC LIBRARY

ASTOR, LENOX AND
TILDEN FOUNDATIONS
R L

two men found him at Scalford, bringing him back to the kennels at 10.30 that night.

One of the best days at the end of this season was from Burton Long Wood, after meeting at Easton Hall, and the line was through Easton Wood, Witham, away past Lobthorpe to Morkary and Clipsham, where he was viewed crawling about in the wood; but unfortunately the pack changed to the line of a fresh one. The whole of the journey is over a rough, wild country, and those who held prominent positions through the run were Miss Laura Willson, Mr. A. Cross, Mr. Allcard, junr., Mr. James Hoyes, and Mr. James Rudkin.

The number of hunting days this season was 115, the number of foxes killed 93.

Season 1880-81

Even cubbing excursions at cock-crow were not always devoid of humour, for one morning when the van stopped at Ancaster Inn by 4 A.M., making it a half-way house for the outlying fixtures on that side, they found in the stable a well-known farmer's horse, which had spent the night on the pillar chain. The occasion was Ancaster feast, and one of great rejoicing; so much so that the owner of this unfortunate horse had been put to bed in his boots and spurs by the landlord. For many a day afterwards Gillard used to pull this young roysterer by the leg about it, when he came out hunting.

Another wet summer, and consequently late harvest, made it impossible to start cubbing before September 9th, and on the second morning out with the dog pack in Knipton Coverts, they made a long day of it, hunting from 6 A.M. to 8 P.M., returning to kennels without tasting blood. The new addition to the hunt staff this season was Arthur Wilson, who came as second whipper-in; and he soon showed his keenness for hounds, taking great notice of them in the kennel, learning much that was of great assistance to him when he became huntsman to the York and Ainstry. Unfortunately, before Wilson had been a month at Belvoir, he took a very heavy fall on his head when riding a young horse over a blind place, and was laid up for a month.

Against the doings of the young entry on a morning in October, the most delightful month of the whole season's sport, Frank records the following: "I never knew a better morning for hounds, now there is a good covert with nettles and briars in Patman's Wood. It proved to be full of foxes. Hounds were kept very busy for an hour before they drew blood, and another half-hour before they got hold of their second fox. Just at the moment the pack were killing him, the other part ran a cub to ground in a short tunnel. All the hounds joined in breaking up the second cub, and then I took them to mark the other to ground, which we bolted and killed after a fifteen minutes' scurry."

In these record-breaking days it would be hard

to find a wetter one than that of October 5th, or a more ardent body of horsemen than the Belvoir Hunt staff, whose enthusiasm was in no way damped by the tremendous downpour. "We left kennels at 8 A.M. for Rauceby, fourteen miles distant as the crow flies. It rained in torrents from morning to night, and we returned to kennels at 8.80 P.M. with one nose to the kennel board. The next day, when we went into the vale of Belvoir, we found it nearly all under water, and the floods round the Thirteen Acre at Allington looked like a sea. We killed a brace of cubs, and on the journey home got another wet jacket."

One of the best-known faces in the hunting-field at this period was Parson Bullen of Eastwell, aged eighty-five; "he was a little bit of a man, a regular Tom Thumb, mounted on a big chestnut horse." On many days that he came out he would ride up to Gillard and ask him where he intended to draw in the afternoon, because he had to return to his parish to take a funeral or wedding as the case might be. The next time he would tell him, "I got back in time, Frank, after that gallop; had to take the funeral in my boots and spurs, could not be helped! it did not matter so long as I was there!" The bitterest pill of all was when the old gentleman had to bury his own parish clerk, to whom he was most attached, and who was used to all his old-fashioned ways. Parson Bullen hunted up to ninety years of age; to the last he used to go, and hated shirking.

This season was one of the wettest on record, but

there was a scent, so that day after day hounds scored excellent runs, making the riding division very keen. Red marks of excellence are placed against the sport of November 10th at Croxton Park, the 13th at Goadby, 17th at Stonesby, 26th at Rauceby, and 27th at Waltham, where we will join the hunt. "This was a hard day for hounds and horses, and we started by riding to Burbidge's Covert, where we cracked our whips before throwing the pack in. A fox was soon away over the river, but hounds did not settle well to his line, and he was headed a time or two, which also puzzled the pack. After threading the Stapleford coverts he went straight for Whissendine brook in a line for Ranksborough Gorse, but was again headed by a man plashing a fence. Turning back over the Burton Flats, hounds again crossed the river and railway by Wyfordby, running by Brentingby and Thorpe Arnold, finally marking to ground near Newport Lodge. It was a difficult fox to hunt, never running straight for more than two fields, and those who rode to hounds had plenty to do to keep near them over a very strong bit of country."

The noble master was prevented hunting much this season owing to rheumatic troubles in addition to gout, but he took the liveliest interest in the doings of the pack, and most mornings before starting out Gillard would ride up to the Castle dressed for the chase and see him in bed. The affairs of the hunt were more often than not discussed under these conditions between Master and huntsman, and whatever turned up in the morning's correspondence, in the way of claims for poultry or damage, was handed over to Frank to deal with. The bye day on Thursday was the time and opportunity to personally investigate all such claims, and the huntsman would jump on a hack, ride off to see what could be done, making an offer to meet such damage as soon as he had heard all particulars. Before parting with any money he always complied with the express wishes of the Duke by asking, "Are you satisfied with what I offer you? You are quite sure that you are satisfied with the amount. We part friends?" No wonder the Duke and his huntsman were so deservedly popular, and Gillard adds, "Claims from the Lincolnshire side were very few." On some mornings the Duke was to be found reading the accounts of the previous day's sport, which often amused him immensely, and referring to the quaint wording, he would say, "I read that yesterday you were hunting a pug; I hope hounds liked his taste when they caught him."

Continuous bad weather was succeeded by a stop for frost during half the month of January, but the first day out hounds scored a nice gallop of thirty-five minutes from Newman's Gorse. Amongst the field out was a fat American gentleman who saw hounds for the first time, and his friends insisted that he should be blooded with all due ceremony befitting so important a debut. Amongst the many presents and tokens of regard Gillard received during his time from friends at a distance, was a jackal's tooth mounted as a scarf-pin, killed by hounds sent from Belvoir to the Blue Mountains of Southern India.

The fastest gallop of the season happened on February 16th from Coston Gorse, hounds racing like wild-fire towards Wymondham, past the villages of Coston, Sproxton, and Buckminster, away in the direction of Woodwell Head, where he turned sharp back to his starting-point. Those nearest to them were Captain Smith, Mr. John Welby, and Will Wells; the big field of the morning, numbering some three or four hundred, being scattered all over the country. Unfortunately this good fox beat the pack near to Stoke Rochford, for next day Will Charity the keeper, and noted terror of the poaching fraternity, picked up a dead one lying in the middle of a field not far from Coston Gorse.

Two nice gallops are recorded on February 19th, the first being a scurry lasting twenty minutes from Old Hills; and whilst hounds were breaking up their fox in covert another was halloaed away from it. His point was to the artificial earths in Grimston Gorse, from which a terrier bolted, and old Fencer getting hold, gave him a good shaking, but he slipped through the pack like an eel, and so saved his brush. The third fox, started from Clawson Thorns, gave the run of the day by Holwell Mouth, Little Belvoir, Welby Church, back by Wartenby stone pits as if he meant the Curate's Gorse. Being hard pressed, he turned for Dalby, and they fairly raced into him after running one hour and a half. Out of a large field those who were best placed were Captain T. Boyce, Captain Smith, Lord Cloncurry, Mr. George Drummond, Mr. H. Praed, Mr. W. Chaplin, and the Duke of Portland, who took two falls during the run.

It was about this time that Lord Doneraile and Lord Queensbury rented the Rectory at Barrowby as a hunting-box, both being very hard men to hounds. During the time of Cooper the huntsman, Lord Queensbury left the navy and started to hunt from Aswarby, riding old screws, which when shoved along in reckless fashion over every sort of country gave their rider some tremendous croppers, but taught him much experience. Lord Doneraile was a great sportsman, having hunted with Lord Henry Bentinck's hounds; and he quoted him on every occasion as the highest authority on all matters connected with the chase. One season his lordship bespoke the whole of the Belvoir draft, and these were duly despatched to Ireland, where he and two other masters were to divide the hounds. For months Gillard never had a line acknowledging their arrival, and when at last information did come, it was to the effect that rabies had broken out in Lord Doneraile's kennel, said to have been imported by the Belvoir draft, and as in the case of a diseased cow, the vendor must bear the loss. A lawyer had to look into the case, which, when investigated, brought a cheque for the full amount by return of post. A curious and sad ending closed this sportsman's career. It was his wont to adopt as a pet a tame vixen fox, which accompanied him everywhere, even when driving in his carriage, and in a frenzy she bit Lord Doneraile and his coachman. Both started off to Paris to undergo Pasteur's treatment. The coachman was not a pennyweight the worse, but Lord Doneraile died.

The season closed with a remarkable hunting run which lasted four hours, and the distance hounds travelled when measured on the ordnance map was 26 miles. This fox was started in the Debdale cover, and he ran through Allington, Bottesford, Belvoir, back to Croxton and Denton Park, being killed in Mr. Beasley's front garden at Harston. The only sportsman who remained to see the finish was Mr. George Drummond. It might be thought that hounds did not keep to the line of the same fox throughout this run, but there was no doubt about it, because it was noticed by several people who saw the find that a piece of fur was missing from the middle of his brush, and this was found to be so when hounds killed him.

Taken altogether it was an average season's sport of 119 hunting days, 105 foxes killed, and 41 marked to ground.

DAHLIA BY SHAMROCK—DILIGENT.

CHAPTER XI

Season 1881-82

Trojan kills a Fox single-handed—Heathcote Covert—Heathcote Hunters, Blue Stockings, Janette, and Miss Coates—Hunting in a Hurricane at Aswarby—Sir Thomas Whichcote's Pony—Will Tidey, the hard-riding Keeper—Mr. Ashmead Bartlett Burdett-Coutts joins the Hunt—A quick burst in Leicestershire—Good Days—Folkingham Big Gorse—Accident to the Rev. Thomas Heathcote—Buying Horses without seeing them—Berserker the Hunter Sire—Mr. "Banker" Hardy—A Run Fox killed by Greyhounds—The gamest Fox ever hunted—Arthur Wilson swims the Whissendine—Devonshire and Leicestershire Rivers compared—Will Wells and Arthur Wilson across Country—Will Wells' Testimonial.

TROJAN.

THE depth of the public purse gives the strength of the pulse for sport. A bad time for agriculture means a thousand-and-one industries suffer, and there is a falling off in capital for investment in sport. Owing to a very wet harvest, for corn stood out in the fields until October, the farmers had a very bad time of it, and the few good samples of wheat touched sixty shillings, whilst barley fit for the maltsters made forty-eight. Consequently, there was a falling off in the following amongst those whose income came from land, and their strength is always regarded as representative of the vitality of sport.

Open weather favoured the schooling of the young entry, who started work on August 22nd, accounting for fifty-two cubs in forty-two mornings. The Duke followed the sport one morning on wheels and saw a pretty finish, which pleased him very much. Two hounds, Fencer and Trojan, dashed out from the pack, and the latter killed his fox single-handed; he was a fast resolute hound, and accomplished this feat several times during his career. Fencer was an elegant hound, much admired by the late Mr. Harvey Baily when master of the Rufford, and he always expressed a wish to possess him should he ever be disposed of in the draft.

This was undoubtedly a great fox year, and we find a note made of thirteen foxes viewed away from a small four-acre blackthorn covert, known as Folkingham Little Gorse, which greatly pleased the owner, the Rev. Thomas Heathcote of Lenton, who was a regular follower of the hounds with five of his family. A tribute must be paid to the memory of two brilliant performers which carried the ladies—Blue Stockings, the favourite mount of Miss Lucy Heathcote for many seasons, and a better, bolder fencer never looked through a bridle, though she was a three-cornered mare in appearance. The other that carried Miss Gertrude Heathcote for nine seasons was Janette, named after the Oaks winner of this year, and she was better known as "the Belvoir Hunt pony," measuring but fifteen hands. Nearly

THE KING OF THE PACK.

thoroughbred, she was very fast and could stay from morning to night, jumping some of the biggest fences in Leicestershire and Lincolnshire during her career. The faithful groom who followed these ladies three and four days a week, and had to ride up to them, was William Freeman, often mounted on a small dark-brown mare, named

Miss Coates, who went very fast at her fences with her head in the air. This mare started life in Yorkshire leading gallops at a training stable, was hunted, steeplechased, won jumping prizes at shows, carried the ladies seven seasons, went well in harness, bred four foals, never saved herself at any time, always being keen and light-hearted—but lived to be thirty.

The October gales this year did much damage to fine timber, whose branches were full of leaf, offering immense resistance to the wind. In one of these hurricanes Gillard set out for Aswarby Park, twenty miles distant, which he reached at eight o'clock. Sir Thomas Whichcote was one of a small field who braved the storm, but after an hour of it, Gillard said, "By Jove, Sir Thomas, I cannot stand this place any longer, the trees in covert are flying about like feathers!" At that moment a huge branch crashed down close to his horse, and up-wind he started for kennels, twenty miles away. All over the country trees were falling about, and the hound van, as it left Grantham, was stopped by masses of debris across the road. Unfortunately, on the last morning of cub-hunting, Sir Thomas Whichcote, who was crippled from gout and many accidents by flood and field, fell heavily from his pony through a stirrup-leather giving way. Like the late Duke of Rutland, this fine old sportsman, on every occasion he fell, always excused his horse.

When Sir Thomas was seeking a hack to take the place of a hunter, Gillard sent him a pony to try or buy if it suited. "I have tried the pony," wrote the old baronet, "and I find he can gallop when he is squeezed, but if I do too much of that I am afraid there might be two of him, and that would never do!" The pony was a flat-sided one and a trifle light through the loin, which did not please Sir Thomas, who liked his hunter cast in the mould as near perfection as possible.

A stout October cub is not far removed from a November fox, and a good morning's sport was enjoyed from Stoke Pastures to Harlaxton, where the market carts were met on their way to Grantham town. A small field included Mr. Markham, Mr. C. Samuda, Major Longstaffe, Mrs. and Miss Hornsby, Mr. Richard Ord, and Miss Turner from Stoke. Again from Kaye Wood, at the end of the month, hounds raced an old fox pointing for Quorn domains, crossing the Smite, which had to be negotiated, one of those who got successfully over being Will Tidey, the late Wiverton keeper. It is not often that a hard-riding keeper is heard of, but Will Tidey was one trained by Mr. Chaworth Musters, who liked his men to ride, and was a friend to keepers out of place through shooting foxes; and in this way he converted many vulpicides from the error of their way.

Curious weather marked the commencement of the season, but much good sport was enjoyed, hounds accounting for their foxes day after day. An old customer was roused in Heydour Southings on November 11th, and hounds raced him through Culverthorpe domains by Kelby and Wilsford

Carrs, where he dwelt a few seconds. His bolt was shot, and he went away again only a hundred yards in front of the pack, who coursed and killed him by Rauceby High Wood after a gallop of fifty minutes.

The brush was presented to Mr. Ashmead Bartlett Burdett-Coutts, out for the first time with these hounds, hunting from Grantham, where he stayed the season at the George Hotel with the Baroness soon after their marriage. Mr. Burdett-Coutts had a good stud of hunters, which carried him well to the front; he hunted four seasons with the Belvoir, and then abandoned the chase, disheartened by a series of heavy falls.

On November 12th the big pack of $18\frac{1}{2}$ couple trotted off to Sherbrooke's Covert, which on this occasion held but one fox. "We were some time in getting him away," said Frank, ransacking the storehouse of his memory; "he made a false start, but at last crossed the Smite and ran in the direction of Hose Thorns, bearing right-handed for Clawson and Hose, and we killed him close to the house in which Mr. Burton used to live. I have no doubt but what he meant going to Harby Hills, but the hounds pressed him so hard he had to yield up his brush sooner. I certainly never saw hounds run harder for 15 minutes, and but four of us were with them, viz. Captain 'Bay' Middleton, Captain Pennell Elmhirst, Will Wells and myself. It was charming!"

Grand sport resulted this season, and amongst many red-letter days there was the run of November

25th, one hour and thirty-three minutes from Brentingby Spinney, hounds running from scent to view across Croxton Park, killing their fox on the grass. The brush was presented to the Hon. Mrs. H. H. Molyneux, who rode her white mare "Grey Goose," a Leicestershire celebrity. On December 5th, a remarkable day's sport was seen from Tippings Gorse, lasting three hours and forty minutes, finishing by marking to ground in a swallow hole near Market Overton on Cottesmore domains. Again on December 7th, with the afternoon fox from Freeby Wood there was a capital gallop of fifty-five minutes, hounds running round by Brentingby Spinnies, Freeby, over the brook by Saxby, past Rickett's Plantation to the hill-top as if Stonesby Ashes was their goal. The hunted one then turned right-handed past Coston, where unfortunately a fresh fox jumped up and led the pack until night was established, and they were stopped in the vale below Market Overton. Out of a large field there were but few left at the finish, and these included the Duke of Portland, Lord Grey de Wilton, Lord Cloncurry, the Hon. H. H. Molyneux, Captain T. Boyce, Captain Tennant, Mr. G. Potchin, Mr. H. Flowers, Mr. Parker, Mons. Coutourie, and two or three strangers.

Heavy going after the frost and rain marked the sport which closed the year, but a good day was enjoyed from Croxton Park. A fox was viewed by Will Wells to jump up out of a furrow, shaking the wet from his brush before he started on a long twisty run. A large field were out, and there were many falls, but hounds scored a kill, Lady Sykes being presented with the brush. On the Lincolnshire side the pack were out on December 27th, setting a big dog-fox going from Folkingham Big Gorse, a twisty hunt of one hour resulting, much to the entertainment of a Bank holiday crowd of foot people. The find at the gorse was unexpected, for the covert had only recently been burnt down, having grown itself out. Unfortunately the day was marred by a bad accident, which happened to the Rev. Thomas Heathcote, the squire of Folkingham, whose horse fell at a fence near to the gorse, broke its own back, and so injured his rider's spine that he died from the effects some eighteen months later, in his seventy-fifth year. The name of the horse ridden on this fatal occasion was Glenthorne, and a rather singular history is attached to him, for he was bought by Mr. Heathcote without seeing him first, trusting to the description in the sale list of Sir Thomas Leynard's hunters at Belhus Park. Mr. Tattersall was entrusted with a commission of £170, and in due course the horse arrived at Lenton Vicarage, to be well criticised by the family, who hunted from that house six strong. Except for a good shoulder, he did not appear to have a point to recommend him, being very much on the leg, possessing a big fiddle-shaped head, long neck, and small quarters. But he proved himself a sterling good hunter, and carried the ladies in turn on the Leicestershire side. We may add, whilst talking about Glenthorne, that the whole of these reminiscences of Frank Gillard are dipped by the writer out of an ink-pot made from one of the fore-feet of this horse, mounted in silver, by Rowland Ward of Piccadilly. Another instance of a good judge trusting to chance when

MR. EDGAR LUBBOCK ON DEERFOOT.

buying a horse was that of Mr. "Banker" Hardy, for many years honorary secretary to the Belvoir Hunt, and one of its keenest followers. Seeing an animal described in Tattersall's sale list that promised well, Mr. Hardy sent a commission and bought him. To his disgust, when he arrived at

Grantham, he proved to be only a three-year-old and entire, so he was passed on to a local dealer for a small sum, but eventually blossomed into the well-known hunter sire Berserker, by Buccaneer, winner of many races. Mr. "Banker" Hardy only survived his friend Mr. Heathcote two weeks, never riding to hounds again after the day of the accident, which completely unnerved him.

The great day of the season occurred on January 20th with the lady pack from Keisby Wood, racing hard to Mr. Heathcote's new covert in seven minutes. A change of foxes took place in that covert, and then the pack ran on to Walcott, checking again owing to their fox making a sharp turn before they swung round by Folkingham Big Gorse, where all trace of their hunted one vanished. It turned out afterwards that a coursing gentleman was riding up the old Fosse grass lane hard by, and his greyhounds dashed away and killed the run fox. So horrified was their owner that he threw the carcase into the hedge and galloped off without saying anything about it. A splendid hunt, to make up for the disappointment of the morning, was in store for the afternoon, a record one as regards pace and cross country work. Folkingham Little Gorse supplied the fox, which started running a few fields towards Laughton, and then turned and ran close to Pointon. In sinking the wind from Pointon, it was evident hounds were pressing their fox, for after travelling round by Horbling at a cracking pace, the fugitive was glad to seek the shelter of a drain. Hounds were but twenty yards behind him when he got to ground, and so surprised were they at his sudden disappearance that they turned and twisted in their eagerness, jumping over one another's backs, each hound seeming to imagine that the other had got hold of Charlie, the reason being that the mouth of the drain was hidden from view by a bunch of rushes. A terrier being applied, the fox was bolted and killed, after a regular race of twenty-seven minutes with no sign of a check, and perhaps hounds never traversed so much country in so short a space of time without casting themselves. The following were the foremost division: Mr. A. Burdett-Coutts, Major Longstaffe, Miss Turnor, Captain Tennant, Captain Cecil Thorold, Major Charles Thorold, Mons. Couturie, Colonel Mildmay, and Mr. Walter Willson.

A good instance of the stoutness of the South Lincolnshire foxes is shown in the account of a wonderful run from Newton Wood. This covert is recognised favourite fox-ground, for a fellmonger's shop is in the district, from which issues savoury odours, poison it may be to the inhabitants of the district, but caviare to the nostrils of a fox, who knows what's good. Gillard records that "he proved himself one of the gamest foxes he ever hunted." At a nice hunting pace he led the field round by Osbournby, Spanby, Horbling, and Billingboro to Folkingham Little Gorse in one hour and twelve minutes. "When I saw him leave the gorse I thought he was done with, but he kept on for twenty-five minutes before seeking the shelter of a drain half a mile below Threekingham. A terrier bolted him, and he actually went on for fifteen minutes more before again getting to ground by Sempringham, where hounds scratched him out and drank the blood they had earned so well." Those up at the finish were Colonel Mildmay Willson, C.B., and Miss Willson, Misses L. and G. Heathcote, Mr. Ernest Chaplin, Mr. A. Burdett-Coutts, Captain Cecil Thorold, Mons. Couturie, and the Rev. "Billy" Newcome of Boothby. The latter was a great friend of the Duke's, who always asked, when hearing the account of a good run, "Was Mr. Newcome there?"

The floods that visited the country by the middle of February filled up all the dykes and made the land ride very heavy. So we find February 15th put down as a very hard day for horses and hounds, and unsatisfactory as regards sport, owing to the number of times hounds changed. Beaten foxes were viewed all over the country, and yet no kill was effected. From Newman's Gorse hounds ran by Saxby, Stonesby, close to Freeby village, into Stapleford Park. When the river Whissendine was reached, Arthur Wilson, the second whipper-in, tried to swim his horse over the ford, very swollen after the night's rain, and he was very nearly drowned, for he turned his horse's head down stream with the consequence both went under. Mr. Brocklehurst too was another hardy diver who made the attempt to follow, but parted company with his horse in midstream and had hard work to get to land. Gillard tells a story of how he swam his horse over one of these mud-bottom Leicestershire streams during the first season at Belvoir as whipper-in under Cooper. The season was one of the wettest on record, and all the rivers were running bank high; but the young Devonshire whipper-in, imagining all streams had stone beds like those of his own country, saw no fear in his ardour to turn hounds, and fortune favoured him, for he was quickly out again on the other side, without getting very wet either. Parson Banks Wright saw the performance, and riding up to him, said, "Young man, you must not try to swim the rivers here, or you'll soon be a subject for a coroner's inquest; that sort of thing may be all very well in Devonshire, but you'll soon get stuck in the mud here!"

On February 24th, a ten-mile point, lasting one hour and six minutes, from Irnham Old Park Wood, is worthy of mention, for hounds killed their fox on the door-step of Belton House, the seat of Lord Brownlow, after a very fast spin across the park.

The weather being very open throughout the season, sport was good, with only six days' stop for frost. Hounds went out 144 days, killed 188 foxes, and marked 55 to ground.

At the end of the season Will Wells left to carry the horn for the Puckeridge. His career with the Belvoir was a short but brilliant one, and the hunt never had two finer horsemen than Will Wells and Arthur Wilson to turn hounds at the same time. Across country they were the delight of the thrusters, who, to this day, cherish the memory of many a good lead they gave during a spell of excellent sport. Both were good in the kennel, and to their quickness and instinctive knowledge in the field many a fine run was due. Sir Thomas Whichcote used to point with glee to the great drains round Aswarby, and say: "Will, I've got a good place for you there!" On one occasion Will got over, but Arthur got in, and in the struggle he split his scarlet coat right up the back, but cobbled it up with the aid of string and black thorns to finish the day's work. When Will Wells left, he was presented with a purse of money and eleven silver hunting-horns from admiring friends.

BIRDS OF PASSAGE.

CHAPTER XII

Season 1882-83 and 1883-84

All the Elements of Danger, Steam, Teeth, and Water—The Hunter "Belvoir Grey Bob" and his end—The fastest Dart of the Season—Lord Grey de Wilton breaks his Leg—Runs from Coston Covert—Tom Chambers the old second Horseman—The Horse Gameboy—Mr. Tom Hutchinson down but not dismayed—A good Run and Mrs. Cecil Chaplin presented with the Brush—Gillard breaks his Leg driving the Hound Van home—Letters of Condolence—Mr. George Lane Fox on Hound-breeding—Acting the Good Samaritan and its Consequences—Harry Bonner the Whip—Mr. Merthyr and Lady Guest—The great Day of the best Season on record—A good Leicestershire Hunt—Horses go in for Swimming—Sir Thomas Whichcote begs a Mask—A fine Field of Ash Wednesday Horsemen.

Evidence of a Good Day.

A PROLIFIC crop of falls are the natural consequence of good sport in a wet time, when the ground rides deep and water-logged. The inconvenience of freshly fallen rain it is possible to make light of, for horses can then splash through the dirt, and it does not hold them, but directly the ground crusts and dries on the top, then it pulls them all to pieces, and every stable has its quantum of cripples. Certainly the season under consideration saw a climax of dirt and good sport, and the weather continued wonderfully open considering hounds were stopped only fifteen days for frost.

A memorable and rather sensational day's sport happened on November 14th from Stubton, when a stout running fox faced all the elements of danger before he was numbered with the slain. The lady pack roused him in the Plantation near the Hall, and he ran a ring for a few fields before he went straight away for Whitehills, through the covert on to the railway, where he was so blown that he lay down close to a passing train. To save the pack from destruction they were stopped, and some plate-layers drove the fox off the line, nearly every hound having a snap at him before he reached Whitehill Covert. Going through covert like a shot, he pointed away as if he meant Barkstone Gorse, but finding the pace too severe, changed his tactics and reached the river Witham with the pack only twenty yards from his brush. Hounds dashed over the river, but never recovered the line again on the far side, so that it was pretty certain this good fox must have drowned after leading the pack for thirty-three minutes.

A heavy fall towards the end of November placed Gillard *hors de combat*, as he hurt the muscles of his neck and was very much shaken. However, he was not so easily knocked out as some people might think, for in a very few days he came up smiling like an old prize-fighter, ready to be at them again. One of his favourite mounts was the old white horse Grey Bob, just the stamp for Leicestershire, standing a trifle under 16 hands on short legs, possessing great beam, bone, and muscular development with unusual freedom. Belvoir Grey Bob earned a place on the scroll of fame, for he carried Frank before a thrusting Leicestershire field for eleven seasons, and that without ever giving him a fall that could be attributed to the fault of the horse. On a certain Ash Wednesday, with an enormous field out, a stranger lady crossed Grey Bob at a fence, and the consequence was upset horse and rider. However, she never stopped to pick him up, and probably thought there were plenty more huntsmen to take his place. In Gillard's opinion the old horse was quite capable of paying his way as a chaser, for he had a great turn of speed. By some mischance he was drafted from the hunt stables, and reappeared the following season carrying his new purchaser. Frank was naturally much distressed at losing his old favourite, and this got to the knowledge of the Hon. Lancelot Lowther, who, without saying any more about it, bought the horse and presented him as a personal gift to Gillard. The only conditions were, that when Grey Bob died his fore legs should be sent to the donor, and this was of course gratefully done, one of the hoofs being again returned to Frank, mounted as the base of a massive silver candlestick bearing a suitable inscription—"'Grey Bob,' ridden by Gillard from November 1881 to April 1892."

Frost came in December, and after that the going was so terribly holding that hounds had the foot of horses, and dirty coats were pretty frequent amongst the riding division. Of the many good days on record we choose that of December 19th at Stubton. An outline of the sport we give in the words of Frank's diary. "Directly we put into Stubton Gorse the pack proclaimed a find by giving us their fine music, which made reynard bolt off in the direction of Fenton, and it soon became evident that we must look pretty sharp if we meant to keep with hounds as they passed to the right of Fenton and Beckingham, direct as we could go to Brant Broughton Upper Covert. We ran two miles beyond it, and then turning to the right made for Brant Broughton village, where we killed him in a stable, thus ending a very good run of one hour and forty-eight minutes to the Low Covert. The pace was good throughout, with but one check of importance which occurred after crossing the Stragglethorpe and Sutton road, and owing to my making a forward cast which recovered the line on the grass, the bulk of the field never caught us again until we reached Brant Broughton Low Covert."

The fastest dart of the season happened on January 6th with $17\frac{1}{2}$ couple of the small pack from Holwell Mouth in the afternoon. Taking a picked line of country under Little Belvoir to the corner of Wartnaby Stone Pit, some navvies headed the fox at that point. From there it was a race with hounds running as if viewing their fox past Broughton close by Hickling to the artificial earths in Kaye Wood, whose friendly shelter saved a good fox's life after leading the pack at best pace for over an hour. Those who got to the end, besides the hunt staff, were Lord Grey de Wilton and Mr. A. V. Pryor, who took a line of their own to the left of the Smite, and old Mr. Willoughby of Broughton took an awful cropper in his attempt to follow. The remaining half-dozen were the Hon. Hill Trevor, Captain Smith, Count Charles Kinsky, Mr. Behrens, and two more.

Amongst the foremost leaders of the chase the late Lord Grey de Wilton was one of the hardest, and nothing would turn him from his purpose when once he had made up his mind to go. Gillard narrates a particular occasion when he was pounded by a very rough briery fence, and wheeling his horse round to find a more practical place lower down, he called out to Lord Wilton, who was coming at it, "to stop," but to no purpose, "for he never altered his course a foot to the right or left." By the time Frank got the right side, he saw a riderless horse, and Lord Wilton down, the holding briers having wrapped round and turned him over. At once he noticed that his boot was twisted back the wrong way, indicating a broken leg, though Lord Wilton was unconscious of the fact, and making vain efforts to scramble to his feet. "Lie still, my lord, your leg is broken," shouted Gillard. "Never mind me; go on with your hounds!" was the reply.

When drawing Coston Covert, from which more

good runs have been seen than any other in the hunt, it used to be the rule to send old Tom Chambers on to wait in readiness to view away. As Frank approached he would blow his horn before throwing hounds in, and the plan generally answered, a fox immediately leaving as old Tom's musical voice sounded out of his very boots, and he had a pair of the longest feet in the hunt. The hounds knew the old man's "Gone away!" and always went to it, so that it was generally a flying start from Coston Covert. A good day resulted on January 24th from this covert to Woodwell Head, away for Freeby, where the first check occurred after a fine gallop of thirty-eight minutes. The remainder was a fine bit of hunting on the part of hounds and huntsmen, ending with a kill at Stonesby, time two hours and twenty minutes. Amongst the field out were Lord and Lady Grey de Wilton, the Hon. H. H. and Mrs. Molyneux, Major the Hon. and Mrs. Stirling, Colonel the Hon. H. H. Forester, Mrs. Sloane Stanley, Miss Turner, Sir Hugh Cholmeley, Captains Tennant, Elmhirst, Boyce, Messrs. Pryor, Burdett-Coutts, Henry Chaplin, Barclay, A. Brocklehurst, J. Hutchinson, Westley Richards, Roy, Couturie, George Drummond, the Rev. J. Mirehouse, and J. P. Seabrooke.

Amongst the horses that carried Gillard well was a little bay called Gameboy, who had a little too much fire to suit the aged Duke, but when ridden in a snaffle and nose band he proved one of the best conveyances that ever carried a huntsman. On a memorable occasion, Gameboy cleared a very wide deep drain by Haverholme, and when in the air Gillard saw Mr. Tom Hutchinson and his horse at the bottom of it working their way up to find a place to get out. Mr. Tom Hutchinson was so delighted at the sight of Gameboy flying over, that he shouted out, "I have a great mind to get out the same side I came in, and have a try at it again!"

February 21st with the small pack at Stonesby was a day worthy of the traditions of the month. A traveller was unkennelled from the Gorse, running a ring round Newman's Gorse over the Rectory lawn at Waltham back to Stonesby Ashes, where the pack divided and ran hard in covert before they again united. Opinion had it that hounds got away with a fresh fox, and he led them at a rattling pace, past Garthorpe, crossing the brook midway between Saxby, leaving Stapleford three fields on the right. The railway was crossed near to Whissendine, and the fox with hounds close at him popped into a rabbit hole. First one hound then another got hold of his nose, but the roots of the fence prevented the pack getting fairly at him, and his punishing white ivories paid them back with interest. After about ten minutes of this give-and-take business he bolted of his own accord, and ran three fields before they caught him, making a good finish to a grand run of one hour and twenty-five minutes. The brush was presented to Mrs. Cecil Chaplin riding her well-known hunter "Pebble," a dark brown mare with white markings, measuring under sixteen hands. A good-sized field started to ride the run, which was a ten-mile point from Waltham Limekilns to the kill, but very few got to the end of it, for the brook at Garthorpe caused a lot of grief.

In summing up the merits of the season, Gillard remarked, "I never knew the Belvoir vale to ride so holding, the ground was somewhat dried on the top, so that horses could hardly lift their feet out of the dirt." The number of days registered was 137, with 113 foxes killed, and 36 marked to ground.

Season 1883-84

Owing to the wet summer, harvest operations were very late, hardly any corn being "stouked" by September 1st, consequently hounds did not begin cubbing quite so soon as in former years. The season was remarkable for its nice hunting weather, hounds being stopped but three days for frost and fog. This fact was all the more trying for Gillard, who had the misfortune to break his leg at the end of October and was in consequence laid by until January 8th, the hounds being hunted in the meantime by Arthur Wilson, the first whipper-in. The accident happened as follows: On October 23rd, after a hard morning's cub-hunting, Gillard was vanning the hounds home from Grantham in company with George Champion, who had come to take the autumn draft from Belvoir to the Duke of Richmond and Gordon's kennel at Goodwood. The van full of hounds, with

Frank driving the unicorn team, got as far as Harston, where the leader was taken off, reducing the team to a pair of wheelers, one of which was an untried underbred horse, who when half way down the hill turned restive, threw himself away from the pole, upsetting the van by running the wheel up the bank. Unfortunately, Gillard could not get clear from the apron which strapped him on, and the van falling on his leg fractured it badly. The two whippers-in escaped unhurt, George Champion bruised his arm, but no damage was fortunately done to the hounds.

Letters of sympathy came from all corners of England, and the concern expressed for the speedy recovery of the Duke's huntsman might well have made an archbishop or a prime minister turn green with envy. Amongst this mass of correspondence we select the letter of the veteran master of the Bramham Moor, who wrote: "These accidents come when we least expect them, and must be borne with patience." Mr. George Lane Fox then went on to talk of hounds and hound-breeding, which must always be interesting, coming from such a source. "The Duke of Beaufort's Render I

Mr. George Lane Fox, M.F.H.

fancied because I had such stout hard workers by Lord Portsmouth's Render. But he is not a stallion hound, too tall and bad about the knees, though a nice-looking hound in the field. The young Renders work hard in the field, and some of them are good-looking. Lord Galway's Clasher has done pretty well for me. I send you one of my hound books, you will see how much Belvoir blood I have. You will observe that my book begins when Charles Treadwell came to this pack, when the hounds were in Lord Harewood's possession. He had to begin with a pack bad in work and appearance, all bred in and in, no lists kept. Treadwell had a good store of hound knowledge in his head, and was a keen man. In my early days I was advised entirely by him."

Another letter of condolence which caught our eye as we looked through some fifty of them was from the Hon. H. H. Molyneux. "I am very sorry for you—also for ourselves. It is very hard lines to be knocked out in that way. Confound that driving unicorn! 'A cobbler should stick to his last,' they say, and a huntsman, I suppose, to his saddle. You must keep yourself patient, and watch your diet well. Going from jolly hard exercise to a sick bed for so horrid a long time, does come a bit unfair on one's stomach."

As might be expected, Frank threw away his lame leg at the earliest possible moment, and as soon as ever he could bear a legging on it, ordered out the easiest horse he had in the stable, old Sluggard the gray, and hacked gently about for an hour or two at a time, whilst Arthur Wilson hunted the pack. On one of these early days of invalidism, old Mr. Vincent took a fall and got hung up in his saddle. To render first aid and act the good Samaritan was Gillard's foremost thought, though he was too much of a cripple to climb down from his saddle, but the timely help averted what might have been a terrible accident. Now it so happened that both were insured in the same accidental company, and when Mr. Vincent applied for an allowance during disablement consequent from the accident, he gave Frank's name as a witness. The result was the agent of the company wrote to the good Samaritan, "What brought you out hunting with a broken leg?" A satisfactory explanation was of course forthcoming, for Gillard was only a spectator and unfit to ride a yard.

Arthur Wilson, in the meantime, was successful in his efforts to show sport, although he nearly met his fate through a fall over wire, which sent him home with hounds by two o'clock, incapacitated for further work that day. The staff were fortunate in possessing Harry Bonner as second whipper-in, and right well he tumbled to the duties of turning hounds to Arthur. After a season or two with the Belvoir he went to the Meath, then to carry the horn for the Tyndale, where he was much liked, and now he is huntsman to the Meynell.

Amongst those who came to renew old acquaintance with hounds were Mr. Merthyr and Lady Guest from the Blackmore Vale, a hunt which must always present a striking and pleasing effect in the field, from the fact that the whole staff are mounted on gray horses. The colour is hard to beat, and where woods abound it is the easiest to find.

On the authority of Brooksby the season was "a best on record for sport," and his charming book under that title, dedicated by permission to H.R.H. the Prince of Wales, gives us the leading events with the Leicestershire packs.

On January 12th, when Gillard was once more in command, the Belvoir were in luck, carrying on the wave of good sport which marked the opening months of the year, and they ran nearly to a standstill in a tremendous gallop backwards and forwards between their own country and that of the Quorn. The day deserved a kill after a fast forty-five minute gallop by moonlight to Asfordby, for then it would have ranked as one of the best things of a wonderful season's sport. Those sportsmen who saw the finish were the Duke of Portland, Captains Boyce, Smith, and Tennant, Messrs. Beaumont, Burdett-Coutts, Crawley, G. Drummond, Foster, Knowles, E. Lubbock, Praed, and Pryor.

On January 26th, after meeting at Hose Grange in the vale of Belvoir, the little pack of seventeen and a half couple had a rattling scent all day. A regular flyer was set going from Sherbrooke's Gorse the second time of asking, and he led hounds at a terrific pace over the vale to Kinoulton, and when ascending that hill to the left of the gorse, the Quorn Hunt were seen, having met at

Lodge-on-the-Wolds. The point was Roehoe Wood, but the fox, finding the artificial earths closed, made an attempt to go to Wynstay Gorse, till a sheep-dog interfered and drove him back through the covert which the Quorn had entered. Mr. Sherbrooke, riding with the Quorn, left that hunt to see the Belvoir kill the fox they had brought from his covert. After slow hunting round the Curate, the fox took a course parallel with the Smite, and got to ground in a rabbit hole by Clawson, from which he was ejected, and being too stiff to run farther, was killed. The time from the find to Roehoe Wood was twenty-five minutes, to the finish fifty-five minutes. The barometer fell during the day, and a southerly wind freshened up into a gale towards evening.

A curious experience befell a sportsman on one occasion when hounds met at Waltham, and the day's operations lay entirely in the Melton district. When riding the line of fences from Burbidge's Covert towards Stapleford, a route interwoven with railway and river, he had occasion to dismount, and his horse thereupon entered the river, swimming across to join the hounds on the far side. No sooner had he reached the opposite bank than a friendly horseman tried to catch him, but he turned round, entered the water again, and swam back to his rightful owner. Was not the latter an unlooked-for act of Providence!

On February 5th, after a good run of an hour and a half, a curious finish resulted with a railway-loving Rauceby fox. After running all over the lordships of Rauceby, Wilsford, and Willoughby, he was picked up on the line by a platelayer, apparently dead beat. This worthy carried him on, but seeing hounds coming, turned him down again, and he ran for three fields before yielding up his brush.

Another run with a red mark of excellence against it we find recorded on February 8th from Folkingham Big Gorse, the pack running very fast by Birthorpe, Billingboro, Horbling forward for Swaiton, back by Newton Gorse, Walcott, and Threekington, to finish near Spanby. A hound called Dextral, a dark tan little bitch, sighted the fox, and running into him, killed before her comrades could come up, after a fine hunt of one hour and five minutes. The veteran Sir Thomas Whichcote was so pleased at the performance that he begged the mask, and he never did so unless it was a run of great excellence. The leading division were Major Amcotts, Captain A. Welby, Captain Tennant, and J. Bellamy. Two days later, in the afternoon, Captain Alfred Welby, Dragoon Guards, met with a crushing fall by Keisby Wood through his horse putting a foot in a rabbit hole.

The Belvoir Ash Wednesday as usual attracted a large field, representative of at least a dozen hunts. A find was proclaimed at Sproxton Thorns, hounds running well to Bescaby Oaks, over the Sproxton brook and out of scent. The afternoon fox was set going from Wymondham Mill, and gave a gallop over a picked line of country worthy of so historical an occasion. Running by Teigh

SEASON 1883-84

village, he came sharp back into Ashwell, where Mr. Alec Goodman, who had galloped forward, viewed him dead beat, and a few minutes later the "Who whoop" sounded in Stapleford Park after a quick thirty minutes without a check. Gillard's remark to the day's sport was, "I never saw a finer field of horseman ride to hounds." He had with him the talent of half-a-dozen shires.

The number of hunting days this season was 145, the number of foxes killed 118.

A LEAD OVER.

CHAPTER XIII

Season 1884-85

The Hound Gambler described, and his Measurements—Canon Kingsley's Description—The Hound Gameboy—Cub-hunting Notes—George Carter the Fitzwilliam Huntsman, and the Puppies by Rubican—Arthur Wilson gets stuck in the Smite—The Belvoir and Quorn Gallop; Rivalry and Kill—The Brush of the Belvoir and Quorn Fox—The Rauceby Pink Wedding—The Belvoir Hunt Steeplechase Course—A Leicestershire Spin—The Marquis of Waterford—A critical Field out for the last Day's Sport.

THE young entry of this season was an exceptionally strong one, with two amongst their number who are destined to become the most celebrated stud hounds of their day. The name of Gambler by the famous Weathergage [1]—Gratitude is one known world wide, for his sons and daughters went to build up kennels throughout the United Kingdom and abroad. A hound of great character and massive appearance, combined with

TOM FIRR.

[1] See Weathergage pedigree, Chapter VII.

beautiful colour and outline, he made a king worthy of such a pack like the Belvoir. His praises have been sung by all who saw him, his portrait painted by more than one artist, and his bones are now set up like those of the great race-horse Hermit. Gillard could not honour him too much, regarding him as the most perfect type of the beautiful Belvoir blood, filling the kennel with his stock. In all parts of a run he was perfect, and he possessed a beautiful voice, which he used freely, resounding through the woods, giving the keynote to the pack, who would fly to it. The best of his stock were hounds of great character, remarkable for their good looks on the flags, and their good hunting qualities in the field; moreover, the breed was everlasting, and never tired. Gambler was probably the sire of more hounds than any other of his day, and lived to his fourteenth season, running with the pack up to a year of his death, when he had to be drafted for deafness. Although Belvoir Gamblers cannot be bred from rule of thumb, the proportions of this remarkable foxhound as taken by Mr. Basil Nightingale, who painted his portrait for the Duke of Rutland, are worth preserving as an example of what symmetry should be. Standing twenty-three inches at the shoulder, from the extreme point of his shapely shoulders to the outer curve of his well-turned quarters he measured twenty-seven and a half inches in length, whilst from elbow to ground his height was only twelve inches. Possessing great depth of rib and room round the heart, he girthed thirty-one inches, and his arm below was eight and a quarter inches round. Below the knee he measured five and a quarter inches of solid bone, while round the thigh he spanned full nine and a quarter inches. The extended neck was ten inches from cranium to shoulder, and the head ten inches and a half long. His colour was of the richest, displaying all the beautiful "Belvoir tan," and his head had that brainy appearance expressive of the highest intelligence. Gambler might have inspired that earnest poet Canon Kingsley when he described the modern foxhound: "The result of nature, not limited, but developed by high civilisation. Next to an old Greek statue there are few such combinations of grace and strength as in a fine foxhound. Majesty is the only word; for if he were ten feet high instead of twenty-three inches, with what animal on earth could you contrast him? It is joy to see such perfection alive." Gambler's own brother, Gameboy, was quite as good in his work, although he had not quite the same dash and swagger, being rather shy with strangers when showing on the flags. "In the field," Gillard said, "both were hard-running hounds, and I often pointed out the two brothers hunting side by side as if they were in couples." Gameboy left some good stock in the Belvoir kennel like his brother did, and both sired many a Peterborough winner for other packs, so that their fame as the stout sons of old Weathergage will never die out.

The tremendous growth of nettles this season

greatly punished the young hounds when covert-hunting, and drought, with great heat, lasted right up to the middle of November, destroying scent, making the ground so hard that the opening day of the season was delayed until the 8th of November. Though rising at cockcrow four mornings a week for cub-hunting, Gillard found time to go to Quorn to judge the puppies for Lord Manners, who succeeded Mr. John Coupland this season. The best morning's sport with the cubs was on September 12th, in that good forest of oak, Ropsley Rice, which always holds one or two litters. A dense white fog brought a great scent, and the pack raced in the open for forty minutes, killing their fox a hundred yards from Belton Park. Very few saw anything of the run, the field riding about all over the country hopelessly lost in the fog, only to learn the interesting details next day. At the end of October there was quite a gathering at Weaver's Lodge, but the ground was almost too hard for anything but covert work. Amongst those present were Lord and Lady Middleton, who drove to the meet and hunted on foot, Mr. Rawnsley, master of the Southwold, Mr. Mansell Richardson, the Rev. Cecil Legard, and the huntsman from the Brocklesby, Mr. Preston and Mr. Holliday from Yorkshire, professedly to see the stallion hounds in their work. The last-named sportsman used to pay an annual visit to Belvoir, coming with old Mr. Hall, a friend of the late Duke of Rutland's. He was a fine type of yeoman, belonging to the old school, when the price of wheat made it possible to keep the stable full of hunters.

It was a pleasure to set Gillard going on a good gossiping scent as he turned to his diary; and the mark of excellence against November 15th, at Hose, revived memories of sport and those who played their part in it. "I gave a mount to old George Carter, the famous Fitzwilliam huntsman, that day, and I think he must have brought us luck, for we ran for an hour on the grass. He came to watch the big dog pack in their work, with the view of a cross for the stout Milton blood, who were sweeping the board of prizes at Peterborough Show. Belvoir Rubican—1870—did the Fitzwilliam kennel a lot of good, and one litter of four bitches and two dogs was especially excellent in the field and on the flags. I must tell you that Belvoir Rubican was a first-season hunter when I came as huntsman, and owing to the lameness of my predecessor Cooper, the pack had gone to the bad, and it was impossible to cross a deer park without their running riot. I had therefore to rebreak the pack, and Rubican was the biggest tartar of the lot, determined to hunt whatever he liked. Patience and five days a week put him right, for he took to fox, and fox only, and when he retired to the stud was used everywhere. In those days I was often at Milton by Peterborough, for the master, the Hon. George Fitzwilliam, knew me very well, and gave me many a mount; he was a relation by marriage to the late Duke of Rutland, having married a niece of

Lord Forester's, so that he came to Belvoir and spent many an hour at the kennels. When I was out with the Fitzwilliam by Caldecott, I asked George Carter how my Rubican puppies were framing for their work, and he replied in his usual dry way, 'Oh, I don't think they are up to much!' so I kept my eyes open, and sure enough saw them dash out, making one or two good hits. 'Well done, Rubicans!' I shouted. 'Well done again, Rubicans!' Old George Carter stared at me and said, 'I don't know how it is, those Rubicans are doing all the work to-day!' 'Of course they are,' I replied, 'they know I'm here!'"

Three days later hounds had another good spin with an evening fox from Sparrow Gorse, when the big field of the morning had melted away and only the chosen few remained. Hounds were stopped owing to darkness by Rauceby after fifty minutes of the very best. All the horses were done to a turn, but those who struggled to the end were Mr. Edgar Lubbock, Mr. T. Robarts, Mr. Peregrine Birch, Mr. Lionel Trower, Mons. Roy, Mr. Richard Hornsby, and that good sporting farmer and judge of stock Mr. J. H. Bemrose, who has seen over a quarter of a century's sport with the Belvoir.

The very pace of the beautiful Belvoir blood will often cause them to flash over the line, and on one memorable occasion they crossed the river Smite when Gillard had evidence that his fox was back and sinking fast. So keen was Arthur Wilson to turn the pack to the huntsman that he attempted to swim his horse over the river. Un fortunately for him, it was one of those dull sluggish streams, yards deep in thick black mud. Arthur would have been no more, but for timely assistance as he struggled in the holding mud with his terrified horse. One of those who rode up to render aid was Mrs. Sloane Stanley, and she exclaimed, "Oh dear, I am sorry for you! If Mrs. Arthur was here now, she would not know you!" It made the whip smile even in his awkward plight, for there was no Mrs. Arthur in those days.

One of the most memorable days' sport in the annals of the pack occurred on Monday, December 22nd, when the Belvoir and Quorn Hunts met in the middle of a run, and joining forces, killed their fox in company. Gillard roused his fox in Harby Covert and had the pack quickly away, running to Kaye Wood by Colston Bassett. Hounds were pressing their fox all the way, and his point was evidently the Curate's Gorse in Quorn domains, but the keeper of the covert heading him off, he made for a small plantation by Widmerpool, entering it after leading the pack at a good pace for one hour and twenty minutes. It so happened the Quorn hounds were in the district, and Tom Firr was casting about for his fox which was lost after a spin; Mr. J. Coupland saw the Belvoir enter the covert by Widmerpool and told his huntsman. Whilst Gillard was standing in the central ride cheering hounds, Tom Firr galloped up with his hounds just as the fox crossed the ride behind the Belvoir huntsman's horse without his viewing him. "Tally-ho!" shouted Firr, "Tally-

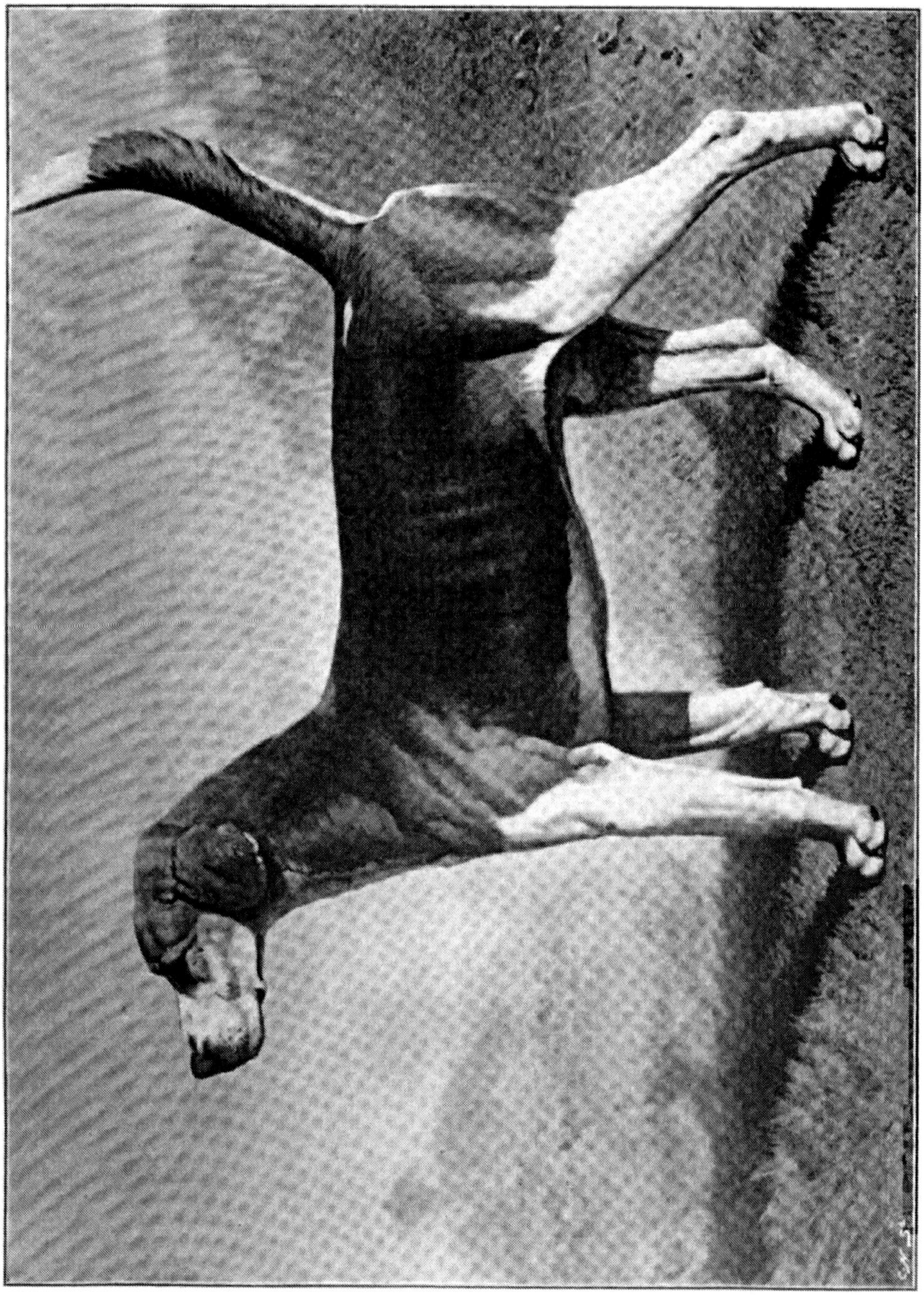

THE NEW YORK
PUBLIC LIBRARY

ASTOR, LENOX AND
TILDEN FOUNDATIONS
R   L

ho! that's my fox!" "Now, Tom, behave yourself," replied Frank, for he saw that it was a critical moment, and did not mean being second best, though on Quorn soil. "I shall be very angry directly, Tom, if you don't let my fox alone, for you know you had no line into this covert!" The two packs settled any further argument by opening on the line, rattling the fox out of covert as they went away together. "It was a very lively run, I can tell you," said Gillard as he brightened up at the very thought of it; "and, as you may imagine, there was a little jealousy between the two hunts, for everybody meant having the first place. Firr took a most awful imperial crowner soon after starting, at a fence with a drop on the landing side, carrying away liberal tufts of grass on his coat-tail buttons for the rest of the day. We had to turn to gap or gate whenever it was possible to do so, for none of the second horsemen had come up, and the pace during the first hour of the run had been sufficient to keep horses galloping along. I rode a little snaffle-bridled bay horse all day, name Gameboy, and he made no mistake, enabling me to be quickest up at the finish. The hounds never wanted much help, as they took the line away for Parsons Thorns to Old Dalby Wood, leaving Grimston Gorse on the left into Saxelby Spinney. Here I viewed our fox, a big gray dog, and not very far in front of hounds, but he was not done with yet, and struggled gamely on to Welby Holt or Lord Wilton's plantation, where they killed him after hunting together for one hour and five minutes, the Belvoir having run consecutively for two hours and twenty-five minutes. I could hear the hounds savaging him in covert, and was quickly off my horse, knowing there was not a moment to lose. Hounds had broken up their fox, but, as luck would have it, they left the brush and mask lying close together, so I picked them up before Firr came, putting the brush in my pocket as I wanted to take it to the Duke, and I was afraid one of the field might ask for it. As Firr made no claim, I thought I would not be hard on him, so said, 'Here you are, Tom, you take the mask, as your hounds helped to kill my fox!' A moment later, to my horror, I heard him tally-hoing and who-whooping in the central ride, with every hound round him and the field looking on, under the impression it was his fox. 'By Jove!' I said, 'this will never do,' and I slipped out of covert, ran about fifty yards down the fence, blowing my horn, waving the brush about. In a moment all the hounds left Tom and came to me, so I cheered and hallooed them till I thought he had heard enough of it, and he said to me, 'Now, Frank, we had better take the pack to that gate and draw out our own hounds.' 'All right,' I said, 'let me jump on my horse first.' No sooner was I in the saddle and said, 'Come on, my lads!' than every one of my hounds came to my horse's heels, including one couple of the Quorn, which I had the pleasure of returning next day. Mr. J. Coupland came up and begged very hard for the brush, saying that he would give anything to possess it as a memento of so remarkable a run, for we had covered twenty-six miles of country. I let him have it, but as his Grace the Duke of Rutland expressed a wish next day to possess it, I wrote to Mr. Coupland, and he very kindly returned it, so that I had it set up in a case and placed in the room at the kennels." The field who rode this run included Mr. Burdett-Coutts, Mr. Edgar Lubbock, Mr. Francis Crawley, Mr. Ernest Chaplin, Mr. Lionel Trower, Mons. Roy, and Mons. Couturie, all from Grantham. Then there were Mr. J. C. Coupland, Mr. Craig, Captain Hume, and the Rev. J. P. Seabrooke to represent Melton; Mr. Fisher of Orston, Dr. Williams of Colston Basset, Mr. John Marriott of Cropwell, and Mr. Henry Smith. To this day the case may be seen at the kennels containing the brush of this memorable fox, and a printed account of the day's sport, with two other trophies. These latter belonged to a fox that was killed the day after Lord Forester's funeral. It was the end of October, but the pack had been stopped for this sad event, and Gillard was only giving them an exercise in the woods round Belvoir. However, they got glued to the line of an old one, who gave them an extraordinary hunt, lasting nearly two hours, before he was rolled over in the cabbage garden not far from the kennels. The mask was one of the biggest we have ever seen, and Gillard always regarded it as one of the family heirlooms belonging to the pack. The other brush in the case belonged to a fox killed by Blankney kennels, December 15th, 1885. Winter and rough weather ushered in the January of 1885, but hounds were out of kennel whenever there was half a chance, and on the last day before the frost a large and distinguished gathering were at Croxton Park to meet them. Amongst those present were the Duke of Rutland, on wheels, accompanied by Sir Frederick Leighton, the late President of the Royal Academy, the Marquis of Waterford, Lord John Manners, and a host of Leicestershire and Lincolnshire sportsmen.

Much good sport was enjoyed during February, and the month was made memorable by the Lincolnshire pink wedding at Rauceby Hall, on the 17th, between two of the best-known followers of the hunt, Major "Fritz" Amcotts, 5th Dragoons, and Miss Emily Willson. The morning was bright, though a powdering of snow covered the ground, a very large field attending the wedding ceremony and the meet at Rauceby in honour of the occasion. The bride and bridegroom joined the hunt, and a fox jumped up off the fallows near to Bully Wells, showing the way nearly to Sleaford town, then twisting back to Rauceby, where he was killed by the Hall, in full view of the wedding party, who were assembled there. Altogether it was a singular occurrence befitting the occasion, for the run lasted one hour and seventeen minutes. It proved a good scenting day, for the evening fox started from Sparrow Gorse gave an eight-mile point.

An interesting run is recorded from Keisby Wood across a fine stretch of Lincolnshire country in the vale below Lenton, where a course was in preparation for the Belvoir Hunt steeplechases, which were instituted this year by Mr. Burdett-Coutts, who won the red-coat race riding his own horse. Twice the Lenton brook came in this charming run, and it is a classical stream that sets a hall-mark of approval on the sport of the day. Of the twenty who rode up to hounds, including Miss Lucy and Gertrude Heathcote, fifteen took a fall before the run finished. The point this good fox hoped to make was Sapperton Wood, but he was unfortunately headed, and ran a ring back by Lenton Pastures to Aslackby Wood, where he beat his pursuers in that big forest.

The month's sport closed with a good day on the Leicestershire side from Sherbrooke's Covert in the morning, and Wartnaby stone pits in the afternoon, hounds being stopped at 6.80 by Kinoulton Gorse.

At the close of the season the Belvoir hold a meet in the town of Melton, the Quorn on the opposite banks of the river which marks the boundary of the two packs. The hunting metropolis is always full this week for the ball, so that both packs have a good following. This occurred on March 4th, and the afternoon fox from Coston Covert gave a remarkably fast spin of twenty minutes before he was pulled down on Sproxton Heath. The brush was presented to the Marquis of Waterford, the mask to Captain King King, whilst Miss Chaplin and the Hon. H. H. Molyneux took pads. There were few men who went harder than the late Marquis of Waterford, or enjoyed their sport more thoroughly. When out with the Belvoir he once jumped a gate on the swing, his horse catching the top bar, giving his rider a terrible fall. Some thought that this fall brought about the serious illness and subsequent paralysis which ended his life.

On the last day of the season, April 14th, at Marston, in weather that savoured more of June, we find a characteristic entry in Gillard's diary: "Rather a nice field were out, there being no less than three masters of hounds, two ex-masters, and one huntsman. They were Lord Harrington, Lord Galway, Mr. C. B. Wright from the Badsworth, Mr. Richard Ord of the North Durham, Mr. Pennington, and Sam Morgan, huntsman to the Grove hounds."

The number of hunting days this season was 139, and 121 foxes were killed.

LORD HARRINGTON, M.F.H.

CHAPTER XIV

Seasons 1885-86 and 1886-87

Six Masters of Hounds out Cub-hunting—Mr. Brockton of Farndon—The big Day of the Season ending at Blankney—Good Hound Work—A Day with Lord Lonsdale's Hounds at Blankney—Blooding Lord William Manners—Mr. Basil Cochrane—The hardest Day of the Season with many Leicestershire Foxes—Home on Foot, all the Horses beat—Three of the Hunt Horses—Frank Beers the Grafton Huntsman—A note about the Brocklesby Kennel—Several good Days—A Run and Kill by the Forty-Foot Drain—A Wedding Special saves the Pack from Destruction—A good March Gallop and Kill in an Ash Tree—A Note of Music in Frank's Diary—The Fowl-House Door opens to the Name of the Duke.

THE STACKER'S ART.

"NO less than six masters of hounds came to look at us one morning during the cubbing season when we met at Croxton Park. They were Mr. Lort Phillips from the North Warwickshire, Mr. Chandos Pole from the Meynell, Mr. W. E. Wemyss from the Burton, Mr. Coupland from the Quorn, Lord Middleton from

Yorkshire, Lord Willoughby de Brooke from Warwickshire, and Lord Lonsdale from Blankney. They could not have come on a worse occasion, for it was very stormy all day, foxes ran short, and we had a poor scent. Late in the day, when they had all left us, we had a nice spin," said Frank, referring to his diary. During the cubbing time hounds did plenty of hard work, "the fifteen couple of youngsters entering well, except Magic and Mystery by South Notts Mountebank. On September 18th, on a very hot morning, we were at Rauceby by six o'clock, and in the saddle twelve hours. Again on the 25th we left kennels at 4 A.M. and returned 4 P.M. What with thorn-hunting afterwards, attending to the lame, and making hounds comfortable for the night, the whippers-in were in hard condition by the time the season proper commenced."

The opening day on November 3rd at Leadenham House was wet, and seventeen and a half couple of the little pack were out, who quickly accounted for a fox in the Hill-top Covert. The second run was started from Colonel Willson's Gorse, and they ran nicely, marking to ground in Wellingore Gorse, one of the Blankney coverts. Lord Lonsdale was out, and he offered to bolt the fox with one of his wire-haired terriers.

A red-letter day resulted from Staunton on 7th. A fine old fox was roused in Cotham Thorns, going away by Bennington and Claypole to Stubton, where the pack divided with a fresh fox in Coddington Plantation, one lot marking to ground, the others going on to Stapleford Moor, where they were stopped. No one went better than the veteran Mr. Brockton and his third daughter riding a thoroughbred, the three sisters being feather-weights, and hard to catch over a country. Mr. Brockton lived at Farndon, on the banks of the Devon, a sterling good sportsman who made his mark as a rider between the flags, besides owning several horses of note, Victor Chief being a sire of many winners on the flat and over a country. In the furtherance of hunting interests his services have been invaluable. A great fox-preserver himself, he delighted to convert those who were not, and generally won his point with the aid of a present in the shape of a pig or the use of his stud horse.

The big day of the season came on December 15th, when seventeen couple of the dog pack found a fox in Lord Bristol's Plantation, and quickly ran him to ground by Temple Bruer. Speedily ejected from his hiding-place with the help of a rocket, he ran past Ashby-de-la-Laund, through the Thorns to Kirkby Green, where he was headed by plough teams and turned sharp back. With patient hunting they followed on by Blankney gardens, and killed him very tired near to the kennels, making a capital finish to a run of one hour and fifty-five minutes. Hounds that came in for particular notice during the run were Fencer and his son Fenian, Stainless by Fallible, Gainer, Gambler, Glancer, Flyer, Newsman and Worcester. The brush of this good fox the Duke had placed in the glass case at the kennels, containing two other trophies of memorable days. The hound Fencer was much admired by the late Mr. Harvey Bailey, who, had he lived, promised him a home in the Rufford kennel when his hunting days were over. Stainless, the son of Fallible, was used by Gillson in the Cottesmore kennel, and he did much for that pack, siring some beautiful bitches. Flyer was a hound who left some beautiful stock in the Duke of Buccleuch's kennel, and his services went in exchange for strong Scotch foxes off the moors, sent by old Shaw the huntsman to turn down in Leicestershire for fresh blood.

On the last day of the year Lord Lonsdale invited Gillard to Blankney to have a day with his hounds from Bloxholm, mounting him on a hog-maned chestnut, which was the favourite colour. Hounds ran well at starting, after which they did little good but drag on after their fox until they came up with him in Crow Bottom Covert, where they killed. "With a scent the pack would have done well," was Frank's opinion, "for they kept their noses down and were quick in casting, particularly Villager, a good-looking short-legged hound well off for bone and very muscular. This hound was used at Belvoir kennels later with good results."

The new year brought frost, in all a forty days' stop to hunting, but on January 14th the pack had a by-day at Goadby, the going in the vale being possible. Those out were the Hon. Mrs. Pennington, Captain and Mrs. Brocklehurst, Mr. John Welby, three sportsmen from Melton, and Messrs. Cecil, Robert, and William Manners. "The latter

I had the honour to enter to hounds, and I painted him, as I thought, fairly well, but he expressed himself disappointed at not being blooded all over his face," was the remark made in Gillard's diary after performing the Baptême de chasse for "Our Billy of Belvoir," as the late Lord William Manners was affectionately termed by his many hunting friends.

The red mark of excellence stands against the doings of February 17th, when hounds assembled at Croxton Park, the day being fine with a keen northeast wind blowing. "Sport commenced with a sharp ring from Coston Covert, but the second time away we ran at a rattling pace by Wymondham Wind Mill to Rickett's Covert, where we changed. Our run fox was viewed by Major Candy, going away with one hound, Niobe, in pursuit. After slow hunting, and difficulties from fresh foxes jumping up, we ran very hard by Waltham Thorns, going round by Goadby, Bullmore, and Harby Hills. Here I viewed him running along the bank of the canal, and on reaching Harby he ran a ring to Eastwell, and killed by the railway after a good hunt of one hour and twenty minutes. Those I noticed going best were Captain Arthur Smith, Lord Hopetoun, Mr. Basil Cochrane, the Rev. J. P. Seabrooke and Mrs. Candy." Of these, Mr. Cochrane hunted up to within four months of his death, which occurred at the ripe age of seventy-eight, in April 1896. A bold determined horseman, he delighted to follow Tom Firr and Frank Gillard wherever they went, often telling them that he preferred this to taking a line of his own. His nerve was good up to the last, although he came in for some awful croppers in his time, breaking his leg at the age of seventy. By the rising generation he was looked upon as a golden link between sport of the past and present, being a fine specimen of a true English gentleman and an officer of the 6th Inniskilling Dragoons. During a long and varied experience, Mr. Cochrane hunted with many packs and in many countries, but always came back to the Belvoir, hunting the best of his time from Grantham.

The best day's sport of the season, one of the hardest for horses and hounds in the annals of the hunt, was on February 20th from Piper Hole. The morning was frosty and the wind south-east, scent lying well on the grass. Gillard had twenty-three and a half couple out, made up from the middle and small packs. Finding in Melton Spinney, hounds ran a bee line to Kettleby; they changed foxes and raced by Scalford Station back to Holwell, where he beat them after a forty minutes' gallop. The second run was from Holwell Mouth with a fresh fox, and he gave a brilliant fifty minutes by Clawson Thorns down to Hose Village, past Sherbrooke's to Little Belvoir. Here he turned sharp back to his starting-point, and, unfortunately, hounds changed again at Piper Hole Gorse. Going away from this covert with a fresh one, the pack ran hard for one hour and forty minutes right into the Quorn country, passing Melton Spinney, marking to ground on the railway at Asfordby, where some plate-layers viewed him just in front of them. Out of a very large field very few remained to see the finish: these were Lord Hopetoun, Captain Brocklehurst, the Hon. A. Pennington, and Mr. Pryor, jun. Both the whip's horses were dead beat, and Arthur Wilson left his at a farmhouse near Asfordby, whilst

GILLARD GOT HIS SECOND HORSE AT THE RIGHT MOMENT.

Gillard left his at Melton in Mr. Pryor's stables. The hounds were brought home by train to Redmile, and the hunt staff footed it with them late that night from the station to the kennels.

Amongst the best conveyances in the hunt stables this season were two by Ripponden, a good hunter sire who stood at Belvoir, and sired Playfair, a Grand National winner. The mare was Whitefoot, a fine jumper, and the horse was Farewell, who made a great name for himself, and in his day jumped the Melton brook oftener than any other horse in Leicestershire. Another good mount was Horn Shy, so called because he was very excitable, and took hold of his bit when he heard the horn. Over the big doubles in the Leadenham Vale this horse was not to be beaten, "and never set a foot wrong."

On April 14th the meet was at Piper Hole, and it was a regular hound day, with twisting foxes very sparing of scent. One of those who thoroughly enjoyed it, regarding it from a professional point of view, was Frank Beers, the Grafton huntsman, who returned with the pack to kennels at 9 P.M. The mention of this fine sportsman's name conjures up ancient history, for Frank Beers followed his father as huntsman, but one thing he lacked in comparison, and that was voice. Old George could ring such a merry tune as would charm the very foxes from their earths. Frank was first initiated under his father with the Oakley, went from there as second whip to the Brocklesby, then to Russia as huntsman to Count Branetski, who, in addition to a pack of foxhounds, had a stud of seven hundred brood mares, together with some well-known English sires. Beers was driven out of the land of the Tzar by the Crimean War, and found his way to Grafton to turn hounds to his father. Talking of the Brocklesby, there is little doubt that these hounds have been kept as a pack in the Pelham family for quite a hundred and seventy years. Moreover, the Smith family hunted them for almost as long a period, the office descending from father to son without any intermission, Nimrod Long following the first break of the Smiths.

The number of hunting days this season was 121, there being ten weeks' stop for frost. The pack accounted for 121 foxes, 1 badger, and 1 otter weighing 26 pounds, killed in Burbidge's Covert, which was set up in a glass case and put in the Duke's room at the kennels.

Season 1886-87

It was a late harvest and a luxuriant autumn, with a wealth of grass and tangle in the ditches warranted to catch even a third-season hunter. One of those who fell a victim to the blindness of the country was Arthur Wilson, who took a very heavy fall on to his head and was in consequence laid up for a month. Hounds went out twenty-seven mornings during the cubbing time, and accounted for nineteen brace. Taken altogether, it was a short season owing to frost and hard going, but excellent sport was enjoyed during November and the greater part of December, hounds running well day after day.

The opening day was bright and scentless, beautiful for agriculture and outdoor exercise, but too gaudy to hunt. In spite of this, hounds managed to mop up a brace of fat foxes, and no doubt the field enjoyed the ride round a charming country with the foliage of September still on the trees.

On November 5th a good day's sport resulted after meeting at Weaver's Lodge, hounds running backwards and forwards between Newton Wood and Dembleby Thorns, unfortunately changing at critical moments. Rain came down heavily in the afternoon, and hounds whipped off at five o'clock just as night was established, having a good fifteen miles back to kennels. On November 15th another good day's sport is recorded after meeting at Bottesford Station, and a brace were killed after giving two smart gallops. A start was made by running a fox very hard from the Debdales, by Shipman's Plantation and Woolsthorpe Cliff, to Casthorpe Covert, where he dodged the pack for half an hour and then crawled into a hollow tree, from which hounds dragged him out and killed. The day ended with Mr. Earl supplying a brace from his osier bed, and one was killed after a smart gallop to Harlaxton Clays.

This particular November was hardly a winter month with its fine weather, and the going was so good that horses could gallop and jump all day on the top of the ground. To give a brief summary of a succession of good days which are doubtless inscribed on the memory of many a man who was lucky enough to ride them, we may mention that of November 27th, forty minutes and a kill from Clawson Thorns with the afternoon fox. December 1st, a good sporting run of one hour and twenty minutes from Goadby Gorse, ending by marking to ground at Sysonby, greatly pleasing a stranger in the field, Mr. Edward D. Adams, a banker from New York. On December 7th a nice gallop from Marston Platts to Carlton, and a better one in the afternoon from Jericho Wood to Marston, a brush coming to hand at the end of each. Under the ban of foul weather during the second week of December all the field melted away in a whirling snowstorm, excepting Messrs. James and Arthur Hutchinson, who stuck to hounds, and went fox-catching to Harrowby Gorse with Gillard when the storm was over.

Another good day's sport was enjoyed on December 15th in very foggy weather with the country nearly all under water. After drawing Sproxton Thorns blank, and killing a fox in Coston Covert, one was bolted from the artificial earths and took a bee line away past Crown Point to Woodwell Head, going through it like a shot, passing to the left of Market Overton and Barrow without checking until Cottesmore was reached. Changed foxes by Exton Park and made straight for Greetham Wood, hunting slowly towards Thistleton, losing all trace in darkness by Morkary Wood. Two days' sport rolled into one, if you will follow it by the map. Moreover, the greater part of the journey was over a wild wet country which carries a scent.

From December 17th to January 21st any number degrees of frost were registered, and people skated on the high roads, which were a sheet of slippery ice. During such hateful periods of inactivity the Belvoir woods were very welcome exercise ground, being nearly always in fair going condition, old hounds so disliking road exercise that they have to be coupled to younger ones.

On February 4th a fine day's sport was enjoyed from Folkingham Big Gorse, a famous fox covert which has given many a good run. Going away past Stowe Green, they ran very fast to Horbling, at the edge of the fen country on the dead level. By the time Swaiton was reached the hounds had travelled five miles in twenty minutes, and a check occurred through the hard-riding field driving them over the line. A successful cast hit it off again, and they sailed away over Helpringham fen and killed their fox handsomely on the banks of the old Forty-Foot Drain, after running for one hour and thirty minutes. In the Middle Ages this famous drain or canal, which was originally cut by the Romans, was the means of bringing stone and materials to build the fine churches which are dotted about all over the fens, and are so useful as landmarks in this featureless country. Another smart scurry with a fox started from Swarby Gorse finished the day, the pack streaming away by the Northing Plantation, Kelby, Aswarby, back to Silk Willoughby, where they killed close to the clergyman's pantry-door after a race of five-and-thirty minutes. The lights at the Belvoir kennels were very welcome to the hunt staff when seen that night about 9 P.M.

Melton Mowbray is always full to overflowing at the spring of the year, and the occasion of a concert given by the hunting folk in aid of the Farmers' Benevolent Society brought a very large field out on February 9th, when hounds met at the house occupied by Colonel Markham. Many thought that it was too hard to ride, but every hour the sun dispelled the frost and improved the going. A find was proclaimed in Burbidge's Covert, the fox crossing the river, running over the Burton flats nearly to the Punch Bowl, where he turned left-handed for Burrough Hill. Scent was good, and they ran well by Thorpe Sackville, unfortunately changing to a fresh one close by Adam's Gorse, running through Gartree Hill Covert, away to the railway at Great Dalby. Hounds ran down on to the line just as the express was due, but most fortunately the signal was up to stop the train to pick up a young couple who had been married that morning, and owing to this fact a bad accident was averted. Gillard narrates in his diary that "on the way home we passed through Great Dalby, and were invited by Mr. Brewitt, father of the bride, to drink her good health, which we did in a bumper, most heartily expressing a hope that the new son-in-law was as good a sportsman as himself."

An awkward fall in a spin from Sproxton Thorns placed Gillard for a few days on the shelf, damaging his ribs and shoulder, but the Ides of March ushered in rough weather and a stop to sport, for perhaps fox-hunting of all sports is the most tantalising, depending as it does entirely on scent, circumstances, and favourable weather. A good day was snatched from the frost on March 5th, the meet being Hose Grange. The turf was in such order that a horse went as if upon springs, and a scent vouchsafed in dusty March, giving a burst over green Leicestershire, is a little gift from paradise. A find was proclaimed in Sherbrooke's Covert, hounds crossing the Smite, making for Hickling, inclining towards Old Dalby and Holwell Mouth, keeping in the vale until Piper Hole Gorse was reached. Here a shepherd dog coursed the fox, and spoilt all further chance of sport, after a good run lasting one hour and fifteen minutes. The second gallop from Goadby Gorse was the better of the two, being a brilliant fifty minutes, ending with a kill. The line taken was past Melton Spinney and Waltham Ashes, up the Chadwell Valley, the brook being jumped three times in quick succession. Hounds threw up by the railway, and after casting about they winded him in an ash tree, quickly pulling him out of his hiding-place—a fine old dog-fox, with a well-tagged brush, which was presented to Lady Gerard. "No check of any importance occurred throughout this splendid gallop, for when the fox turned a bit sharp the pack cast themselves before the field could catch them up, and went running on. When this fox was roused in Goadby Gorse it was a quarter past four in the afternoon, so that only a few remained to see it. Those who went well were Mr. Leatham, who had a fine stud of Yorkshire-bred horses, Mr. Praed, Mons. Roy, Mr. Edgar Lubbock, Mr. Birch, Mr. Saunderson,

Captain King King, Mr. Brocklehurst, Mr. Hatfield Harter, and Lady Gerard."

With the genial warmth imparted by a good day's sport still upon him, we can in imagination see Frank penning the following note of music in the diary before turning into bed:—" During the last run in Boothby Wood, it was splendid to hear the charming cry of hounds; not that they used their voices more than they usually do, but the rarefied atmosphere and still evening brought the music to our ears sweetly and distinctly."

A capital hunt of forty-five minutes is recorded on March 30th, when hounds met at Croxton Park, finding their fox in Newman's Gorse, going over the Melton brook, round by Melton to within half a mile of Newport Lodge, where the pack doubled back and marked their fox in a fowl-house. The farmer, Mr. Josiah Wood, closed the door in the face of the hounds, but directly he heard they belonged to the Duke of Rutland the door flew open like magic, thus giving the pack the blood they deserved.

The number of hunting days this season was 115, and 104 foxes were killed, 63 being marked to ground.

Music.

CHAPTER XV

SEASONS 1887-88 AND 1888-89

Gillard's Family—Frank Gillard, junior, joins the Hunt Staff—A good Run from Sapperton Wood; Mr. John Gubbins presented with the Brush—Mr. Cecil Rudkin goes hard—Hunting till Dark—The Belvoir and Cottesmore Hounds come together in the Field—The Hound Cottesmore Prodigal—The Kennels to which Frank went for Blood—Old Sir Thomas Whichcote's Opinion of the Day, and his Letter—The late Duke of Clarence—Death of Mrs. Willson of Rauceby—Dangers of a Swallow-Hole—Mr. Otho Paget jumps locked Railway Gates—Death of the Master, the Sixth Duke of Rutland—Succession of the Seventh Duke of Rutland—Stud Hounds, the Entry and Nominal—Good Hound Day by Culverthorpe—Aswarby Foxes—An Accident to the Hound Van—Mr. Jolland wins a Fen-Land Fox's Brush—Count Zhrowski—Lost Hounds finding their Way back—Ash Wednesday drops out of the Fixtures—Mr. Richard Fenwick presented with a Brush—A Lady of eighty-six presented with her first Brush—Captain Pennell Elmhirst's Tribute to Gillard's Vigour and Keenness at the end of his nineteenth season Huntsman.

GORDON, BY GAMBLER, 1885.

"WHAT'S bred in the bone comes out in the flesh," and, as might be expected, the girls and boys of Frank Gillard's numerous family, reared within sound of the kennel, all wished to adopt hunting as a profession. Everything was game that walked about their home, from the breed of fox-terriers, for which Frank was celebrated, to the fowls, which were as good as it is possible to get. Very wisely Gillard discouraged the idea of the family following his footsteps, knowing the hard work attending the calling of a whipper-in, and the keen competition for the higher berth in these days, when so many gentlemen prefer to carry the horn themselves, instead of paying a professional. But the eldest son, Frank, was so keenly bitten with the sport that he left a business, and came this season as second whipper-in to his father; the other two brothers going to the Royal Veterinary College of Surgeons, where they completed a course with distinction. Arthur Wilson leaving to carry the horn for the York and Ainstry, was succeeded by Will Jones, so that the new staff had the geography of a large country to learn.

A big day in the season's sport was December 2nd, when a large field met hounds at Weaver's Lodge, one of the best fixtures on the Lincolnshire side of the country. A find was proclaimed in Sapperton Wood, the pack going screaming away for Haydour Southings and Dembleby Thorns. Turning from Newton Wood a check occurred, but a halloa supplied the missing evidence, and a man informed Gillard that his fox had gone by twenty minutes ago. Consequently, it was slow hunting up to Swarby Gorse. From this covert hounds got away close at the brush of their fox, simply racing for thirty-five minutes, the field having to ride their hardest to keep them in view, running a ring by Rauceby, Silk Willoughby, Aswarby Park, Culverthorpe, ending with a kill in the open near to the Northing Plantation. The brush was presented to Mr. John Gubbins, an ex-M.F.H. from Ireland, driven away by agrarian agitation to Grantham's gain, for he built stables and kept a fine stud of hunters. Mr. Gubbins, who won the Derby of 1897 with Galtee More, was a heavy weight, hard to beat across country, pounding the field on several occasions, the Bottesford Beck being one big place which gave him the coveted ambition of being alone with hounds. The mask of this good fox went to another very determined thruster of the farmer division—Mr. Cecil Rudkin of Sapperton, and custodian of that reliable covert. During the run he took three falls, the first being in an attempt to charge through a great bullfinch black as Erebus, the thorns wrapping round the horse instead of giving way, sending him end over end. The second fall was at a trappy fence with a double dyke, which caught fifteen riders all in a row. And the third was near the finish, when the heavy plough knocked the wind out of the horses, and each fence brought them down like ninepins.

The sport we see before Christmas turns is far better than what falls to our lot after, for we love the short, dark, dirty days which characterise November and December. This particular month was full of good things, and on December 14th we find recorded that the pack assembled at Croxton Park, starting a good hunting run from Sproxton Thorns, ending by marking to ground in a rabbit burrow by Stonesby. The second was a very fast ten-minute burst from Coston Covert, with a mark to ground in the artificial earths at Sproxton. A third gallop finished the day, from Bescaby Oaks, hounds being stopped by darkness at Piper Hole Gorse. "Though it was late, about thirty horsemen remained to the finish, though darkness made it difficult to distinguish who they were," wrote Gillard; "but I found Mr. Gubbins, his nephew (Mr. Dring), the steeplechase rider (Mr. Beasley), and Mr. James Hutchinson."

"The day the big pack of $21\frac{1}{2}$ couple met at Easton Hall, December 19th, is one to be remembered, first because we hunted in two inches of snow, and secondly because we joined with the Cottesmore. A find was proclaimed in Easton Wood, and when running to the left of Witham big wood the cry of the Cottesmore hounds was heard, each pack running within a field of one another, coming together in Cabbage Hill Wood, after which they ran in company to Castle Bytham. Scent was fair, which enabled them to run hard at times, and on two or three occasions I pointed out to Mr. Baird that several Belvoir hounds were running at the head of the combined pack. Gordon, General, and Nightdew put the others right when difficulties arose. In Castle Bytham village much confusion was caused by villagers who headed us, and then we were unlucky enough to get on to a fresh fox, which took us back to Witham Wood, where we lost, so there was nothing for it but to divide the packs. We had no difficulty doing this, William Neil riding one way and I the other, our hounds following each of us." On a former occasion in 1881, when the Belvoir and Cottesmore

LINCOLNSHIRE FATHERS OF THE HUNT. 1896.

nearly clashed out hunting, three hounds of the latter pack joined the Duke's. One of these was Prodigal, and Gillard saw him do such capital work that he rode over to Barleythorpe the next non-hunting day to look at him on the flags, and arranged for a visit. He was an extraordinarily good hound, and was bred at the Milton kennel, being in the sale list when a draft of the Fitzwilliam were sold at Peterborough, where Mr. Baird bought him, to the immense advantage of the Cottesmore pack, as about half of it traces to him now. His son Traitor lived to be the oldest hound at Belvoir, and so his worth can be taken for granted. Gillard did not go out of his usual path when he used Prodigal, for he was by a Grafton sire out of a Fitzwilliam bitch. The Pytchley Comus of 1876 and Mr. Hammond's Stormer are perhaps the only two hounds for which the Belvoir huntsman might be asked for an explanation, for in twenty years Frank Gillard only used two kennels freely, namely the Fitzwilliam and the Grafton. In all he did not go to more than eight, and the number of visiting stallion hounds were not much over a dozen.

The work of hounds is again noted in the doings of December 21st, when they ran from Sproxton Heath Gorse and killed between Wymondham and Woodwell Head. Gillard remarks: "I never saw hounds hunt better, old Playmate and Caroline distinguishing themselves frequently by picking up the line on the fallows. So did Constant, Toilet, Forecast, Dashwood, and his son Dominic, all good hounds who helped to catch many a fox."

Frost ushered in the new year, and a doubtful day's hunting resulted at Rauceby in a partial thaw and rain. The diary records "that a move was made to Aswarby to see if the outlook was any better there, and of course we had to call at the Hall and see old Sir Thomas Whichcote, whom I asked whether he considered it fit to hunt. 'If

I were a young man I should have said it was fit!' he said; to which I replied, 'Then we will hunt, to fancy ourselves young again.' Amongst Gillard's large correspondence is a letter from the baronet, dated Aswarby Park, March 1888: "I have had a gouty cough. I know myself the cause of the ailment. The liver has been allowed to get torpid from not having had a gallop. Directly I can sit on my cob again, the old clock will begin to tick and the whole of the works will act as well as ever. Thank goodness the wind has gone out of the east."

A visit from Prince Albert Victor the late Duke of Clarence, who was the guest of Lord Brownlow at Belton Park, causes a red letter to be affixed to January 16th, when hounds met at Scrimshaw Mill. The Prince, who rode a gray horse, was late in arriving at the meet, but directly hounds tried the Rectory Covert they started a fox and ran well in the direction of Elton, taking a ring back to the starting-point. The line of country is pronounced by some as hardly fit to ride, so strongly is it fenced, but the Prince went gallantly.

Hunting was stopped at the end of January, owing to the death of Mrs. Willson of Rauceby Hall, who had been one of the keenest followers of the pack for many years, and left a large family, who, by preserving foxes, furthering the interests of the sport, and riding with hounds on every occasion possible, deserve the gratitude of the whole hunting community.

In a day's sport during February, Gillard had thirty couple of hounds to hunt the Easton Coverts.

The day was too warm for scent, until the cool of the afternoon, when the pack roused a fox in Burton High Wood, and ran him very hard to a swallow-hole in Witham Wood. A serious accident was only just averted by prompt assistance, the pack crowding down into the bottom of the deep hole, so that those underneath were nearly smothered. Three were got out stiff and motionless, lying as if dead on the bank, but they came round in time, joining in the worry breaking up that fox with a demon-like ferocity.

The big day of the season occurred on February 8th, with a regular flyer in the afternoon who went away from the west corner of Melton Spinney with sixteen and a half couple of the middle pack close at his brush. A hard-riding field were soon stirring up the mud in the brook, and then the railway with its locked gates confronted them. These Mr. Otho Paget boldly charged, got well over the first, but came an awful cropper at the second. Before the gates could be opened he was on his horse and away with a start of the flying squadron, though hounds were at least three fields in front of him going like pigeons, not a straggler to be seen. Before the Melton and Kettleby road was reached, Mr. Otho Paget came down at a big place and was put out of the run. Every horse was sent along at his best pace, but it was of no avail, they could not live with hounds, who streamed silently away to Welby Holt, leaving that snug covert with a point for Grimston Gorse. A mile farther on they checked, huntsman and field catching them after they had been running for twenty minutes unattended. There was scarcely time for horses to catch their wind before the line was cleverly recovered by a young dog-hound Drastic, who had been "walked" by Mr. James Rudkin of Hanby. He was a bit the quickest getting through the fence, and was half-way across the next field before his voice was heard. Three fields farther on a sharp right-hand turn took the hunt to the left of Cant's Thorns, and then a beaten fox was viewed only a field ahead of the pack. Unfortunately an open drain in the bridle-road midway between Kettleby and Wartnaby saved his brush. Time of this brilliant gallop, forty-five minutes. Rough wintry weather stopped hunting operations in March, but on the 3rd of this month, when fifty couple were exercising, they met Major Amcotts, Mr. E. Lubbock, Mr. F. Crawley, the Rev. J. P. Seabrooke, and a few more, who declared it was fit to hunt, and hunt they did, finding in the Rectory Covert running fast to Jericho where they killed.

A sad sad day for the Belvoir Hunt was Sunday, March 4th, when the sixth Duke of Rutland passed peacefully away after holding the mastership for thirty seasons. The heart was out of the season after that, and the hunt staff wore crape bands round their left arms to the finish.

The number of hunting days this season was 109, foxes killed 83, hounds were stopped hunting 40 days for frost, 8 days for death.

Season 1888-89

"The King is dead, long live the King." Lord John Manners, seventh Duke of Rutland, succeeded his late brother to the mastership this season, and sport continued the even tenor of its way on the

THE REV. J. P. SEABROOKE ON TOP-BAR.

same lines with Frank Gillard at the head of affairs. Cub-hunting was sadly hindered owing to the hot suns of a St. Martin's little summer baking the plough lands to the consistency of iron.

Three couple and a half of stallion hounds this season in the kennel were by Weathergage, namely,

Glancer, Worcester, Gameboy, Gambler, Triumph, Forecast, and Commodore. It was said of Glancer that he was a tremendous driver, and, like his ancestor, the Osbaldeston Furrier, an excitable hound on a catchy scent, he sired some good-looking daughters for Lord Galway's kennel. Worcester, the same age as Glancer, was not so handsome though an excellent hound, much resembling his sire Weathergage in appearance. Gameboy and Gambler were the choice of all masters and huntsmen. Triumph, of the same year, was beautifully bred on his dam's side, Tutoress being by the renowned Fallible. Then there were younger sires who blossomed out later into celebrities, namely, Gordon (1885) by Gambler in his third season, and judged the fastest hound in the pack; Talent, another son of Gambler; Pirate (1885) by Proctor. Two old stallion hounds by Fallible were General and Garnet, out of Governess, a Weathergage bitch. Another Fallible sire was Dashwood—nearly the oldest hound in the pack—a model as to feet and legs, and he was used much both at home and elsewhere, siring two sons in the entry of 1887, named Saxon and Shamrock.

Gambler was the favourite sire at Belvoir this season, and of the young entry the best was his son Nominal—Needy by Syntax, son of Grafton Silence, her dam was Needful by Fallible. A grand young hound—all quality, truly made about his back, loins, and ribs, with bone right down to his toes, and straight as a rule. Whipster by Newsman was the best hound in the pack to carry a line down a road—his dam Warlock by Founder the son of Fallible. Narrator by Glancer—Nightwatch by Founder, her dam Narrative by Saffron son of Senator. Also a quick young hound was Gaylad by the Rufford Galliard—Constant. The Belvoir bitch entry this season were considered perfect and of great beauty, the Weathergage blood being very noticeable. They were Decorous, Definite, Dipple, Dimple, Goldfinch, Specious, and Sequel, all daughters of Gambler; Redcap, Rachel, Royalty, by Glancer. Three beautiful sisters, Tropical, Tolerance, and Trophy, by Traitor out of Syren who was by Syntax.

On the first day of hunting, November 7th, good sport was enjoyed in Culverthorpe coverts, where hounds ran a fox for three hours and forty-five minutes, killing him on the north side of Culverthorpe Hall after meeting on the south side. "The hunt was never farther than four or five fields from Dembleby Thorns, and brought out much good hound work. Pirate in particular made many fine hits at a time when it looked as if our fox had beaten us, and this occurred generally on fallows. His splendid voice came most welcome at those critical moments. Others of the pack who all did their share were Spartan by Fallible, Worcester, Gambler, Gameboy, General, Garnet, old Traitor, Gordon, and young Nominal, who recovered the line when it looked hopeless."

During November north-easterly gales prevailed, the wind attaining a tremendous velocity, for we read of a poor hansom cabman being blown off his perch. It was a credit to our stiff old soil that any trees were left standing; but after such a gale the country always rides better; for wind and rain—Nature's hedgers and ditchers—do their work well.

We waited the arrival of hounds at Aswarby on November 23rd, for it was most unusual for them to be after time at a meet. The reason for delay on this occasion was the breakdown of the hound van, so that Gillard and his whips came on with the pack, riding the three horses of the team in their harness, minus saddles. When business did commence there was no lack of sport, for the Aswarby foxes have long been noted for their stoutness, and Gillard always said of them "that they were the biggest he ever handled." In the afternoon a fox was set going from Swarby Gorse, who took us back in the direction of Aswarby, but on reaching Osbournby he entered an old woman's house and went upstairs. Young Frank Gillard, the second whip, and Bellamy, the well-known universal horse-provider, got him into a sack and brought him on horseback to turn down, but he beat them through an interfering terrier joining in the chase.

A good run, measuring eleven miles on the map into the Cottesmore country, was recorded on December 10th, after meeting at Easton Hall. Hounds kept going all the way at a nice hunting pace, threading several large coverts but wearing their fox down, eventually killing him handsomely by Exton Park. The Cottesmore had met there that morning, going over some of the same ground, but right well did the pack hunt the line, the newly ploughed land keeping their heads down, and at the finish every hound was there.

After the break up of the frost in December, a serious accident happened to Captain Lathom Cox, for many years the popular adjutant to the Militia at Grantham. His horse slipped upon the half-frozen snow, when jumping a stone wall, and falling on his rider's leg, caused a compound fracture, laying him by for the rest of the season.

The morning of December 28th was spent at Rauceby Hall, scurrying about the home coverts with a whole litter of foxes afoot, but in the afternoon the scene was changed to a stiffer country round Aswarby. Getting away with a fox, who set his mask for the fen-lands, the field being soon confronted by the yawning chasm known as the Burton Padwadine drain, one was found to sacrifice himself and horse, like Horatius Curtius—Mr. Jolland of Newark, famous as the owner of that good horse Clawson, winner of a big stake at Newmarket, who twice attempted to capture the Grand National Steeplechase. Riding a wonderful jumping cob, he sent him at the wide drain, landing as a matter of course in the middle of it, but luckily getting out the opposite steep bank with nothing worse than a thorough ducking and the consolation of being the only one up when they marked to ground in an earth by the railway on the south side of Helpringham. The fox was bolted and speedily killed, the brush being presented to the plucky horseman. It was five o'clock when hounds killed, on a short dark December afternoon, and kennels were a good twenty-five miles distant, but the pack trotted back with their sterns up, and ate their meal when home was reached at 9.15 as though they had only been a short exercise.

The big day of the season came off on January 16th, with the afternoon fox roused in Melton Spinney. His line was by Scalford past Old Hills, where a shepherd dog joining in, caused him to change his plans. After a check, hounds recovered the line and recrossed Melton brook, driving along at a great pace by Abb Kettleby and Wartnaby to Grimston Gorse—time, fifty minutes from the find. Here a fresh fox jumping up caused confusion, but a signalman in his box viewed the hunted one near the station, and hounds ran on by Thrussington Grange, marking to ground in the stick heap of a rabbit warren. Time of this good gallop was one hour and fifty minutes, distance a nine-mile point. There was much grief in crossing the brook; Count Zhrowski, one to have a cut at anything, generally showing a hard-riding field his back, got into deep water near Potter Hill.

A long tiring woodland day was January 25th, when the pack ran a brace of wild foxes through the big chain of forest stretching from Keisby to Bourne. Gillard had to whip off at dark, a good 22 miles from kennels, which were reached at ten o'clock with two and a half couple missing. All but one found their way back to kennels that night, shelter and food always being left out in readiness for the lost ones on their return.

A new departure this season from old traditions was the Ash Wednesday hunt dropping out of the fixtures, due to the refining influence of a Duchess at Belvoir; and in a very short time all other packs of any importance followed suit.

A curious termination to a fine run of one hour and thirty minutes happened to a fox set going from Grimstone Gorse. Running on the Midland Railway near the Curate's Gorse he was cut to pieces by a passing train.

Another good gallop lasting an hour and fifteen minutes is recorded on February 4th with an afternoon fox roused in Croxton Banks, hounds streaming away at a great pace by Shipman's Bogs, Bescaby Oaks, to Herring's Gorse, where he wheeled round for Saltby, and the pack had to be stopped owing to darkness. Those who were with them at the finish were Mr. Ernest Chaplin, Mons. Couturie, Mr. Birkbeck, Mrs. Amcotts, Major Longstaffe, and Lord Robert Manners.

On February 26th another capital run occurred with one of the stout Stubton foxes, who was roused in Reeves Gorse and headed away for Fenton, giving the field the river Devon to swim over. The brush of this good fox was presented to Mr. Richard Fenwick, hunting with his two brothers and Miss Fenwick from Grantham. His name is famous in the annals of sport as the owner of Mimi, winner of the Oaks in 1891.

The meet at the Lenton cross-roads on March

15th brought a good day's sport, a fox being roused in Lenton pastures, setting his mask for Ingoldsby Wood, which brought the Lenton brook into the gallop. The lead over was given by Major Longstaffe, but in the valley below Sapperton all trace of the hunted one vanished. With the afternoon fox from Folkingham big gorse we had one hour and thirty minutes of the very best going by Scot Willoughby, Quarrington, Bully Wells, to the Northing Plantation where they pulled him down. Those who saw the best of this fine gallop were Major Longstaffe, Major Amcotts, Mr. E. Lubbock, Mr. Fenwick, Mr. T. Heathcote, Mr. J. Hutchinson, Mr. A. Hutchinson, and Miss Carter. The distance hounds ran was quite 16 miles by the ordnance map.

A rather singular coincidence happened at the finish of a good hunting run from Peas Cliff to Ropsley, where hounds killed their fox in front of Mrs. Smart's house, a lady eighty-six years of age, a tenant of the Duke's, who always had a good walk for a foxhound puppy. Gillard presented her with the brush, and she then told him that she viewed in the distance from her house, the day before, the fox killed after a run from Boothby Wood. This was wonderful, even in her long life, and a proud moment too, even if rather late in the day!

On April 6th a large field were out, including Captain Pennell Elmhirst, and as " he was the only rider with a pen behind his ear," we quote him. "The meet was Three Queens, and until three o'clock hounds were searching the heath for a

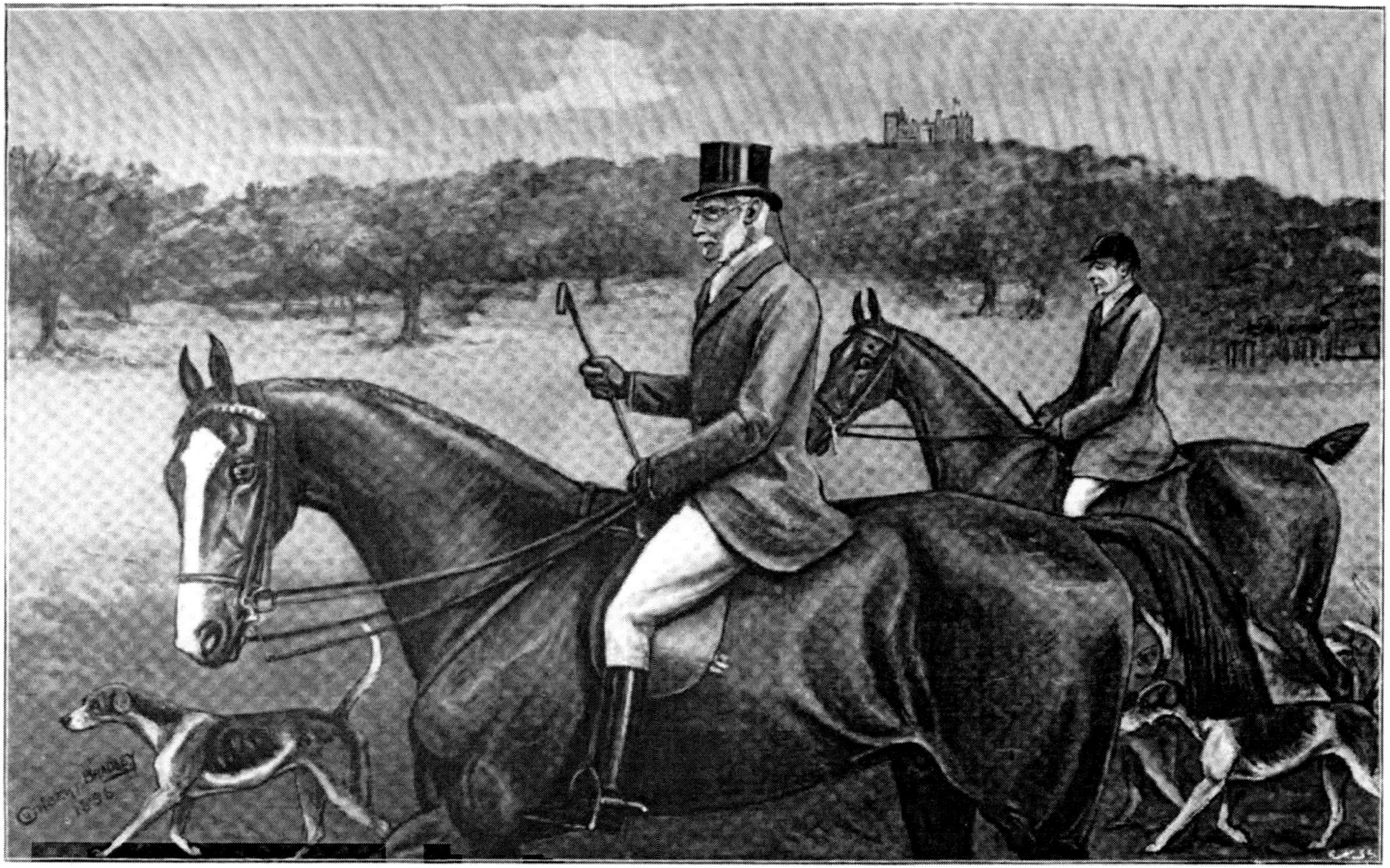

rumoured lamb-killer, who was probably curled up till dark at his master's fireside! Most of Melton had gone to see Donovan win the big prize at Leicester, but of those out were Lady Augusta Fane on a mealy bay, Miss Constance Gilchrist on a gray, Count Zhrowski, who held a pioneer's place when hounds did run; Mr. Knowles, Mr. R. Pryor, Mr. B. Lubbock, Mr. W. Chaplin, jun., Mr. and Mrs. James Hornsby, Mrs. R. Ord, Sir Hugh Cholmeley, Major Longstaffe, Major Pennington, Mrs. Sloane Stanley, Captain Warner, Mons. Roy, Mr. Salvin, and the Rev. J. P. Seabrooke.

"Melton Spinney supplied a good fox which gave a rattling twenty-five minutes over the brook by Scalford to Holwell Mouth, where scent failed on a newly-sown field. The bit of east in the wind helped them; there was all the scent they wanted while near their fox, and on the grass, which rode to perfection. Was there ever such a hunting April? Was there ever a brighter finish to a long good season? By Holwell Mouth, Gillard chose the oxer in preference to the wolly place, and his good mare Dublin Lass went gaily over and afterwards. No sign of age in horse or man yet! they might be whipping in to John Musters for vigour and keenness, and they are about the only couple who forget to knock hard at the binders, or to sound the shallow ditch," wrote Brooksby at the end of Gillard's nineteenth season huntsman.

The season finished on April 20th, with 115 days, 91 foxes were killed, and 17 days hounds were stopped by weather.

CHAPTER XVI

SEASONS 1889-90 AND 1890-91

The Demand for Gillard's Whippers-in—Accidents to Hounds in the Field, on the Line, and over a Cliff—Tree-climbing Foxes—Mrs. Edgar Lubbock presented with a Brush—Before Christmas Sport—A Ride Home on a very dark Night—A Curious Accident to Mr. Edgar Lubbock's Horse—The Weight of a Fox—The Election and Fox-hunting Candidates—Gillard's Coming of Age, Season 1890-91—Lord Edward Manners, M.P., Field-Master—The Season's Entry and Favourite Sires at Belvoir—Captain "Jim" Barry presented with the Brush—An awkward Accident to Mr. Cecil Rudkin—Recovery in Time to win a Steeplechase—Accident to the Pack crossing a Frozen Canal—A Day at Staunton, Mrs. Phillips presented with the Brush—A Kill on a Railway Station Platform, Countess de Clairemount presented with the Brush—A fast Spin from Coston Covert—Arthur Wilson sets a Hound's broken Leg—Fox up a Chimney—A Fox commits *felo de se*—Gillard wins the Melton Town Plate with Gunby.

DOWN THE CHIMNEY.

NOT only did masters of hounds look to Belvoir as the fountain-head and home of the thoroughbred foxhound, just as Newmarket occupies the premier position in the racing world, but the first whippers-in serving in such a good school under Frank Gillard were in demand to fill the posts of huntsmen everywhere. Consequently changes in the hunt staff were of frequent occurrence, and Will Jones left this season to become huntsman to the North Pytchley, his place being taken by Kane Croft from the Hertfordshire, a fine horseman, "lang and leet," built on the lines of the immortal James Pig. Promotion came for him after a season or two, to carry the horn, first in the Isle of Wight and then for the South Dorset hounds.

A series of accidents befell the pack this season. In Harlaxton Wood a young hound, Chorister, fell down a dry well, but fortunately used his voice to some purpose, and was rescued by a woodman next day. On December 21st three hounds were run over by a coal train, Prospect being killed on the spot, whilst Delight and a second season hound were badly injured. Another serious railway accident is recorded on January 14th, when Governor, always to the front and a nailing little hound in his work, own brother to the famous Gordon, met his fate on the line below Leadenham hill-top. Gillard tells the sad story of how in his anxiety he climbed down on to the line, and picked the hound's head up cut clean off as if done with a knife, and until he found the body could not recognise which hound it was. The other serious accident which befell them was on the last Lincolnshire day of the season when hunting a fox in the Ancaster Quarries. It was after a smart scurry from Wilsford Carrs, hounds killing their fox in Ancaster Quarries on the very edge of a pit from fifty to sixty feet deep. "I jumped from my horse and tried to get hold of the fox which hounds were worrying on the brink of the precipice, but before it was possible to do so three couples rolled over and lay on the rough stones as if lifeless. Though much hurt, all fortunately recovered from this nasty accident with careful nursing."

Rough weather this season probably caused many of the varmint to take up their quarters in hollow trees, though in some districts, such as Stapleford Park, this climbing propensity is attributed to the light shelving nature of the soil, and the fear of being easily scratched out by hounds or stray dogs. On February 5th, "we went to the willow tree by Wyfordby and for the second time found Charles on his perch, so comfortable that he refused at first to be dislodged; but Mr. Spreckly, the occupier of the land, at last drove him off, and away he went in view crossing the railway. Unfortunately, when roused again a few days later he ran into the pack, who were out of sight behind a hedge, and so ended his career." Another instance is recorded on March 10th, when hounds raced a fox from Tipping's Gorse, and he popped into the trunk of an old oak tree at Croxton Banks. Curiously enough when Bob Knott, who had succeeded Tom Chambers, climbed up the tree he poked out a brace.

The opening day of the season was November 4th at Three Queens, the Duke of Rutland and the Marquis of Granby being two of the large field out. A fox found in Tipping's Gorse gave a sharp scurry of fifteen minutes before he surrendered his brush, which was presented by the noble Master to Mrs. Edgar Lubbock.

A long ding-dong gallop of over an hour happened on November 15th, after meeting at Newton Bar. A fox was chopped in the turnips by Birthorpe, another going away past Folkingham Gorse to Osbournby hill-top, where, says Gillard, "it looked fifty to one on hounds killing him, but a fresh one jumped up in front of the pack—or rather ten couples, for seven and a half couple (with the whips) were left behind at Aswarby,—and they dashed over Aswarby Park, close at his brush, running on to Cliff Hill and Rauceby. Here they had the bad luck to again change, and after a good dusting on the heath they ran to Brauncewell, where, finding I had but nine and a half couple, no whips, and only two sportsmen left, viz. Mr. Francis Crawley and Mr. Chapman of Frieston, I stopped these stout hounds. The distance as the crow flies would be quite 15 miles, and the line hounds ran about 25."

A bad day's sport round Elton and Bingham is summed up as follows: "For want of scent and better luck, hounds never stuck to the line very well, and to make more difficulties, our fox crossed a bad country—nothing but railways, drains, and the river Smite."

A stop for frost this season came before Christmas, very few days being registered during December, and it calls to mind a characteristic story told of Mr. Nicholas Parry, Master of the Puckeridge, who when on his deathbed was asked, "If you could live your life over again, what should you do different from what you have done?" "I should put in a few more days before Christmas," was the reply; and they are worth all the sport we see after, say we.

A long woodland day on January 10th ended up in Bourne Wood. Gillard remarks: "In all my experience I never knew such a dark night, for after leaving Ingoldsby our horses kept getting off the road; consequently, we borrowed a candle and lantern, which proved useful. I kept sounding my horn to give people warning of our approach, and we found a horse and carriage quite lost in the pitchy darkness, not daring to move!"

A meet at Weaver's Lodge, though of late years it has appeared to bring frost, at one time of day always drew a large field from two counties. On the occasion of January 17th, when hounds assembled there, a curious accident happened to a sportsman on wheels. When going down Newton Hill, the horse that Mr. E. Lubbock was riding crossed its legs and fell, sprang up again and galloped away riderless. In its mad career it cannoned broadside against a pony-cart and upset the whole concern with its occupant, though fortunately doing little damage.

A fine day's sport is mentioned on the last day of January, after meeting at Bitchfield. "The first fox was found at Irnham, running nearly to

Grimsthorpe, and killed after a good hunt. Ingoldsby Wood supplied the second, who gave a capital gallop to Humby, away to the left of Boothby Hall, where Major Longstaffe gave the lead over the brook, and kept it till we reached Stoke Tunnel. Here the good gallop ended, for we changed to a fresh line, though I saw our beaten fox cross the middle ride of Stoke Park Wood, but could not get the hounds back before he had gone, leaving no scent."

The weight of a fox is often a matter for discussion, and Gillard records a big mangy dog-fox, killed by hounds, which turned the scale at $17\frac{1}{2}$ pounds. "That was, I think, one of the biggest I ever handled," he remarked, "the Aswarby foxes being hard to beat for weight."

Amongst good days, that of February 22nd must take a place, for finding at Melton Spinney, hounds ran for fifty minutes to Holwell Mouth. Changing foxes there, they ran for an hour and fifteen minutes back to Melton Spinney, going on to Thorpe Ashes, past Chadwell and Goadby Gorse, finishing a hunt of two hours with all the horses done up, the first whip having to leave his at Scalford all night.

A damaged leg and frost kept Gillard out of the saddle for ten days at the end of February, but we were not without excitement, for the election of the Stamford division of Lincolnshire was in full swing, through the promotion of Mr. John Compton Lawrance to the judge's bench. The two candidates, Mr. Cockayne Cust and Mr. Arthur Priestly, were both well-known followers of the hunt, it was therefore suggested they should ride it off to save the worry of an election. The poll day was Friday, March 8th; and by common consent a non-hunting day, for every good fox-hunting Conservative sported his "pink," and went to see Mr. Cust returned by a majority of 282 votes. A monster meet in honour of the occasion took place in April at Belton House, where Lord and Lady Brownlow, the uncle and aunt of the successful candidate, extended a hearty welcome.

On the last day of the season hounds killed their nineteenth Rauceby fox, their total being 86, and 49 marked to ground. Number of days, 127. Stop for frost, 17 days.

Season 1890-91

This season Frank attained his majority as huntsman to the ducal pack, rode 11 stone 11 lb., and had a son Frank junior to turn hounds to him. For the first time during his tenure of office he had the assistance of a field-master, Lord Edward Manners, M.P. for the Melton division of Leicestershire, the Duke of Rutland's second son, and late of the Fourth Battalion Rifle Brigade.

The favourite hound sire at Belvoir this season was Nominal (1888), a 28-inch hound, with tremendous length of haunch, and his shortness from the hock to the ground was remarkable. He was just as level as his sire Gambler, and the same sort of worker. Old Glancer (1881), by Weathergage, headed the list of stallion hounds, being in his eighth season, and much used by other packs, some of his best progeny going to Lord Galway. Gambler and Gameboy (1884), in their sixth season, were bred from more than any hounds of their day. One of Gambler's first sons, Gordon (1885), out of Spangle, by Saffron, son of Senator, was another sire much talked about. He was a grand

THE PARSON GIVES THE LEAD.
1. The Rev. J. P. Seabrooke. 2. Lord Edward Manners, M.P. 3. Mr. Horace Peacock.
4. General the Hon. H. H. Mostyn. 5. Mrs. E. Lubbock.

foxhound, with the shoulders of a Leicestershire hunter, and bone right down to his very toes. His son, Sampson (1889), was considered the crack hound at Quorn, he won at Peterborough, and Tom Firr swore by him in the field. Pirate of the same year was another favourite, considered by some as the best stallion hound in England. He was a red tan, a good-bodied hound, deep in ribs, and wide in loin, standing on capital feet and legs. He had but one fault, and that was he never liked to leave off hunting, on more than one occasion giving considerable trouble to the hunt staff to stop him at the end of the day from hunting a fox in the dark on his own responsibility. When the order was given for home, Pirate was at once coupled to another hound, much to his indignation. His two sons, Prodigal and Painter (1890), did much good to the kennel. Shiner by Lord Portsmouth's Sailor out of Gamestress was used with great success by the Cottesmore, also Sapphire by Stainless out of Gertrude, and Dominic by Dashwood, son of Founder, by Fallible out of Ruin.

In the breeding of the entry this season, Gillard kept very close to the two hounds he considers the best he ever saw on the line of a fox, namely, Weathergage and Fallible; and it was through the grandsire of the former—Wonder, sire of Warrior—that he got more tongue into the pack, with this advantage to other kennels, that all the descendants of Weathergage are good workers, and say plenty about it, no matter how hard they are running. In an entry of seventeen couple, a beautiful litter was that by Shamrock (1887) out of Constant, by Weathergage, her dam Countess by Fallible, they were Columbine and four dogs, Cruiser, Counsellor, Cardinal, and Chancellor, all of whom grew into stud hounds of note. The brothers were beautiful in colour, dark Belvoir tans, much reminding us of Stainless. The two brothers, Pompey and Pilot by Pirate (1885) out of Sunshine, were different hounds to look over. Valiant and Vengeance, by Gameboy the son of Weathergage out of Vanity by the Blankney Villager, were perhaps the pick of the entry. The young dog measured 24 ins., an inch over regulation height, and his sister had size enough for the big pack, but with all the quality of a 21-inch bitch. Her neck and shoulders were beautiful, and her turn of loin, quarter, length of haunch, perfect legs and feet were all in harmony. Another good litter by Gambler out of Dimple were Duplicate, Dainty, and Dimity. By old Glancer in his eighth season, out of Nicety, were Symphony and Solitude, and two other daughters out of Tolerance were Traitress and Trifle, his best daughter being Surety out of Special, a long, low one, with a rare lot of stuff and bone. The visiting sires were "Grafton" Deputy, Finder, Duncan, and "Grove" Harkaway, two couple of their get being put on.

The ground during cubbing time was as hard as that of 1870, and many hounds were lamed in consequence. In Gillard's opinion this was one of the worst seasons on record for sport, owing to a continued stop for frost from December 13th to January 25th.

A good day's sport is recorded from Harby Covert on November 15th over the cream of the Belvoir Vale. Amongst those out were the field-Master, Lord Edward Manners, Lord Robert Manners, Lord W. Bentinck, Captain J. Barry, Captain King King, Mr. and Mrs. John Charlton, Lady Augusta Fane, Mrs. Sloane Stanley, Major

Amcotts, Mr. J. Fullerton, Mr. V. Hemery, Mr. T. Robarts, the Rev. J. P. Seabrooke. Running by Hose Gorse and Sherbrooke's, hounds passed to the left of both coverts, and on approaching Broughton Bridge got close at their fox, who made a point for Holwell Mouth, but being very hard pressed he turned very sharply and crossed the Smite, hounds killing him close to Nether Broughton. Gillard goes on to remark: "Hounds deserved great praise for the way in which they stuck to the line, considering scent was not very good. The fox was turned first one way and then another by work-people, and twice coursed by sheep-dogs, so that he was a very difficult customer to hunt. Time of this run, an hour and two minutes, Captain 'Jim' Barry being presented with the brush."

During a run from Swarby Gorse, on the afternoon of November 21st, Gillard took two heavy falls, his old mare Black Bess breaking some rails, coming down heavily, damaging her rider's ribs; but he pluckily stuck to his post, and saw the run out until Abney Wood was reached, when Kane Croft handled the pack, and he rode off to be patched up by Dr. Willson of Grantham. Talking of falls brings to mind a serious accident which happened to a hard-riding farmer this particular week—Mr. Cecil Rudkin. After a day on the Leicestershire side, he was steering a course for home some twenty miles distant, at Sapperton, on the Lincolnshire side. To cut a corner he jumped a few small fences, and his horse, being probably tired, blundered and put him down, breaking his rider's leg. His first idea was to crawl from the lonely spot to a farmhouse, but he soon found out the pain was too great, and there was nothing for it but to sit still. By a providential dispensation the horse galloped on, and finding a line of gates open, turned into the stack-yard at the farm, where the men, who had just finished a day's thrashing, saw him, and what is still more wonderful, followed for the best part of a mile the track of his footmarks back to the hedgerow where Rudkin sat. Making them put him in the saddle, he very pluckily rode back to Grantham and got it set, going home the other 10 miles that night on wheels. For weeks he lay in bed mending, getting well just in time for the chases which wound up the season; there he rode this same horse Billy which had given him the accident, and received a tremendous ovation on winning the heavy-weight farmers' steeplechase. Subsequently the horse was sold to Sir John Lawrance, and hunted by his daughter, who with her mother were ardent followers of the chase when not too busily engaged with Primrose League work.

Winter and rough weather made many days a very doubtful matter hunting, and one of these was December 1st, when hounds were busy running in the neighbourhood of Woolsthorpe. The fox crossed the frozen canal, the ice being strong enough to bear him; but when the pack attempted to follow, some ten couple became submerged, and as they fought smashing at the broken ice, it was with great difficulty that all were landed safely, and the neighbourhood was promptly given a wide berth. The next day a complimentary meet was held at Fulbeck Hall in honour of Colonel Francis Fane's return from Canada on Government business. The day's sport resulted in three nice gallops, the second run being five-and-twenty minutes of the very best, over the cream of the Leadenham lordship, the brush of this good fox being presented to an American visitor.

Owing to the heath country being frozen and unfit for hounds' feet on December 8th, they trotted down into the vale, and drew Normanton Thorns, where they found, and ran well for half an hour, ending by marking to ground in Mr. Phillips' artificial earth at Staunton. The second fox was bolted from an earth in Cotham Thorns, giving a capital gallop of thirty-five minutes to Elston in the South Notts country, where hounds caught him. Very few got to the end of this second run, but amongst these were Lord Edward Manners, Lord Robert Manners, Mr. and Mrs. C. J. Phillips, who was presented with the brush, Mr. Stevens, Mr. Campbell Dick, Mons. Roy, Mr. E. Lubbock, the Rev. J. P. Seabrooke, and the Hon. Bernard Petres who took a bad fall.

The first day's hunting in the new year, owing to frost, was January 26th, when hounds met at Bottesford Station. A good beginning was made by Bob Knott viewing an old gray customer from Normanton Thorns, and he led the pack at a great pace over the stiffest line of Belvoir country, nearly to Foston. Swinging round, a return was made to the starting-point, and this time they ran at a great pace to the Debdales, turning before entering this covert, going away straight for Elton. Just skirting these coverts he took a sharp left-hand wheel, reaching the Rectory Covert in forty-five minutes from the second time of leaving the Thorns. For some ten minutes a very tired fox puzzled hounds in covert, then he was viewed by Mr. Fisher stealing away towards Redmile Station, and hounds rolled him over on the platform after a brilliant gallop of fifty-five minutes. The number of dirty coats and crushed hats testified to the severity of the gallop, and amongst the fortunate few with hounds were Mr. James Hutchinson, Mr. F. Crawley, and Mons. Couturie. The Rev. J. P. Seabrooke, cutting out the work on his well-known gray Top-Bar, took a fall over timber, Mr. Arthur Hutchinson ruined a hat, Major Amcotts fell at stiff timber, whilst the Countess de Clairemount, in taking a fall, parted with her safety skirt for a time, but got to the finish, and was presented with the brush.

Against the doings of February 4th, Gillard remarks, " One of the most brilliant gallops I ever saw from the famous Coston Covert. Instead of putting the pack into covert, I blew my horn, moved an old dog-fox who broke the S.E. corner, and clapping hounds on his line, we went at a tremendous pace, leaving Wymondham on the left, turning sharp right-handed, running to the left of the Rickett's, wheeling round and passing to the right of Saxby, nearly reaching Freeby Wood, where the pack crowned their smart gallop by racing up to their fox, killing him by the keeper's lodge, in twenty-three minutes from the start." Reviving his riding recollection of this fine burst, Frank remarked: "On jumping out of the Sproxton and Wymondham road, I got the lead on old Farewell and kept it too, though Mr. Alfred Brocklehurst drew up to me once or twice, but near the finish, as we were both riding for a gate out of the field, I saw some cattle running up to it, and turning quickly, had the fence whilst he got penned at the gate."

A curious accident happened to a hound called Student in a day's hunting round Leadenham; jumping off the parapet of the railway bridge, he fell a distance of forty feet, fortunately landing on some grass, and beyond being shaken was little the worse. On another occasion, when a hound Garnet did a similar thing he broke his leg, which was immediately set with a piece of stick by Arthur Wilson the first whip; and so well was it done that it mended, being difficult to see next season that it had ever been broken.

A memorable day's sport occurred on February 13th, when hounds found a fox in Aswarby Coverts, and raced him so hard that he was glad to seek the shelter of an open cottage door at Swarby. A baby lay on the hearth-rug, over which the fox jumped and went up the chimney, the mother of the child fortunately being just in time to slam the door in the face of the pack. We then had the curious sight of Kane Croft climbing on to the roof of the cottage, peering down the chimney-pot at the fox, who was secured by "Gentleman" Cox below, carried out into the open black as a sweep, given a start, but speedily rolled over. The evening fox from Sapperton Wood gave a charming hunting run over a grand country to Grimsthorpe, where he committed *felo-de-se* down a well. This was a really good point of one hour and ten minutes, being nearly a straight line on the map. It was 5.30 before the run ended, and hounds did not reach kennels that night until 10 P.M.

A special village meet for Kirkby Underwood was arranged, which drew all the natives out of the fens as spectators. "A wretched day: scarcity of foxes, absence of scent, and fourteen perambulators counted at covert side," remarked Gillard.

During March two nice days' sport worthy of mention resulted, a gallop of thirty-five minutes from Melton Spinney ending with a kill at Sysonby; and a merry thirty-five minutes' spin with a Stubton fox.

At the end of the season Kane Croft left to go as huntsman to the Isle of Wight foxhounds, and Frank Gillard, junior, went as huntsman to a pack in Pennsylvania, taking with him a large draft of Belvoir hounds.

The winner of the Melton Town Plate this season was found in Frank Gillard's good-looking bay horse Gunby, son of the Cottesmore Hunt horse Muleteer. Quite an ovation was given Frank when the horse returned to weigh in, and he credited his owner with three chases before being sold to Mr. Flowers. Subsequently he was sent up to Tattersall's with the stud, and was bought by Miss Margaret Tennant, now Mrs. Asquith, who hunted him a season or two, and he passed on to Mrs. de Winton.

Though the season was a short one, there were more than an average number of historical runs. The number of hunting days was 110, stopped by frost 33 days, whilst 80 foxes were killed, and 62 marked to ground,—the latter large number being explained by the dryness of the drains, the shortness of the cubbing season, and the scarcity of foxes in the home district.

UP THE CHIMNEY.

CHAPTER XVII

Seasons 1891-92 and 1892-93

Reduced to a Four-day-a-week Pack—An exceptionally good Lot of young Hounds by Belvoir Pirate and Rufford Dancer—Lord Willoughby de Brooke's opinion of Fallible—Boys and Girls entered to Hounds—Visit of H.R.H. Princess Beatrice of Battenberg—Death of Sir Thomas Whichcote and Mourning for H.R.H. the Duke of Clarence—A Burst from Coston Covert—Old Farewell gives Frank a Fall—Lord Lonsdale saves Mr. Pidcock's Life—Father O'Flynn, the Grand National Steeplechase Winner—Vigilant wins a Chase for Gillard at Melton—Funeral of Mr. J. Nicholas Charlton—The young Hound Tapster and his End—Good Gallops in November, one voted the best seen in three years—A Record Stop for Frost—A Hunt in Freeby Church for a Fox—A Nine-Mile Point in the Fog from Aslackby to Weaver's Lodge—A Race from Staunton Thorns to Normanton Covert—The best Run Gillard ever saw—The Rain Register in a dry March—Lenton Brook—Two Runs into Haconby Fen 1865 and 1893.

THE HUNT SPECIAL.

TO the regret of all sportsmen, the noble master of the Belvoir found it necessary to hunt his hounds four instead of five days a week. As the saying is, "Needs must when the devil drives"; and the devils to drive this stage were the depreciation in value of the ancestral acres owing to agricultural depression. The noble owners of Belvoir had hunted a vast country in the most liberal way for so long a time, and maintaining the prestige of the Belvoir, benefited every hunt in England through what may be termed a national pack. The strength of the kennel remained the same, being still three packs, made up of sixty-two couple.

A capital hunting song was composed and sung by a local sportsman, marking the change in the number of hunting days, the following being a couple of verses.

> Let us stroll to the kennels that lie in the grounds
>   Of good old Belvoir.
> To talk with Frank Gillard and look at his hounds—
>   The good old Belvoir.
> How deep is each chest, how strong is each thigh,
> How broad is each muzzle, how gentle each eye;
> But see them from Sherbrooke's across the vale fly,—
>   Good old Belvoir.
>
> Then, hey, tally-ho! a-hunting we'll go, but not Monday
>   next week;
> On Saturday, too, you may ride the vale thro', but
>   Gillard in vain you'll seek;
> From South Notts to Cottesmore, from Lincoln to Quorn,
> You my hearken in vain for the sound of the horn.
> Each fortnight from Friday till Tuesday's morn,
>   The hounds grow sleek.

That Gillard thought the world of Gambler and also of old Glancer, sons of Weathergage, is proved by the fact that there were three stallion hounds by Glancer, namely Rupert, Narrator, and Nobleman. Six by Gambler in the following:—Nominal, Galloper, Dryden, Graphic, Grasper, and Gordon. Glancer himself was drafted, but old Gambler was still in office with sixty consorts sent to him in this his eighth season.

The entry numbered seventeen couple, seven and a half of dogs to nine and a half of bitches, and good judges pronounced them the best "put on" in the last five years. Of these Gambler was the sire of five couple, namely, Buxom, Brave, Damper, Dalesman, Guardsman, Galloper, Gracious, Guilesome, Regulus, and Racquet. Pirate, in great demand for other kennels, had three couple "put on"—Careless, Prodigal, Plaintiff, Painter, Rocket, and Daphne. The beautiful Shamrock came out strong, and a great sort he was, being by Dashwood son of Founder son of Fallible, who was the son of Fitzwilliam Furrier. Of Fallible, Lord Willoughby de Brooke said in a letter to Gillard, dated from Warwick, March 20th, 1888, "I think Fallible the best dog in England, and I have been to nearly every kennel. He is far superior to Melton Spanker. I am in the position of one, as it were, forming a new pack. I find I can get quality nowhere except from you and Brocklesby." Others who subscribed to Fallible's work were the Duke of Grafton, who sent Frank Beers to try and buy him, the price mentioned being £500. Old George Carter, when he came to look at Fallible, the son of his champion dog Furrier, said, "If you will let me have the young dog I will walk all the way back to Peterborough with him; I won't risk taking him by train."

The dam of Shamrock was Symbol by Traitor, son of Cottesmore Prodigal, whom we have mentioned in a previous chapter. The dam of Symbol was Speedwell, by Woodman brother of Warrior the sire of Weathergage. The young Shamrocks this season out of Diligent the daughter of Grafton Dancer and Gamestress by Weathergage were Druid, Daphne, Dahlia, and Dowager. All the entry were by home sires excepting two and a half couple by Rufford Dancer, who was poor Mr. Harvey Bayley's Cup puppy during his last season, and he was by Galliard, who had Belvoir blood in his veins. Their dam was Specious the daughter of Fallible and Special. Special was the daughter of Spinster, a sterling good bitch who worked in the kennels until she was twelve years old. She was the daughter of Syren, who belonged to Mr. George Lane Fox, who said that "Syren ran at the head of my pack until she was thirteen; the breed is everlasting and never tires." With such blood in their veins it was not to be wondered that the litter by Rufford Dancer and Specious were an exceptional lot, their names being Dancer, Dolphin, Donovan, Danger, and Durity. Gillard used to say of them, "They are a most valuable new strain, and perfect in their work. On more than one occasion I saw Donovan, Dolphin, and Dancer all together at the head of the pack, and all speaking to the line on cold scenting plough. Donovan was the hardest runner and best jumper in the pack—he would sweep over everything in chase; such a driver too, with beautiful nose and voice, both of which he used to the best advantage."

The two new whips this season were Bob Cotesworth and Fred Powell from the north of England. A whole batch of young people were duly blooded by Gillard, and entered to hounds during the cubbing time; they were the Master Amcotts, two little fellows wearing scarlet frocks made from their father's old pink coat; the Hon. Brownlow Cecil, home for the holidays, now the Marquis of Exeter; also the daughter of Captain Thorold of Boothby, Miss Marguerite, now the Hon. Mrs. Maurice Gifford; Miss K. Hodgson; and Miss Victoria Heathcote, the youngest of a sporting quintette of sisters who all hunted together from Newton Hall.

On December 9th a large field assembled at Croxton Park to welcome H.R.H. the Princess Beatrice of Battenberg, who drove in an open carriage with the Duchess of Rutland, and Gillard, mounted on old Farewell, had the pleasure of pointing out the hounds to her.

During the season sport was stopped twenty-four days for frost and death, another link being severed with the past when Sir Thomas Whichcote, the seventh baronet and mighty hunter, went to his long rest. The untimely death, also, of the Duke of Clarence and Avondale cast a gloom over the season, for the sight of a Leicestershire field of some three hundred horsemen all clad in black struck a chill to the heart of all who rode with hounds. Such skeletons at our feasts are a wholesome reminder that our scene on the stage of life is but a short one.

The best day of the season was February 10th, after meeting at Croxton Park, a regular Belvoir burst resulting from Coston Covert. "According to our usual plan, I sounded my horn instead of putting hounds in covert, thus rousing a fine fox, who went away, bold as a lion, to Bob Knott's musical halloa. Clapping the pack on his line, they ran with a rattle to the left of Woodwell Head, past Crown Point, and forward to Gunby Gorse, which was reached in twelve minutes. We were not very long here before hounds showed us a line away, and ran at a reduced pace to Gunby Warren, where they marked to ground in a stone quarry—time, twenty-five minutes in all. We had a monster field, who meant riding hard; but I never saw hounds make such an example of them, for they always had the lead, and I never saw so many dirty coats at the finish—my own included. The good horse I was riding, old Farewell by Ripponden, was trapped in one of those deep, narrow Gunby ditches completely hidden by silvery grass, which grows rankly in this district. Poor fellow, he fell on his head, all but breaking his neck, which was twisted for many a day afterwards! Major Amcotts was nearest to me until he fell near the finish when jumping into a muddy lane. Amongst others who had the best of this fine gallop were Lord Lonsdale, Lord Drumlanrig,

Colonel the Hon. H. H. Forester, Captain Blair, Captain Lee Barber, and the Rev. J. P. Seabrooke." A trappy fence caught Mr. Pidcock, lying in great peril under his horse, who threatened any moment to kick his brains out. Lord Lonsdale averted a bad accident by promptly whipping his own saddle off, putting it round the head of the prostrate rider, whose struggling horse at once cut the panels to pieces with his iron heels, showing how near a miss for a fatal accident it had been. The mended saddle Lord Lonsdale afterwards sent as a present to Mr. Pidcock! In this good gallop the veteran of the hunt, Colonel the Hon. H. H. Forester, was amongst those who registered a fall.

During the season two or three unlucky falls laid Gillard by, and in his absence Bob Cotesworth was successful in showing sport, learning much that was useful to him when he subsequently became huntsman to a pack of hounds in Hertfordshire.

Much more of the lion than the lamb characterised the debut of March, the scene being semi-Siberian, and the atmosphere almost Arctic; but in spite of this a good forty minutes was scored in the Vale of Belvoir on the 3rd. On the following Saturday, when hounds met at Piper Hole and snow fell at intervals, a rare good fox left Sherbrooke's Covert, and raced without a check to Little Belvoir in fourteen minutes, from there giving a ten-mile point all down wind to Cossington Gorse in the Quorn country, the distance being covered in seventy minutes, a sufficient tribute to the pace and dash of the beautiful Belvoir blood. Those who saw the best of this gallop were Lord Edward Manners, Major Amcotts, Mr. de Winton, Mr. V. Hemery, and the Rev. J. P. Seabrooke.

The result of the Grand National Steeplechase this year came as a distinct honour to Leicestershire, for Father O'Flynn was trained at Melton Mowbray, and his owner, Mr. Gordon Wilson, was one of the foremost of the fox-catching division. Whilst talking of steeplechasing, which always usurps hunting interests in the spring of the year, we are reminded that Gillard won for the second year in succession a good chase at Melton with Vigilant. A speedy mare bought for hunting, she had a trick of putting her rider down the moment a leg was thrown across the saddle, so her attention was turned to chasing, where her fine turn of speed won a few nice stakes for the Belvoir huntsman.

The sport seen during April savoured of straw hats, white waistcoats, cloudless skies, dusty fallows, and intense heat, but the season finished at Stathern Point on the 17th in a whirling snowstorm.

The number of hunting days was 86, the number of foxes killed 87, with 44 marked to ground.

Season 1892-93

It fell to Frank Gillard's lot to attend the funerals of many members of the hunt as a last mark of respect. His greeting as he joined the sad

The Royal Meet at Croxton Park.

1. The Duke of Rutland.
2. H.R.H. the Princess Beatrice of Battenberg.
3. The Duchess of Rutland.
4. Colonel Forester.
5. Frank Gillard on Farewell.

THE NEW YORK
PUBLIC LIBRARY

ASTOR, LENOX AND
TILDEN FOUNDATIONS
R   L

procession was characteristic, "This is a sorry meet, sir!" On one occasion only, and that in the summer of '92, did he attend such a ceremony in scarlet, the funeral of Mr. Nicolas John Charlton, of Chilwell Hall, Notts. It will be remembered by those who were there as one of the most picturesque and touching sights they ever witnessed. The coffin, covered with a scarlet cloth, was conveyed in a farm waggon drawn by a white horse, the sides of the vehicle being decked with blooming gorse. Upon the coffin, which bore a large number of wreaths made of flowers and gorse, the deceased's hunting-whip and spurs were placed, and he was carried to his last resting-place in the green and leafy churchyard of Attenborough by fifteen hunt servants in scarlet, representative of the Belvoir, Quorn, Rufford, South Notts, and Badsworth kennels.

Mange was an evil that had to be reckoned with this season, as many as five litters of cubs being destroyed in the home coverts. The best of the entry this season were Harlequin, Noble, Phillis, Sensitive, Skilful, Tapster, Trueman, and Tempest. Perhaps of these, the hound that eventually did the pack most good was Tapster by Pirate—Twinkle. He greatly pleased Will Dale, who came with Lord Yarborough from Brocklesby to enjoy a morning's cub-hunting, and was not slow to note Tapster in his work. Poor fellow, he met his fate in 1897, being run over on the line at Ancaster Station, where he had returned to meet "the special," which was then an institution.

Two good days' sport occurred on November 9th and 10th, the first being from Brentingby Spinney, commencing at hunting pace but ending with a race down to Melton brook. During the run much disaster occurred, Lord Lonsdale and Lord William Manners getting in the brook, whilst Mrs. Sloane Stanley was dragged out of the saddle through her habit catching on a fence. The pace was fast by Scalford round to Old Hills, ending with slow hunting to Piper Hole Gorse, where the late hour made it necessary to whip off. One of the few who remained to the finish was Mrs. Hildyard of lawn tennis fame.

The next day an excellent hunting run started from Boothby Little Wood over a fine line of country by Ingoldsby, Osgodby, and Irnham, as if the point was Aslackby forest. This good fox then twisted back down the valley to Lenton, where hounds unfortunately got off the line, and were stopped at dusk in a meadow known as Paradise by Ingoldsby. Those to the front in this fine run were the Rev. J. P. Seabrooke, Mr. E. Long, Mr. James Rudkin; and the ladies who stayed to the finish were Mrs. E. Lubbock, Mrs. C. J. Phillips, the four Miss Heathcotes, and Miss K. Carter. The run fox was viewed by Mr. James Hoyes as he rode homewards, and he opinioned, "he was so tired he had only five minutes more run left in him."

Capital sport was enjoyed during November, a good finale to a nice hunt of an hour from Newton Gorse to Folkingham Little Covert being the presentation of two brushes to two young ladies wearing their hair down, and riding ponies, Miss K. Hodgson and Miss Victoria Heathcote.

A run voted the "best seen in three seasons," a nine-mile point from Harby to Staunton, came off on the 14th of December. The cream of the gallop was up to Jericho, which was reached in twenty minutes, the full time to the finish at Allington being one hour and a half. The leading division were Mr. W. de Winton, Mr. James Hutchinson, Mr. V. Hemery, Mr. E. Lubbock, Mr. Noel Fenwick, Mr. Basil Cochrane, Mr. Gordon Wilson, Mr. T. Hutchinson and Mr. J. Brewster, whilst Mr. Grey Fullerton and Bob Cotesworth fell at wire. The plough lands by Jericho were very deep after the frost, so that a check was welcomed, for the little Belvoir bitches had the foot of horses all the way. When Bob Knott signalled the fox away on the Staunton side, those who kept closest to hounds were Lord Lonsdale, the Hon. L. Lowther, Captain Burns, and Mr. Gardner Muir, many opinioning this to be the best run seen in three years.

A cloudy sky and a mild moist air gave promise of a scent lying on December 17th, when hounds met at Three Queens, and they went away on the back of their evening fox from Coston Covert with a point for Wymondham. The pioneers of the gallop were Captain Lee Barber riding a gray, Mr. Arthur Hutchinson, on his well-know cream-coloured, with Gillard on old Farewell. Quickly flew the golden minutes of pleasure as hounds streaked across a sea of grass, and on reaching the valley Gillard was laid low, Miss K. Hodgson having the pleasure of giving the lead over. The point this good fox evidently intended was Sproxton Thorns, but being headed he turned back to Coston, and up to Waltham it was but slow hunting. Reynard had evidently rested, for scent suddenly became breast-high as hounds skimmed away over the turf towards Chadwell, and it was a stern chase for the field up to Goadby Bullmore, where a sheep dog joined in and spoilt the finish. Time, seventy-five minutes, and it only wanted a kill to make it first-class.

A stop for frost of thirty-two days, beginning December 24th, pretty well established a record which no hunting man wishes to see beaten, but when hounds started again on the 26th of January they tapped a good vein of sport. A very large crowd assembled at Croxton Park, and Newman's Gorse supplied the first fox, who ran by Waltham Thorns to Freeby with the two visiting masters of the day, Lord Lonsdale and Mr. Fernie, in close attendance. The inevitable pastoral scourge, the sporting sheep-dog, caused complications near to Freeby, all trace of the hunted one vanishing in the churchyard, so that the whipper-in entered the sacred edifice in search of the fox. The evening gallop from Melton Spinney was a regular steeple-chase across a stiff line of country to Bescaby Oaks, with Lord Lonsdale, Lord Edward Manners, Mr. V. Hemery, and Mr. J. Fullerton riding as if between the flags. On reaching the covert, hounds turned their attention to a badger, which they killed.

A remarkable red-letter day resulted with a straight-necked fox from Aslackby Wood on February 3rd, who made a nine-mile point in one hour and ten minutes before he surrendered his brush by Weaver's Lodge. The day was very foggy, so that only a fortunate half-dozen who got away with hounds saw anything of this fine gallop, the rest of the field, riding about for two hours, were completely lost. The line hounds ran was by Lenton to the left, away by Humby for Ropsley nearly to the Hurn, turning to the right over Haceby hollow, killing their fox handsomely on the roadside by Weaver's Lodge. The fortunate few who rode to them were Mr. James Hutchinson, Mr. Edgar Lubbock, Mr. F. A. Soames, Mr. T. Heathcote, Miss Lucy Heathcote, Miss K. Carter, Mons. Roy, Messrs. Casswell, and Messrs. Grummitt. The brush of this good fox was presented to Miss Carter, and a pad to Miss Heathcote.

A regular Belvoir burst occurred next day with the third fox from Staunton Thorns, one of Mr. C. J. Phillips' coverts. Getting a good start, the pack raced for a couple of miles across a stiff bit of country to Normanton Little Covert. Mr. E. Lubbock, Mr. S. K. Marsland, Mr. C. Hodgson, and Mr. Brockton rode a regular steeplechase to keep within touch of hounds, but Frank Gillard managed to arrive at the covert first, winning with very little to spare, and possibly the distance has never been compassed in shorter time, or offered anything more exciting whilst it lasted.

"I think the best of all the good gallops I ever

rode was on February 25th this season," said Frank Gillard. "We went from Harby Covert to the edge of Dalby Wood in forty-five minutes, eleven miles—I measured on the map afterwards the way hounds took." A fox was well found at Harby Covert, and for fifteen minutes the pack raced as if glued to his brush, taking a beautiful line of country by Hose Thorns and Sherbrooke's Covert. The fences are big and strong, but the sound turf offers the best take off, and the Rev. J. P. Seabrooke, with Captain Barry, acted as excellent pilots up to Holwell Mouth. As they galloped at topmost pace down into the vale, the reverend gentleman took a most awful cropper, and up the hill to Dalby Wood the gray horse Macnab, who carried Gillard, turned a complete somersault over a tall unyielding fence. "Confound those lawyers," said Frank, as he scrambled to his feet again, "I always call those briery fences lawyers because they cling to you so!" Amongst the second division pegging along in this brilliant gallop was Mr. Brockton and his daughter, the latter going gallantly on an own brother to St. Gatien, Mrs. Cook, riding a gray, Mr. C. Hodgson, and Mr. Serecole. Being headed by a labourer, this good fox turned for Six Hills road, entering Saxelby Spinney, and here occurred the first check in a gallop of forty minutes. Hunting carefully on to Grimstone Gorse, they turned back to Saxelby Spinney with all the dash and vigour of the start, and racing past Shoby, rolled their fox over in the middle of a grass field near to Hoby in Quorn domains. The field were the wrong side of a big unjumpable drain at the finish, watching a beaten fox die gamely, and so fierce were the pack for blood after running one hour and forty minutes, that they worried the brush and mask before any one could get to them. Gillard remarked in his diary, " I never saw hounds run more freely or fast over a fine line of country with such unchecked, unaltered pace."

During March the rain register was 0·63, none falling for a period of twenty days, comparing with the March of 1878, 1880, and 1885. On the 10th a nice spin resulted with an outlier viewed by Humby Wood, and he went by Humby and Ropsley, turning back to a well-known fox drain made by Mr. "Banker" Hardy near to Ingoldsby. Being ejected from his hiding-place, he made straight for Lenton brook, and the first over was the top weight, Mr. Joseph Wilders, riding a powerful bay horse. Others who jumped the brook successfully were Mr. E. Lubbock, the four Miss Heathcotes, Mr. Measures, Mr. A. Pick, and Mr. Bernard Casswell. Those who were unfortunate to get in were Mr. T. Heathcote, Mr. S. K. Marsland, and the Rev. J. P. Seabrooke, but there was plenty of time to get out again, for the hunted one sought the refuge of a rabbit warren on the opposite bank.

The experiences of March 17th, after meeting at Keisby, revived the memories of a similar day's sport, thirty years previous, when Cooper was huntsman. The run on both occasions was down to Haconby Fen, and Gillard had never followed a fox there since the days he turned hounds to

Cooper. Two gentlemen of the hunt who rode both runs were Captain Cecil Thorold, who as a boy remembered taking a fall, and Mr. James Hutchinson, whose horse died four days afterwards from the severity of the run. After marking to ground we returned to Dunsby Wood, and there encountered two garrulous old woodmen who had a vivid recollection of the great run in December 1865, "and the sight of 'osses as never got 'ome after it, though the gents dried the only public-house by givin' their mounts an alarmin' sight of beer." The distance of that great run was 17 miles from point to point, the time being two hours and forty-five minutes at a good holding pace without much of a check. This stout fox was roused in Ancaster Gorse, and ran by Welby Hazels, Ropsley, Lenton, Laughton, crossing the London and Lincoln road at the 103 mile-stone. Passing through Rippingale, the father of Sir John Lawrance, Q.C., viewed him going for Haconby Fen. Cooper the huntsman remarked that every hound but one was up at the finish, including five couple of that year's entry. Returning to the present, Frank fulfilled the traditions of the past by whipping off at Osgodby Coppice when it was dusk.

The number of hunting days this season was 100, and 86 foxes and a badger killed, with 50 marks to ground.

CHAPTER XVIII

Seasons 1893-94 and 1894-95

THE HEATHCOTE PATENT SAFETY.

DATES of commencing Cub-Hunting—Foreign Hay—The Hounds Old Gambler, Skylark, the Daughter of Druid—Too many Foxes killed in a Morning—Sir George Whichcote—The Hunt Honorary Secretaryship—Lord Lonsdale takes the Mastership of the Quorn—Frank Gillard's Contemporary Tom Firr—The Old Hunt Horse Oscar carries Miss Robinson—Mr. Arthur Hutchinson, Mayor of Grantham, and the Meet at the Guild Hall—The Fifteen-mile Stubton Run, Mr. S. K. Marsland presented with the Brush at the end of it—Mr. and Mrs. C. J. Phillips' Coverts at Staunton—The Three Shire Bush—Mrs. Bend, the Wife of the Earth-stopper, presented with a Brush—Two good Days before the Frost—A good Run from Heathcote's Covert with a Bobtail—Miss Gertrude Heathcote wins the Belvoir Hunt Red Coat Race—The Heathcote Patent Safety Habit—The Entry 1894—Mr. W. Theobald Maud on Canvas and in the Field—Death of the Hound Nominal—The Revival of the Folkingham Meet and a great Day's Sport—Lord Willoughby de Eresby presented with the Brush—Pulpit Allusions—Bad Falls—Harry Maiden hunts the Pack—The Duke of Rutland's seventy-sixth Birthday—The long Frost—A good Run and Kill at Newton Hall—Another good Run and Kill at Lenton Vicarage—The Melton Contingent.

An extract from Frank Gillard's diary gives the dates he commenced cubbing from August 1870. The autumn of 1874 was the earliest start on record, after a blazing hot summer, and a consequently early harvest, hounds commencing on the 12th of August. This season under consideration was the second earliest, bracketed with 1884, as in both years hounds commenced on August 21st. During seven years from 1886 to 1892, which were wet, the dates were respectively September 13th, 5th, 19th, 5th, 4th, 11th, and 8th, which clearly proves how closely the interests of sport and agriculture are allied.

The drought and heat this year were excessive, so that the hay crop entirely failed, and our hunters were asked to eat a foreign importation from America and Russia. As an example of the price of English-grown hay for hunters, the order for the Quorn stable was one hundred tons, for which one thousand pounds was paid by Lord Lonsdale. Hounds also suffered much from heat and thirst when drawing thick covert, all the ponds and dykes being dry or choked with black mud. The grass land, too, was brown as the road, and of the same consistency, so that stock were unusually troublesome in breaking fence, and cub-hunting operations practically confined to walking exercise.

This season Fred Powell was promoted to first whipper-in, the new hand being Harry Maiden from the Linlithgow and Stirling—quick to turn hounds and cheery as a blackbird. Old Gambler, the king of the pack, in his twelfth year, stone deaf, otherwise sound, received an honourable pension to roam about the kennel precincts, enjoying a day's sport when the fixtures were near home, and not in big woods. Of the young hounds Gillard pointed with pride on a cubbing morning to Skylark, walking at his horse's heels carrying a cub's mask. She was the daughter of that promising stud hound Druid (1890) the son of Shamrock and Diligent, pronounced by Mr. Henry Chaplin, the Squire of Blankney, to be worth £1000. What a grand fellow he was—symmetrical, deep of girth, remarkable in neck and shoulders, even in Belvoir kennel, nippy as a kitten, and good as he looked. Unfortunately Druid died of inflammation this year, but he left five couple which were all considered good enough to "put on," viz. Captive, Costly, Dinah, Gainer, Guidance, Monarch, Render, Romeo, Regal, and Skylark.

A useful morning's work resulted at Leadenham, though Frank remarked in his diary, "we killed too many foxes, two and a half brace." The late duke would always grumble when he heard of more than a leash being killed in any one day's work, and Gillard stood true to old precedent. A brace were first killed in Leadenham Hill-top Covert, and another in California Covert, the fourth being a fine old dog-fox quite eight years of age, and the last a green cub started from Tiger Holt. Strange to say, in his hurry to bolt through the first fence, he ran his nose against a big flat stone with such force that his neck was broken, and hounds had only to eat him up.

At Aswarby this season a new squire reigned,

Sir George Whichcote, nephew to the late Sir Thomas Whichcote, "a father of the hunt"; and the young baronet, true to his breeding, showed that "fox-hunting was the foremost passion of his heart." A change too came in the Honorary Secretaryship of the Hunt, which had been so ably undertaken for many seasons by Mr. James Hutchinson, who retired, and was succeeded by Mr. Charles Parker, the grandson of Mr. "Banker" Hardy, who in his time acted in the same capacity to the hunt. Amongst changes with the neighbouring packs, the most important was the appointment of Lord Lonsdale to the mastership of the Quorn, Gillard and a strong Belvoir contingent throwing in their lot at Kirby Gate on the opening day. Tom Firr carried the horn and started his twenty-third season huntsman to the Quorn, Gillard exceeding him by one year with the Belvoir.

Certainly the season 1893-94 was ushered in at Kirby Gate by a splendid pageant, and the eyes of the whole fox-hunting world were centred upon it. The occasion was Frank's first visit to Kirby Gate since he carried the horn for the Quorn in 1869; but they did not carry silver whistles and hunting hatchets in those days!

December 20th was the wettest day of the season, but the small field that met hounds at Croxton Park scored quite a nice hunt. Melton Spinney, the first draw, responded to the call, hounds getting away with a fox down wind to the Scalford Brook. The lead over was given by Gillard, riding Farewell, who took it in his stride regularly every Wednesday during the season. Mr. V. Hemery on King Charles was next, followed by Miss Miriam Barlow on her clever black cob, Mr. Ernest Long on a bay, and his wife riding that wonderful performer Game Cock. Then the stream as usual was quickly dammed by struggling horses and riders.

Talking of horses brought to mind a sharp little bay, with always a leg to spare, named Oscar, who carried Gillard well for many seasons, and when he was drafted from the hunt stables, went to carry one of our accomplished lady riders. "Miss Robinson learnt to go to hounds on Oscar," said Frank; "directly I blew my horn the old horse knew me; he would collar his bit and come close after me, so that several times I had to ride hard to escape being jumped on."

A memorable meet this season was that of December 26th, at the Guild Hall, Grantham, on Boxing Day, by special invitation from the fox-hunting mayor, Mr. Arthur Hutchinson. To Lord John Manners, the present Duke of Rutland, belongs the credit of being the first to plead for the establishment of national holidays, anticipating Sir John Lubbock in this respect, so that it was only to be expected that his superb pack of hounds should accept the invitation to give a Bank Holiday crowd so healthy and inspiriting a spectacle. A fox quickly roused in Harrowby Gorse gave a nice spin to Abney Wood, in full view of the assembled crowd, and it was remarked that thirty-eight falls were registered, including one taken by his Worshipful the Mayor off the gray mare.

A long spell of ill luck in the Lincolnshire vale was broken on January 23rd, when hounds scored the red-letter day of the season after meeting at Caythorpe. The air was crisp, with a sharp catch of frost, and the ground did not really ride until midday. A visit was first paid to the Beacon, from which covert Mr. R. Bemrose viewed a fox away which gave a nice hunting run to Hough Gorse; but the run which put into the shade all other performances was that of the afternoon. By consulting the map it will be seen that it took the form of a big loop, measuring 15 miles from Stubton Rookery nearly to Brandon, out round Brant Broughton, the farthest point, back by Beeckingham to Stubton Coverts, where they marked to ground, bolted, and killed him. It is a big country to ride, and the pace too that hounds travelled was sufficient to try the best horses in this run of one hour and twenty-five minutes. Gillard, on a clever old roan mare, piloted the way, whilst in the vanguard Mr. and Mrs. Edgar Lubbock, Lord Edward Manners, Mr. F. A. Soames, Mr. F. Worsley, Mr. S. K. Marsland, Mr. J. Hutchinson, Mr. A. Hutchinson, Mr. F. Parker, the three brothers Rudkin, and Mr. R. Dowse with Powell were conspicuous. Grief and disaster there was all along the line, the river Brant coming twice into the run, but at the finish Lord Edward Manners presented the brush to Mr. Marsland, who well deserved the honour, having gone gallantly on the old chestnut Alabaster. It was a great hound performance, for they never wanted touching the whole time, and there was only one slight check at Brandon, where the fox had run the road.

The coverts round Staunton Hall were a great

KIRBY GATE, 1898.

1. Frank Gillard. 2. Tom Firr. 3. The Hon. Mrs. L. Lowther. 4. The Hon. L. Lowther. 5. Capt. T. Boyce. 6. Mr. A. V. Pryor. 7. Lord Lonsdale, M.F.H. 8 and 9. Mr. and Mrs. James Hornsby.

stronghold this season under the guardianship of Mr. and Mrs. C. J. Phillips. Sir Walter Scott has immortalised Staunton Hall, the old fifteenth century house, in his novel *The Heart of Midlothian*, when he makes Jeanie Deans come there after leaving the shelter of Jericho Covert—the latter is good fox ground on the arch of the Great Northern Railway tunnel. A very interesting covert, too, is Cottam Thorns, marked on the map as the Three Shire Bush, because the three shires of Nottingham, Leicester, and Lincoln meet there. Half a century ago the spot was the scene of many a prize-fight, and the shire drain hard by is a deep sepulchral trench dug by the ancients to map out the border of the two counties. The custodian, too, of the neighbouring Normanton Coverts was quite a character, Mrs. Bend, the wife of the earth-stopper, who also combined rat-catching as a profession. This good lady was a keen follower of the chase, driving about in a pony-cart, delighting to give a shrill view halloa when she viewed a fox away. Gillard took the opportunity to blood her with the brush one day when up at the finish. "I could not make her face much prettier, for she carried a good colour," Frank gallantly remarked.

Two good days' sport preceded the stop that came for frost in February. The first of these was on Wednesday, 14th, after assembling at Croxton Park. A fox set going from Coston Covert headed for Wymondham over a grand line of country, and those nearest to hounds were Mr. V. Hemery, the Duke of Marlborough, Captain Standish, Mr. A. Brocklehurst, the Rev. J. P. Seabrooke and Mr. F. Crawley, the two latter registering heavy falls during the run. With a good holding scent hounds raced their fox to Stapleford, where he was hallooed by navvies who turned him. A forward cast by Garthorpe recovered the line across to Freeby Wood, and getting on better terms again, hounds raced their hardest to Waltham Thorns, where they effected a kill. The afternoon gallop of forty-five minutes was even better, the line from Brentingby Wood to the Waltham Spire being a most inviting one. Those nearest to hounds were Lord and Lady Henry Bentinck, the Duke of Marlborough, Mr. W. Lawson, Mr. Muir, Mrs. Lubbock, Miss Parker, Mr. Holland, and Mr. Fenwick.

On the 16th a nice run is recorded on the Lincolnshire side, the best part of it being by Lenton Pastures, with Mr. Edgar Lubbock, Mr. F. Crawley, and Mrs. Royds leading. Leaving Lenton village on the left hand, the pack swung down the line of grass fields to the brook, Mr. F. Soames being first over with Snowflake, followed by Miss Emily Heathcote, who got the right side with a fall. Others followed, more left it alone, and some got in, including Gillard, who parted company with his horse.

A capital day's sport was enjoyed in March with a bob-tailed fox started from Folkingham Little Gorse, the Heathcote family fox covert; hounds rattling along over a charming country out by Birthorpe and Sempringham, finally killing by Aslackby after a pretty gallop of fifty minutes. The brush, which was no bigger than a sheep's tail, was presented to Mrs. E. Long, and the mask, covered with old scars won in marauding and courting excursions, went to Mr. Frank Heathcote, who had gone gallantly on a hireling.

The name of Heathcote was to the fore, as well it might be with a family of seven hunting from

Newton Hall. At the finish of the season Miss Gertrude revived the memories of old Sir Gilbert Heathcote's colours by winning the Belvoir Hunt Red Coat Race with her good horse "Bob," ridden by Mr. V. Hemery. Her eldest sister Miss Lucy invented and patented a safety skirt which is called "the Heathcote Patent Safety," and being the outcome of much experience across country, it has proved its worth.

Taken altogether, it was not a good scenting season, though an open one, hunting only being prevented on 13 days. The number of hunting days was 120. Foxes killed, 101; marked to ground, 49.

Season 1894-95

This season's entry was fourteen couple, and by experts the young dog hounds were pronounced the best seen in the famous kennel for twenty years. The entry was entirely made up by home sires, as follows: two couple by Gambler, the same number by Druid (1891), and two and a half by Wonder (1890), three couple by Donovan (1891) son of Rufford Dancer, one and a half couple by his brother Dolphin (1888), two couple by Hermit (1890) son of Grove Harkaway, and by Nominal, Prodigal (1890), and Valiant (1890), each a single hound. Hermit's one family from Vanquish, a daughter of Nominal, were the best of a good lot containing two dogs Vanquisher and Vaulter, two ladies Vigilant and Varnish, the Belvoir tan showing richly on their shapely forms. Another beautiful family was that of Donovan's, from Royalty a daughter of Glancer, viz. Rebel, Regent, and Rueful, and by those whose judgment is never much at fault Rebel was considered one of the truest-shaped dogs ever seen. Two very striking young dogs, almost unbroken in colouring, were the couple by Shamrock from Diligent by Grafton Dancer, by name Donegal and Deemster, another couple by the same sire from Rampish by Gameboy were Rusticus and Ransack. Those by Wonder were Welbeck and Wrestler. Of the ladies perhaps the best was Novelist by Nominal; she stood magnificently, and had a strong symmetrical frame. Druid was represented by Dulcimer and Density, Wonder had a daughter Decimal, Gambler a couple of daughters Gravity and Gossamer.

The hunt was immortalised by a large picture of a meet at Rauceby Hall, painted by Mr. W. Theobald Maud, the distinguished war correspondent and artist to the *Graphic*. Lincolnshire bred and born, he was one of the keenest bitten for sport, thrusting along after hounds, taking falls with the greatest equanimity.

On a morning in October, when a rich pea-soup fog enshrouded London, nothing worse than a white mist hung about the Harby Hills waiting for the sun to melt it away. Hounds, after rousing the echoes in Piper Hole Gorse, were marking to ground, with old Nominal leading the pack as usual. Tumbling over one another in their eagerness to get hold of the cub, they jammed

Nominal in the earth, and a quarrelsome hound seizing him was the signal for all to worry before help could arrive. Poor Nominal was sent home by train with a whipper-in, but died in kennels that night, and the culprit was drafted to the United States of America.

A capital day's sport was enjoyed after meeting at Hose Grange on November 17th, and Gillard remarks: "I never knew hounds run better." After finding in Hose Thorns the pack went away over Penn Hill, turning to Sherbrooke's Covert, running a ring back, making a good finish by killing their fox handsomely. Over the Smite Mr. Cecil Grenfell gave the lead, and but very few struggled to the end—these including Mr. Edgar Lubbock, riding that good mare Carlton, Mr. Guy Fenwick, Mr. V. Hemery, Mr. de Winton. Another really good hunt of over two hours was that on the 21st, from Burbidge's Covert, a fox running into Cottesmore country. After slow hunting, a return was made to Burbidge's Covert, and hounds getting on quick-scenting grass, fairly raced over the flats by Burton, away for Great Dalby and Ashby Pastures in Quorndom, where a good fox saved his brush by getting to ground. Those who saw the best of this fine gallop were Lord Edward Manners, Mrs. E. Lubbock, Count Zhrowski, Rev. J. P. Seabrooke, and Mr. W. Gale.

A meet in the market square of Folkingham on 23rd was a revival this season of an old fixture in 1805, when Shaw was huntsman, and Sir Gilbert Heathcote lord of the manor of Folkingham.

Hounds assembled opposite the house of the squire and his wife, Mrs. Thomas A. R. Heathcote, the day being a red-letter one for sport. A summary of it is as follows: a nice hunting run of an hour with the morning fox, a quick dart middle day with fox No. 2, in the evening forty minutes at racing pace and a kill in the open. Sapperton Wood had been in great form this season, and on this occasion supplied the evening fox, who took the desired line of country, first with a point for Hanby, then away over the grass and Lenton brook to Ingoldsby Wood. The brook, as usual, sifted out the field. Mr. F. A. Soames on his chestnut horse Kedar gave the lead, which was followed by Mr. E. Lubbock, Lord Willoughby de Eresby, and the Hon. Claude Willoughby de Eresby, the latter losing his hat, finishing the run bareheaded. Mr. T. A. Rudkin, the hard-riding vet., was one of those who nicked in, and though encumbered with a bag on his saddle full of blister bottles and lotion, he rode at the brook and got the right side with a fall, breaking all his bottles. Before this good fox could reach his goal, Ingoldsby Wood, hounds pulled him down in a stack-yard close by, after giving forty minutes of the very best. To Lord Willoughby the brush was presented by Gillard, and to Miss Lucy and Emily Heathcote, each a pad, the mask going to Mr. T. A. Rudkin. The day did not end there, for the following Sunday the vicar of Folkingham took for his text, " Evil shall hunt the wicked," knowing that his congrega-

T

tion were red-hot on the subject of fox-hunting, cleverly bringing home a telling parable.

A good spin of something over an hour from Buckminster, and a ring out to Gunby Gorse, was attended with much disaster. Those nearest to the pack up to Crown Point were Lord Edward Manners, Lord Lonsdale, Major Charles Thorold, Mrs. E. Lubbock, Mr. Gordon Wood, Mr. J. Brewster, and Mr. Bowman. A heavy fall incapacitated Gillard during the run, though he pluckily remounted and finished; the Rev. J. P. Seabrooke and Harry Maiden also came to grief in the run. The next day Maiden had to hunt the hounds, and he was so badly served by his horse that he took two falls in seven minutes; however, he had the satisfaction of slaying a brace of foxes, besides marking one to ground. The brush of one of these, an old gray fox, was presented to Sir G. Whichcote, who went well on his big gray horse.

On December 12th the Duke of Rutland celebrated his seventy-sixth birthday by joining the large field that met hounds at Croxton Park, and a good day's sport was experienced after a heavy night's rain, which had filled the brooks and rivers bank high. The first fox led the field gallantly, and finished his career by drowning in the river by Egerton Lodge, after he had sought refuge in a greenhouse. Amongst those who had the best of the good things the line of country had to offer were Lord Edward Manners, Mr. G. P. Evans (Master of the Cambridgeshire), Mr. Alfred Brocklehurst, Mr. H. T. Barclay, Mr. V. Hemery,

Mr. C. Hodgson, Mr. Ricardo, Mr. R. Fenwick, Mr. Foxhall Keene, Captain Rennie, and Mr. W. Gale. The fox of the afternoon did his best to drown the field, swimming the river Whissendine, which had a flood tide. Three young subalterns, who had evidently been practising swimming their chargers, plunged boldly into the stream. The horses got out of their depth or got caught by a hidden wire, for all bobbed under and parted company with their riders. Harry Maiden was one of those not to be headed by cold water, and it was bad luck for this band of hardy divers that hounds checked on the opposite bank.

The fates were very unkind to the hunt staff, for just before Christmas turned Gillard was again incapacitated by a heavy fall, and Harry Maiden, his first lieutenant, hunted hounds, though himself sore and crippled, being credited with twenty-five falls up to that time. The second whip, Fred South, had extinguished his chances early in the season by jumping into a stone-pit, so that Bob Knott was looked to as the mainstay of the pack, until he was knocked out of the saddle in a gateway.

Harry Maiden had the luck to score a gallop of great excellence from Coston Covert to Gunby Gorse on December 19th, the time being twenty-five minutes. The line was about the best that could possibly have been taken, and so quickly were hounds away with their huntsman, that only six lucky men got with them—Mr. Foxhall Keene, Mr. Ricardo, Mr. V. Hemery, Mr. Tom Rudkin, and Mr. W. Gale, whilst Mrs. W. Lawson was the foremost lady.

During January and the whole of February we experienced a frost of such duration and intensity as had never been seen in this country since the season 1860-61. Only four very doubtful days' hunting were registered between December 30th and March 1st. The first day out, hounds met at Newton Bar, and two first-class hunting runs resulted. After an uneventful morning a fox was set going from Culverthorpe domains, giving a good chase of fifty minutes to Newton Hall, where he was killed on the lawn, and the brush presented by Lord Edward Manners to Mrs. Heathcote. The second gallop was from Sapperton Wood with the evening fox, who again took us the desirable line by Hanby, turning for the grass down to Lenton brook. Mr. V. Hemery gave the lead over on Shining River by Tiber, followed by Mr. James Hutchinson, Mr. Soames, and Mr. Cecil Rudkin—the bulk of field finding an easier place by halving it at the ford. After crossing the brook, we turned sharp to the left and ran parallel with it below Lenton, where the pack divided, some running into the Vicarage garden, where they killed. Gillard with the others cast on over the brook up to Osgodby, where they checked, and it was a curious sight to see Ben Baxter, the shoeing smith, riding up with the dead fox over his shoulder, and the six couple who had effected the kill at the vicarage. It was a good thirty-five minutes and an excellent ride.

SEASON 1894-95

March this season was one of the wettest and dirtiest months on record. Melton, as usual, was very full for the wind up and the Leicestershire chases. Amongst those who had house parties for the occasion were Prince and Princess Henry of Pless, the Duke of Marlborough, Mr. and Mrs. W. Lawson, Captain and Mrs. Burns Hartopp, Mr. and Mrs. de Winton, Mr. and Lady Augusta Fane, Colonel and Mrs. Baldock, Mr. and Mrs. Alfred Brocklehurst. At Croxton Park chases, Gillard was the only one of the hunt staff off the sick list able to keep the course and wear a tall hat.

The season, which finished on April 23rd, was a short one of 87 days, and 98 foxes were killed; 48 marked to ground.

A BELVOIR RED LETTER DAY 40 MINUTES AND A KILL

CHAPTER XIX

Season 1895-96

Stud Hounds at Belvoir Kennel—Gillard relating the Merits of each Hound—The Families of Gambler, Shamrock, and Pirate compared—Hard Ground—The Fox-hunter's Wedding—Opening Day—The Buckminster to Edmonthorpe Gallop—Record Time—The Pack and Huntsman's Horse—Another Buckminster to Woodwell Head Gallop—Continued good Sport in Leicestershire and Lincolnshire during January—Retirement of the Duke of Rutland—The Meeting of the Hunt in Grantham—The Hunt Committee—Frank Gillard's last Leicestershire Day a brilliant one—A Kill in Ranksboro Gorse—The Horse Farewell—The number of Foxes killed in twenty-six Seasons—The new Master, Sir Gilbert Greenall—A Tribute to Gillard's Care of the Pack—The Testimonial to the retiring Huntsman—Sir William E. Welby Gregory's Speech—Frank Gillard's Farewell.

PORTRAIT OF A LADY.

THE concluding chapter, like a beautiful sunset, necessarily has a tinge of sadness, because it brings us to the first break in the mastership of the house of Manners, whose family pack the Belvoir had been since its institution. Though the sun certainly set and a new day began for the Belvoir, it was full of reflected glory, "for when Frank Gillard retired with his noble master the Duke of Rutland, he left behind such a number of superb stud hounds as has probably seldom if ever before been assembled in this famous kennel. Some few—very few—kennels in England may show you six stallion hounds worthy of the title. Belvoir can show you twenty." We are quoting the outside opinion of so high an authority as Brooksby, who goes on to say: "The wherewithal to strengthen a pack, to maintain its bone, to improve the type of its brood bitches, is to be found in quantity and variety. It merely remains to ask yourself which lines of blood you prefer. For instance, if that of Weathergage and of Lord Henry Bentinck's Dorimont attract you, and it is an object to get increased substance, how can you do better than appeal to the massive and successful Valiant (1889)? If, again, you are not averse to that of Rufford Dancer, how can you leave the notable brotherhood of Dancer, Dolphin, and Donovan (1891)? All three have made their mark in many a kennel, but the greatest of these is Donovan, who has worked such wonders for the Grafton. If, again, you have a fancy for the great Proctor—Struggler—Ruler—Nelson family all are well proven, and their names are respectively Prodigal, Painter, Pensioner, and Tapster (1886). Prodigal has been most used at home, but Tapster, a year younger, is, to the ordinary observer, one of the most desirable and magnificent stud hounds in the kennel. He should, with proper opportunity and luck, be able almost to build up a kennel of himself. Or would you aim at breeding a second Dexter (1894), you will take Watchman (1892), to give you the blood of Weathergage and Milton Solomon; while to obtain that of the Grove Harkaway upon that of Fallible and Weathergage, you may turn to Harlequin (1891). Then there is Resolute (1894), a third-season dog, a son of Dolphin (1891), and quite one of the most beautiful hounds at Belvoir, his dam being a daughter of Pirate; Resolute should, indeed, set any kennel on its legs. Donegal (1893), a son of Shamrock (1887), being noticeable among other good points for his immense depth of brisket. Others that might do credit to any kennel are Vanquisher (1893), by Hermit, Welbeck, and Wrestler (1893), by Wonder. From such hounds as Valiant, Donovan, Tapster, and Resolute I should expect to lay in a store of brood bitches such as might last for a decade to come!"

One advantage breeders had when using Belvoir sires was Gillard's way of relating the merit of every particular hound—whether they drove, used their tongues freely, or were good road hunters. He had particular families in each line of duty, and he recommended the Weathergages for both tongue and drive, as he specially bred for the former quality when he came to Belvoir and used Wonder (1865), a hound with a beautiful note, and he was the sire of Warrior (1870), the sire of Weathergage

(1876). The Belvoir kennel is one family bred out into branches that are by no means remote from the parent tree, and the Gamblers come first for consideration. Apart from the well-known colours, far-famed legs and feet, they have remarkable substance, power, and weight in proportion to their height, and their ribs have a tendency to be deep rather than round. All the Gambler stock are rather a long hound, low and level, with immense muscular development and bone, brainy-looking heads, whilst in the field their characteristics are thorough trustworthiness, pace, and extreme stoutness; they can hunt as well as gallop. A pack of hounds like the Belvoir, which have been bred for nose and sterling hunting qualities, will cover more ground in less time than the most galloping lot without it. The Shamrocks, 1887, a family largely used with the Gamblers, give us another type of hound, all throwing strong family likeness into their get. A very gay family this, with punishing-looking heads, rare necks and shoulders, depth of girth, with not quite the power of the Gamblers behind. Their depth of girth makes them appear a trifle light in their back ribs, till you see the cause of the deception. Rare hounds all of them are in their work! and two grand matrons of the sort are Dahlia and Daphne (1891).

Another group were the Pirates (1885). They had not quite the Shamrock's length of neck or quite the muscular development of the Gamblers, but were a slashing powerful family, and fox-catchers every inch of them. Prodigal and Painter

(1890) were two sons of Pirate. Gillard said, "Prodigal was a remarkable hound when a fox ran the road, often setting the pack right on these occasions."

This season, 1895-96, owing to the hard state of the ground, which retained all its August consistency right into the month of November, it was found impossible to start in the shires until Monday, November 11th. When we say that scarcely a drain-pipe ran since the snows of the previous spring melted, it is easy to realise how hard the ground was, and how low was the stock of surface water in ponds and dykes. Consequently cubbing work was delayed, and one of the worst for damage to hounds' feet. A pad of the first cub killed, Gillard had mounted as a paper-knife, and gracefully presented it to Miss Lucy Heathcote on her marriage, September 12th, with the writer of these pages. The wedding was from Newton Hall, where a representative Belvoir following, including the chaplain of the hunt, the Rev. J. P. Seabrooke, and the huntsman, assisted at the ceremony, Mr. W. T. Maud being best man.

On the opening day, November 12th, good sport was enjoyed from Fulbeck, for after a welcome rain the plough lands in the vale carried a holding scent, and hounds made the best use of it. The little square covert, Parson's Thorns, held a fox of the right sort, leading the way over the Leadenham and Wellingore Vale to within a field of the famous gorse. Then wheeling round past Broughton, he crossed the river and made straight for Leadenham, where he sought the shelter of a drain. A fox-terrier bred by Gillard, and the property of Mr. J. Reeve, bolted, a kill being speedily effected after a good hunt of fifty minutes.

By the last week in November most of the forward division with hounds had registered a fall, the greasy state of the going being held responsible for so much tumbling about. Scent was very moderate until December 2nd, when the ground had somewhat settled, and hounds scored a fine day's sport after meeting at Bottesford. "Unfortunately," Gillard remarks in the diary, "it was our first visit to Normanton little covert, for during the cubbing time the ground was so hard it was not safe to take hounds there. Consequently the cubs clung to 'home, sweet home,' but after a lot of ringing about we got one away over the river Devon, and ended by marking to ground near Orston. After that, Normanton big covert supplied a fox which gave one of the fastest fifteen minutes on record, ending with a mark to ground and kill by Staunton. The Duke of Rutland was one of the field on this occasion, riding his gray cob."

A red-letter day resulted after meeting at Buckminster Hall on December 18th, and few things are more enjoyable in life than to be with the Belvoir when they run over the closely-fenced meadows of their Melton country. A fox was quickly on the move by the Hall, and ran straight for Coston Covert, going hard all the way to save his brush. Fortune and a quick look-out enabled seven good men to get away with them, the rest of the field having a stern chase. Nearest to hounds, though never within half a field of them, was William Gale, so well known between the flags, Lord Charles Bentinck, Mr. de Winton, the Rev. J. P. Seabrooke, Mr. Edgar Lubbock, Mr. V. Hemery, Mr. H. T. Barclay, with Gillard and his two lieutenants, Harry Maiden and Sam Gillson. Hounds did not falter for a moment as they streamed by Wymondham, but nearing Woodwell Head they checked slightly, and gave the crowd the first opportunity to catch their leaders. The pack were soon away again in the valley below Market Overton and Teigh, but at Edmondthorpe the gallop was over. The time from Buckminster Park to Woodwell Head was twenty-three minutes, with another seventeen minutes to the check at Edmondthorpe; "the record" from the first two points named is seventeen minutes, which is pretty good proof of the excellence of the gallop under consideration. The pack for the day was $18\frac{1}{2}$ couple of the big dog hounds, and the horse that carried Gillard so well up to them was "the Miner," a bay with always a leg to spare, a big, bold jumper, but one who was "a bit nappy" to ride. At the end of the season, when all the hunt horses were sold, the Miner only fetched 12 guineas!

The next day we had a pretty bit of cross-country work across by Irnham and Ingoldsby, the gallop being led by Mr. Soames and Mr. E. Lubbock, whilst of the lady division Miss M. Heathcote was to the front for the Belvoir, and

BANK HOLIDAY.

"We 'unted with the Dook's 'ounds."

THE NEW YORK
PUBLIC LIBRARY

ASTOR, LENOX AND
TILDEN FOUNDATIONS

Lady Mary Willoughby, well carried by her good gray, upholding the honours for the Cottesmore. At the end of the day hounds killed a fox in a barrel drain under the North Road by Stoke. Nearly the whole pack followed and broke him up in the drain, one hound afterwards bringing out the mask and another the brush.

To start the new year with a red-letter day augured well, and this was the luck of the Belvoir after meeting at Croxton Park. The run was nothing less than a repetition of the famous gallop of December 18th from Buckminster. A hard-riding field had as good a country as the heart of man could wish, with the big dog pack again streaming away over quick-scenting grass to Woodwell Head. Only a small band of riders were with them, and these included Lord Edward Manners, the Rev. J. P. Seabrooke, Mr. and Miss Musters, Mrs. Cecil Chaplin, Mr. and Miss Hodgson, Mr. F. Worseley, Mons. Roy, Mr. Heldmann, Captain Rennie, Mr. James Hutchinson, and W. Gale.

Accounts agreed from all parts of the kingdom in pronouncing the month of January this season a good one for scent, so that long and straight runs were the order of the day. The mercury stood for an exceptionally long period phenomenally high, frost did not interfere, and rain came latterly. In the diary Gillard placed the mark of excellence against the doings of the 1st, 10th, 11th, 14th, 15th, 17th, 20th, 25th, and 31st.

Referring to the incidents of the 11th, we find

that after meeting at Piper Hole it was the last gallop from Old Hills which crowned the day. A good fox led the field at a great pace nearly to Scalford, turning to Melton Spinney, following the brook to Welby osier beds, where he got to ground with fifteen couple up out of a pack of eighteen and a half. This gallop of about an hour was very fast, and tailed off the field, only Mr. Gordon Canning and Mr. Chaplin, jun., being up at the finish. Gillard lost both his whippers-in, and rode back to kennels in the dark with only seven and a half couple of hounds, but all the rest found their way back to kennels during the night.

On the 17th the scene of the morning was pounding across the vasty deep of fen plough-land country, which carried a good holding scent, a fox leading us from Aswarby domains round by Sempringham and Helpringham, where he got to ground, but, when bolted, gave another ring over much the same country, beating us at the finish, after a hunt of one hour and forty minutes. The leaders of this fen-land hunt were two sturdy yeomen, products of Lincolnshire soil—Mr. Dickens, riding his wonderful yellow cob, and Mr. Cecil Rudkin. The run of the evening, from Spanby Gorse, by Folkingham and Walcott, a fine line of hunting country, to Newton, finishing at Osbournby, was a far better performance, and offered an excellent ride. Those of the lady division who enjoyed this fine gallop were Mrs. Cuthbert Bradley, the four Miss Heathcotes, and Miss Laura Wilson. It will always stand out as one of the finest and truest days of hound work, the big dog pack hunting most persistently with only a moderate scent, although they were the same hounds which had scored the fastest gallops over Leicestershire. It was moonlight when they whipped off, and the distance back to kennels was eighteen miles.

On the last day of the month a fine hunting run in the shape of the figure 8 was started from Sapperton Wood, making Ingoldsby Wood the centre and Grimsthorpe Park the farthest point. The line was chiefly on grass, and measured fourteen miles, with the far-famed Lenton brook coming in the outward journey. Those who had the best of this fine gallop were Lord Edward Manners, Mr. J. E. Platt, Mr. C. Hodgson, Mr. V. Hemery, Mr. F. A. Soames, the Miss Heathcotes, Mr. F. Schwind, Mr. Gibson, and Mr. H. Timson.

The all-absorbing event of this season, and one which claimed the attention of the whole hunting world, was the retirement of the seventh Duke of Rutland from the mastership of his family pack. It is said, "Happy is the nation that has no history," and this also applies to the fox-hunting community, for the fewer the changes the greater the chance of success. The Belvoir had been most fortunate both in masters and huntsmen, the house of Manners providing sport for over two centuries to the dwellers of Leicestershire and Lincolnshire, with only seven huntsmen in their service from 1790 to 1896. The retirement, therefore, of the

Duke of Rutland meant a disruption of associations which existed since fox-hunting commenced. Up to this time it was a remnant of that powerful splendour which enabled the old feudal lords to carry into battle their own followers, and to keep a troop of armed cavaliers always ready under their own roof. When the necessity for this ceased, fox-hunting sprang into life, ancient history recording that in the reign of James I. the owners of Belvoir Castle displayed sporting proclivities, amusing the merry monarch. The earliest hounds at Belvoir are supposed to have been kept to hunt deer in the forests around, and a painting still exists of them hunting a stag in the year 1689, in the time of the tenth earl, the first Duke of Rutland. Foxhound lists and pedigrees were first kept at the kennels about 1750.

A meeting was called in Grantham on February 27th by Lord Brownlow, Lord-Lieutenant of Lincolnshire, to express regret at the retirement of the Duke of Rutland from the Mastership, and consider how the country could best avail itself of his Grace's offer to lend the hounds and kennel. The following committee was formed, representative of the good sportsmen, covert-owners, and farmers who resided in his Grace's kingdom, to consider the offers of candidates for the mastership:— Colonel Mildmay Willson, C.B., Mr. Edgar Lubbock, Mr. Montague Thorold, Lord Willoughy de Eresby, M.P., Mr. Thomas A. R. Heathcote, Lord Edward Manners, M.P., Mr. John Welby, Mr. A. V. Pryor, Major Paynter, Mr. Charles

Welby, Major W. Longstaffe, Sir George Whichcote, Colonel Forester, Sir Hugh Cholmeley, Mr. T. Hutchinson, Mr. H. B. Minta, Mr. Cecil Rudkin, Mr. T. Hack, Mr. J. Hoyes, and the hon. sec., Mr. Charles Parker.

Except for this one sad incident, the season, being wonderfully open, was excellent for sport, bringing more than an average number of red-letter days. All the Leicestershire packs wound up their season unusually early, not one of them hunting an April fox, owing to the hard season's work and early spring. It would be difficult to find the record of a more brilliant gallop than that which fell to the lot of the Belvoir on March 25th, being a run of one hour and twenty minutes from Burbidge's Covert, ending with a kill in Ranksboro Gorse. By all it was acknowledged a fine performance on the part of hounds and huntsman, and the field on this occasion was a most distinguished one, including Lord Edward Manners, M.P., in command, Lord Lonsdale, Master of the Quorn, Mr. W. Baird, Master of the Cottesmore, Mr. Austin Mackenzie, Master of the Woodland Pytchley, Mr. Gordon Canning, late Master of the Ledbury, The Hon. Lancelot Lowther, Lord Cecil Manners, Lord Robert Manners, Sir Gilbert Greenall, Mr. Cyril Greenall, Captain Richard Ellison, the Rev. J. P. Seabrooke, and Tom Firr. This was the last occasion that Frank Gillard hunted hounds in Leicestershire, $18\frac{1}{2}$ couple of the big dog hounds being the pack for the day. "At a critical moment the young hound Tapster hit off the line of the fox, and carrying it through a narrow planting, his splendid voice quickly brought his comrades together, and their music put life and dash in the whole thing again," is a remark we take from Gillard's diary for the day.

Two more days' sport went to finish the season, which ended at Staunton with the big pack on the 28th, and singularly enough the last horse that carried Frank Gillard as huntsman was old Farewell. When the whole stud was sent up for sale at Leicester at the end of the season, the Duke of Rutland made Frank Gillard a present of Farewell, the son of Ripponden, and half-brother to Playfair, winner of the Grand National Steeplechase, the old horse winning a good steeplechase at Colwick Park for his new owner.

The number of foxes killed this season was 79, making the grand total of 2709 from 1870 to 1896.

An *embarras de richesse* of substantial offers to hunt the country were placed before the committee, their choice being Sir Gilbert Greenall from Cheshire; and Frank Gillard decided to retire at the same time with the house of Manners. Letters of regret and sympathy were addressed to him from all parts of the kingdom, all striking the same note; the following, from a master of hounds, being a specimen of many others. "It is sad news the Duke of Rutland giving up the Mastership of the Belvoir, and I can well realise what you must feel at the change that is coming after being such a long time with the Belvoir. I quite think that it is a national calamity. There is one satisfaction that you will have, and that is that at a time when all hounds have improved very rapidly, and are considered to have made more progress than anything else in the last twelve years, the Belvoir are still standing quite alone in appearance, and doing every kennel good that goes to them."

A testimonial befitting the occasion was set on foot by Mr. James Hutchinson, nearly £1300 being subscribed by Frank Gillard's admirers, in addition to a silver ink-stand presented by the ladies of the hunt. The presentation was made at the Grantham Show during the summer by Sir William E. Welby Gregory, "the father of the hunt," who, in a sympathetic speech, awakened many memories of a glorious past. He said: "Frank Gillard, the hunt is grateful to you for your untiring and successful efforts to show them sport, to consult their convenience, and to meet their wishes in every way. They are proud of the way in which you have kept up the reputation of the pack, and maintained the traditions that have been handed down to you from the days of Newman, Shaw, Goosey, Goodall, and Cooper, under whom you began your career. Of the personal qualities which you have brought to bear on the execution of your duties, the best testimony lies in the continuance of that cordial spirit and kindly feeling towards fox-hunting which has existed so universally throughout the Belvoir country for so long. This testimonial, which I am about to present to you, is only one of innumerable proofs of the extent of that cordial and kind feeling, and of the great personal share which you have had in the maintenance of it."

In replying to the presentation speech, after a spontaneous outburst of enthusiasm from the assembled crowd, Gillard said: "It is gratifying to feel that I have so many kind and true friends, not only in the Belvoir Hunt, but also in many others far and near. I have participated in the sport for many years, and had the honour of hunting the noble Duke of Rutland's famous pack for the long period of twenty-six seasons. It seems but yesterday, though forty years ago, that I started a long career in my native country—sweet Devonshire—first with the harriers, and then with the foxhounds. During this long period I have served under five masters, of whom I have the most pleasant memories, viz. Captain Willett, the Hon. Mark Rolle, Mr. John Chaworth Musters, the late and the present Dukes of Rutland. You may therefore conclude that I have had a long and most enjoyable innings, and I assure you that I greatly feel my severance from the Belvoir Hunt."

FINIS

Printed by R. & R. CLARK, LIMITED, *Edinburgh*.